Rethinking Regionalis

Rethinking World Politics

Series Editor: Professor Michael Cox

In an age of increased academic specialization where more and more books about smaller and smaller topics are becoming the norm, this major new series is designed to provide a forum and stimulus for leading scholars to address big issues in world politics in an accessible but original manner. A key aim is to transcend the intellectual and disciplinary boundaries which have so often served to limit rather than enhance our understanding of the modern world. In the best tradition of engaged scholarship, it aims to provide clear new perspectives to help make sense of a world in flux.

Each book addresses a major issue or event that has had a formative influence on the twentieth-century or the twenty-first-century world which is now emerging. Each makes its own distinctive contribution as well as providing an original but accessible guide to competing lines of interpretation.

Taken as a whole, the series will rethink contemporary international politics in ways that are lively, informed and – above all – provocative.

Rethinking Regionalism

Fredrik Söderbaum

First published 2016 by
PALGRAVE

Palgrave in the UK is an imprint of Macmillan Publishers Limited, registered in England, company number 785998, of 4 Crinan Street, London, N1 9XW.

Palgrave Macmillan in the US is a division of St Martin's Press LLC, 175 Fifth Avenue, New York, NY 10010.

Palgrave is a global imprint of the above companies and is represented throughout the world.

Palgrave® and Macmillan® are registered trademarks in the United States, the United Kingdom, Europe and other countries.

ISBN 978–0–230–27240–8 hardback

ISBN 978–0–230–27241–5 paperback

This book is printed on paper suitable for recycling and made from fully managed and sustained forest sources. Logging, pulping and manufacturing processes are expected to conform to the environmental regulations of the country of origin.

A catalogue record for this book is available from the British Library.

A catalog record for this book is available from the Library of Congress.

Printed in China

To Björn Hettne, friend,
colleague and pioneer of new regionalism

Contents

List of Tables

Foreword

Until very recently International Relations in its traditional realist form could be criticized – and was – for being fixated on states, preoccupied with anarchy and insensitive to economics or change. Yet even before the end of the Cold War refashioned the international system and along with it the way in which IR scholars were now prepared to look at the world, the discipline was already in a state of flux. During the 1970s, for instance, International Political Economy made its entry into the subject. At around the same time, writers like Nye and Keohane also started to rethink liberalism and how modern liberalism shorn of its opposition to power politics might help explain the sources of order in a post-hegemonic age. And a few scholars, inspired largely by the work of Hedley Bull and the so-called English School, began to deploy the notion of an international society in an effort to take the debate within IR beyond realism without necessarily rejecting the insights of realism entirely.

But it was also in the years before the end of the Cold War that regionalism began to be taken seriously within IR – as Fredrik Söderbaum shows in his wide-ranging and analytically rigorous volume. In large part this was the result of a success story: the European project which in spite of its limited ambitions back in the 1940s ultimately transformed what had once been a zone of extremism and conflict into one of peace and prosperity. And where Europe led many others followed. Indeed, as Söderbaum shows, if the widening and deepening of the European experiment through the vehicle of the European Union was the most prominent example of regionalism, it was not the only one; and through the last decade of the twentieth century there was a revitalization or expansion of many other regionalist projects as well, such as the African Union (AU), the Association of Southeast Asian Nations (ASEAN), the Economic Community of West African States (ECOWAS), the North American Free Trade Agreement

(NAFTA), the Southern African Development Community (SADC), and the Southern Common Market (Mercosur). What began in Europe clearly did not stay in Europe.

But how to make sense of the varieties of regional organization? Here Söderbaum is at his conceptual best, showing us all how we should be thinking – or more precisely rethinking – the vast array of regional organizations which exist from Europe to South East Asia, Latin America to Africa; and why such organizations now form an essential part of the international system. Certain great powers may rise while others may fall, as Paul Kennedy has argued. But regionalism, it is now clear, is here to stay.

Professor Michael Cox
Series Editor
Director, LSE IDEAS

Preface

The writing of this book was triggered by dissatisfaction with the way we think and study regions and regionalism. There are many diverse theories and studies about specific aspects and contexts of regionalism but there are few convincing approaches that provide the 'big' picture about why and how regions are made and unmade. I have tried to provide answers to these questions in the past, but this book is my most comprehensive and ambitious attempt.

Originally, the plan was to co-author the book with Björn Hettne. Unfortunately, Björn's deteriorating eyesight interrupted and ultimately thwarted our intended collaboration. Initially, we tried a number of technical solutions as well new ways of dividing the work between us, ranging from finding new responsibilities all the way to having myself or Björn's wife, Birgitta, do the reading and writing on the basis of Björn's sharp mind and verbal skills. Gradually and with great reluctance however, we began to accept that both joint research and co-authoring had become impossible. This was a great sadness for us both. Even if this book tries to complete several of our original ideas, it is a different book than if we had written it together. Still, my long and intense collaboration with Björn around 'the new regionalism' is quite visible in the book. In the most general sense, the origin of my four components of 'rethinking regionalism' lies in our earlier discussions. And to some extent, the very first thoughts elaborated in this book pre-date our joint discussions, originating in Björn's earliest definitions of the new regionalism approach prior to 1996, when I became a PhD student under his supervision.

Apart from Björn Hettne, I owe large amounts of gratitude to a range of other scholars and friends, especially those with whom I have had the privilege of co-authorship. Some of my thoughts in this book were developed in collaboration with Ian Taylor, Philippe De Lombaerde and Andréas Godsäter. Other co-authors also positively influenced my thinking about regionalism, albeit that our collaboration was not as intense as with those mentioned first. Here, I am grateful to Francis Baert, Jakob Granit, Andrew Grant, Jim Hentz, Alberta Sbragia, Tim Shaw, Michael Schulz, Patrik Stålgren, Rodrigo Tavares, Luk van Langenhove and Joakim Öjendal.

At various points in time, drafts or parts of most chapters have been discussed at many seminars, workshops and conferences around the world. I gratefully acknowledge the participants and discussants at these meetings. Comments from two anonymous reviewers provided important stimuli and assisted me in improving an early version of the manuscript. Many thanks to Royden Yates for much help with 'language cleaning' and also with 'cleaning' my arguments. I am also deeply indebted to both Steven Kennedy and Stephen Wenham at Palgrave for their support, professionalism as well as enduring patience in the midst of delays in completing the book. A big 'thanks', as well, to the rest of the editorial team at Palgrave. Finally, my greatest thanks to Lisette, for love, encouragement, support as well as considerable patience.

Kungsbacka, May 2015
Fredrik Söderbaum

Abbreviations

ACOTA	Africa Contingency Operations Training and Assistance Program
ACP	African, Caribbean and Pacific group of countries
ADB	Asian Development Bank
AER	Assembly of European Regions
AFC	Asian Financial Crisis
AfDB	African Development Bank
AFRICOM	US Africa Command
AGOA	US Africa Growth and Opportunity Act
AL	Arab League
ALBA	Bolivarian Alliance for the Americas
ALTA	Latin American and Caribbean Air Transport Association
AMIS	AU Missions in Sudan
AMISEC	AU Missions in Comoros
AMISOM	AU Missions in Somalia
AMU	Arab Maghreb Union
APEC	Asia-Pacific Economic Cooperation
APF	Anti-Privatization Forum
APSA	African Peace and Security Architecture
APT	ASEAN Plus Three
ARF	ASEAN Regional Forum
ASEAN	Association of Southeast Asian Nations
ASEM	Asia-Europe Meeting
AU	African Union
BSC	Baltic Sea Cooperation
CACM	Central American Common Market
CAN	Andean Community of Nations
CAR	Central African Republic
CARICOM	Caribbean Community and Common Market
CARPHA	Caribbean Public Health Agency

CFA	CFA Franc Zone
CFSP	Common Foreign and Security Policy
CIS	Commonwealth of Independent States
CJEU	Court of Justice of the European Union
CLME	Caribbean Large Marine Ecosystem and Adjacent Areas
COMESA	Common Market for Eastern and Southern Africa
CoR	Committee of the Regions
CMI	Chiang Mai Initiative
CSDP	Common Security and Defence Policy
DC	development corridor
DRC	Democratic Republic of Congo
EAC	East African Community
EAEC	European Atomic Energy Community
EAFTA	East Asian Free Trade Area
EALA	East African Legislative Assembly
EASWN	East African Sustainability Watch Network
EC	European Community
ECA	United Nations Economic Commission for Africa
ECLA	United Nations Economic Commission for Latin America
ECLAC	United Nations Economic Commission for Latin America and the Caribbean
ECOSOC	United Nations Economic and Social Council
ECOVIC	East African Communities' Organization for Management of Lake Victoria Resources
ECOWAS	Economic Community of West African States
ECSC	European Coal and Steel Community
EEAS	European External Action Service
EEC	European Economic Community
EFTA	European Free Trade Association
EMU	Economic and Monetary Union
EP	European Parliament
EPA	Economic Partnership Agreement
ESCAP	UN Economic and Social Commission for Asia and the Pacific
ESCWA	UN Economic and Social Commission for Western Asia
EU	European Union

FDI	foreign direct investment
FOMUC	CEMAC Mission to the Central African Republic
FTA	free trade area
FTAA	Free Trade Area of the Americas
GATT	General Agreement on Tariffs and Trade
GCC	Gulf Cooperation Council
GDP	gross domestic product
GEF	Global Environment Facility
GLR	Great Lakes Region
HELCOM	Baltic Marine Environment Protection Commission – Helsinki Commission
HCT	British High Commission Territories
IADB	Inter-American Development Bank
IFI	international financial institution
IGAD	Intergovernmental Authority on Development
IMF	International Monetary Fund
IOC	Indian Ocean Commission
IR	international relations
ITFGPG	International Task Force on Global Public Goods
IWRM	integrated water resource management
JAES	Joint Africa–EU Strategy
LAFTA	Latin American Free Trade Association
LAIA	Latin American Integration Association
LVBC	Lake Victoria Basin Commission
LVEMP	Lake Victoria Environmental Management Project
LVFO	Lake Victoria Fisheries Organization
LVI	Lake Victoria Initiative
MDC	Maputo Development Corridor
MEP	Member of the European Parliament
Mercosur	Southern Common Market (Mercado Común del Sur)
MONGO	My Own NGO
Mozal	Mozambique Aluminium Smelter
MRC	Mekong River Commission
MRU	Mano River Union
MWENGO	Mwelekeo wa NGO/Reflection and Development Centre for NGOs in Eastern and Southern Africa

NAFTA	North American Free Trade Agreement
NAPE	National Association of Professional Environmentalists
NATO	North Atlantic Treaty Organization
NBI	Nile Basin Initiative
NGO	non-governmental organization
NORDPOOL	Nordic energy market
NRA	new regionalism approach
OAS	Organization of American States
OAU	Organization of African Unity
OECD	Organization for Economic Cooperation and Development
OSCE	Organization for Security and Cooperation in Europe
Osienala	Friends of Lake Victoria
PPP	public-private partnership
RBA	region-building approach
RBO	river basin organization
REC	Regional Economic Community
RTA	regional trading agreement
SAARC	South Asian Association for Regional Cooperation
SACCAR	Southern African Centre for Cooperation in Agricultural Research
SACU	Southern African Customs Union
SADC	Southern African Development Community
SADCC	Southern African Development Coordination Conference
SANASO	Southern African Network of Aids Service Organizations
SAPP	Southern African Power Pool
SAPSN	Southern Africa Peoples' Solidarity Network
SARS	severe acute respiratory syndrome
SARS-CoV	SARS Coronavirus
SATUCC	Southern African Trade Union Coordination Council
SDI	spatial development initiative
Sida	Swedish International Development Cooperation Agency
SIJORI	Singapore-Johor-Riau (Southern Growth Triangle)

TICAD	Tokyo International Conference on African Development
TNC	transnational corporation
TSCTI	Trans-Sahara Counter-Terrorism Initiative
UDEAC	Central African Customs and Economic Union
UEMOA	West African Economic and Monetary Union
UK	United Kingdom
UN	United Nations
UNASUR	Union of South American Nations
UNECE	United Nations Economic Commission for Europe
UNEP	United Nations Environment Programme
UNU/CRIS	United Nations University/Comparative Regional Integration Studies
US	United States of America
UNU/WIDER	United Nations University/World Institute for Development Economics Research
USD	United States Dollar
WAHO	West African Health Organization
WANEP	West African Network for Peace
WESSA	Wildlife and Environment Society of South Africa
WHO	World Health Organization
WOA	world order approach
WTO	World Trade Organization
ZAMCOM	Zambezi River Basin Commission

1

Introduction

Why Rethink Regionalism?

Since the return of regionalism in the late 1980s, there has been a global upsurge of various forms of regionalist projects. The widening and deepening of the European Union (EU) is the most prominent example, but there was a revitalization or expansion of many other regionalist projects as well, such as the African Union (AU), the Association of Southeast Asian Nations (ASEAN), the Economic Community of West African States (ECOWAS), the North American Free Trade Agreement (NAFTA), the Southern African Development Community (SADC), and the Southern Common Market (Mercosur). More or less every government in the world is engaged in regionalism, but regionalist processes also involve a rich variety of business and civil society actors, resulting in a multitude of formal as well as informal regional processes in most fields of contemporary politics.

The basic motivation for this book is that more than six decades of academic debate has failed to generate satisfactory answers to questions about the origins, logic and consequences of regionalism. Regionalism means different things to different people in different contexts and time periods and, for some observers, regionalism may not mean much at all. There are also fundamental disagreements regarding how regionalism should be studied and compared, not least over whether regionalisms in different parts of the world are unique and discrete phenomena, or part of a broader and more universal logic.

This book seeks to rethink regionalism and so transcend the deep intellectual and disciplinary rivalries that have limited our understanding about what regions are, how they evolve and consolidate, how we should compare them and what significance they have in a world in flux. Any rethinking of regionalism is closely connected to the way we study, conceptualize and theorize regions and regionalism. This book offers a comprehensive yet general approach for thinking about regions and regionalism rather than a fine-tuning or 'testing' of dependent/independent variables within a parsimonious but often reductionist theory. The ambition is not to build a grand theory of regionalism, but to deal analytically and comparatively, in a non-reductionist way, with a multidimensional phenomenon.

The rethinking of regionalism offered here is built on four interacting perspectives: regionalism viewed historically, spatially, comparatively and globally. These four interrelated ways of rethinking regionalism are rooted in reflectivist and constructivist scholarship. The argument is not by any means that rationalist and mainstream theories are wrong. Rather, this book argues that formulating alternative perspectives is both possible and relevant, not least to provide answers to fundamental questions demanding alternative and arguably more creative answers. Prevailing rationalist theories, of course, are social constructions and are based on particular ways of theorizing, language, power and culture. By implication, there are always complementary ways to understand and explain regions and regionalism. Subsequent sections of this chapter outline and motivate the four components of rethinking regionalism. Before this, a few core assumptions and concepts need to be elaborated.

One weakness in previous scholarship (especially that rooted in liberal thought) is that too often regions are considered desirable and 'good'. That regionalism can solve a variety of collective action dilemmas is indisputable, but it is equally clear that it may sometimes be exploitative, reinforce asymmetric power relations or lead to a range of detrimental outcomes. Hence different theories point in different directions and from a normative point of view it should not be assumed beforehand that regionalism is either positive or negative.

The concern of this book is with so-called 'world' or 'international' regions, which are viewed to be territorial (in contrast with non-territorial) units or subsystems larger than the 'state' but smaller than the 'global' system. Such regions come in many varieties and may group two or more countries and sometimes even whole continents, such as Africa or Europe. These world regions should be distinguished from subnational regions that exist between the 'local' and the 'national' level, such as Flanders or Quebec.

'Regionalism' represents the body of ideas, values and policies that are aimed at creating a region, or it can mean a type of world order. Regionalism in the first sense usually is associated with a regional project or regional organization. 'Regionalization' refers to the process of cooperation, integration and cohesion that creates a regional space (issue-specific or general). In the most basic sense, it may mean no more than a deepening or widening of activity, trade, peoples, ideas, or conflict at the regional level (Fawcett 2005a: 25). There is a strong tendency in this field of study to focus on state-led regionalism and regional organizations in contrast to the processes of regionalization. This is problematic since there is a need to better understand the processes by which regions are made and unmade (i.e. regionalization and region-building).

In terms of scope, this book has the ambition to be relevant to a range of policy areas in most regions of the world – even if the concrete and empirical evidence necessarily is limited. In order to strike a balance between width, depth and focus, the main empirical illustrations deal with the policy fields of trade and development, peace and security, the environment and social policy in the most widely debated regions and sub-regions of the world, such as Africa, East and Southeast Asia, Europe, North and Latin America, and to some degree also the Middle East.

Rethinking Regional History

History is the first component of rethinking regionalism. Fawcett (2015: 1) is correct in that 'work on regionalism rarely adopts a sustained historical perspective except in an introductory and incomplete way'. A common but misleading notion that regionalism is a phenomenon that 'commenced' in Europe after the First or Second World War has prevented scholars from understanding both its deep historical roots and its 'global heritage' (Acharya 2012). The short time horizon in most scholarship has exaggerated the role of formalized regional organizations at the expense of more fluid types of regionalization and region-building around the world.

Even if the common distinction between old and new regionalism has inserted some historicity into the debate, there is considerable confusion in the study of regionalism about what is 'old' and what is 'new'. The distinction between old and new regionalism has been both badly misunderstood and misused, which has reinforced existing divisions in the field.

It is plausible to distinguish between old and new regionalism in a temporal, empirical, as well as theoretical sense (Söderbaum 2004). However, there are both continuities and similarities between 'old' and 'new' regionalism, which obviates rigid temporal distinctions. Many regional projects and regional organizations were initiated in the era of old regionalism (1950s–1970s) but were then renewed or re-inaugurated during the new regionalism (late 1980s–1990s), often under a new name or with an expanded membership. Under such circumstances, it is difficult to separate the historical from the contemporary. One of the pioneers of the study of new regionalism, Björn Hettne (1999: 8), argued that instead of identifying a new era or new wave of regionalism, 'I find 'the identification of new patterns of regionalization (coexisting with older forms) more relevant'; that is, new regionalism in the empirical instead of the temporal sense. A third meaning of new regionalism is related to theory. Often the adjective 'new' is added to distinguish theoretical novelties from older frameworks, as seen in the usage of 'new political economy', 'new political science', 'new security studies' and so forth. 'New regionalism' is employed by a wide range of scholars from different theoretical traditions (Söderbaum and Shaw 2003; Shaw et al. 2011), who try to move beyond 'old' (classical and orthodox) assumptions and methodologies. It follows that contemporary scholars who continue to draw on earlier and orthodox approaches only rarely adhere to this meaning of the new regionalism. Indeed, orthodox scholars sometimes seek to distance themselves from new regionalism scholarship.

As the next chapter makes clear, ideas and theories (and to some extent even concepts) of regionalism must be related to the political context in which they develop. Indeed, at least to some extent, theories of regionalism are historically contingent. For instance, neofunctionalism was the most influential theory during the old regionalism, and its origin should be understood in the context of two 'European' world wars and scepticism about the nation-state. This is not to deny the continued relevance of neofunctionalism either in Europe or in a broader and comparative sense (Mattli 2005). Obviously, ideas and theories may diffuse through time and across regions.

Rethinking Regional Space

The second component of rethinking concerns space and scale. A territorial focus on the nation-state in mainstream thinking (i.e. methodological nationalism) has resulted in many superficial representations of spatial horizons and practices. Often, and especially in political science and economics, regions have been taken as pre-given, and in a rather reductionist sense, been reduced to states-led regional organizations and mechanisms.

The heavy focus on inter-state or supranational organizations is closely associated with rationalist and problem-solving research into what types of (pre-given) regions are the most functional, instrumental and efficient to 'rule' or 'govern'. This perspective views regions and regional frameworks as 'rational' and interest-based responses to a number of 'objective' problems, such as security, development, trade or, more generally, globalization. Integral to this reasoning is the view that regions exist 'out there', identifiable through objective material structures, regional organizations and regional actors. This book by no means claims that pre-given regions and issues of institutional design are irrelevant. The fundamental problem is that the orthodox, fixed assumptions about regions and the prevailing, 'problem-solving' and 'rationalist' focus on regional organizations, crowd out alternative questions and answers as to how and why regions are formed, their inner logic and their significance for global politics.

Rethinking regional space implies transcending the simple view of regions as 'aggregations of states' sharing some degree of interdependence (Nye 1971). It also implies rejecting the view that regions are 'containers' or locations for social processes, dominated by state actors. One benefit of avoiding 'the territorial trap of the state' is that other spaces and scales receive more recognition (Agnew 1998: 2). Insights from critical geography and sociology teach us that regions simply are not backdrops, containers or locations, nor are they autonomous and fixed constructs operating above actors (Emerson 2014). Instead, regions are deeply embedded in the social dynamic of society: 'They shape activities, ideas and decisions, which in turn shape conceptual and functional compartmentalizations of space' (Murphy 1991: 13; also see Paasi 2001). From this perspective, regions are constitutive of society itself, are viewed as social constructions and are held together by historically contingent interactions, shared beliefs and identities, norms and practices.

From such a constructivist perspective, the research puzzle is to understand and explain the process by which regions come into existence and are consolidated – so to speak, their 'becoming' – rather than describing a particular set of (problem-solving) activities and flows within a pre-given region. In other words, in the rethought perspective offered by this book, there are no 'natural' or 'given' regions. On the contrary, they are porous and made as well as unmade – intentionally or unintentionally, endogenously or exogenously – by collective human action and by shared beliefs and identity formation.

Viewing regions as socially constructed implies simultaneously that they are politically contested. And because regions are political and social constructs, devised by human (state and non-state) actors in order to protect or transform existing structures, they may fail, just like other social projects. Regions can be disrupted from within and from without, often by the same forces that built them up. Such political dimensions of regionalism draw attention to agency, which is crucial for any understanding of region-formation (Lorenz-Carl and Rempe 2013). Regionalism may emerge in order to achieve and protect crucial values, such as economic development, ecology and peace. Sometimes regionalism will help states to protect and achieve such values, whereas at other times the values are not ensured by the state. As a result, the nation-state will not necessarily be the main or only object of political allegiance (although sometimes it may be).

Furthermore, acknowledging that there are both winners and losers from regionalism and that regions can be manipulated for private gain, both by state and non-state actors, is also crucial. This implies that regionalism becomes a political struggle between various social forces over the definition of the region, how it should be organized politically, and its insertion into the global order. Alternative, transformative and counter-hegemonic visions of regionalism may emerge in response, depending on the dominant form of regionalism and who sets the agenda. In turn, this implies that nearly always there are a multitude of strategies and ideas about a particular region, which mingle, merge and clash. This book provides the tools to understand such heterogeneous processes.

Rethinking Regional Comparison

There is an urgent need to rethink how to compare regionalism. Despite a growing number of specific comparisons of selected aspects of regionalism (especially regional institutions, regional complexes and regional orders) in selected regions (principally Europe and Asia), there is only a weak intellectual debate about the fundamentals of comparative research in the field (see De Lombaerde et al. 2010; De Lombaerde and Söderbaum 2013; Börzel and Risse 2016). There are deep contestations of what to compare, how to compare, and even why to compare at all, which limit our understanding of regions and theoretical innovation as well as the generation of cumulative knowledge. One of the main problems lies in the unresolved tension between universalism and particularism, which too often has resulted in Eurocentrism and parochialism. The third element in rethinking regionalism offered in this book will transcend these two pitfalls in favour of a non-Eurocentric and non-ethnocentric approach to comparative regionalism.

Eurocentrism can be understood as one of the systematic weaknesses in the study of regionalism (Acharya 2012; Söderbaum 2013). During the 'old regionalism', regional integration theories were developed for and from the European experience and then more or less re-applied or exported around the world. Different types of Eurocentric generalizations continue to influence and shape the research field. To some extent, the widening and deepening of the EU has led to worse Eurocentrism in comparison to the old regionalism. For many scholars European integration in general, and today's EU in particular, has become a marker, a model and a paradigm from which to theorize, compare and design institutions as well as policy in most other regions of the world.

Indeed, anyone engaging with literature and policy on regional integration will detect that too often many other cases of regionalisms are compared – implicitly or explicitly – against a backdrop of European integration theory and practice. From such Eurocentric perspective, European integration is usually considered as multidimensional, sophisticated and highly institutionalized – both a descriptive and prescriptive contention – whereas regionalism/ regional integration elsewhere is seen only as atypical, weakly developed, weakly institutionalized and usually reduced to either an economic or security-related phenomenon (or an instance of 'regional cooperation') (Christiansen 2001a).

The Eurocentric bias lies in how underlying assumptions and understandings about the nature of European regionalism (which most often stem from a *particular* reading of European integration) condition perceptions about what regionalism in other parts of the world does and should look like. Indeed, heavy emphasis is placed on the economic and political trajectory of the EC/EU or on a particular definition of 'regional integration'. Several realist or intergovernmental and liberal or institutionalist approaches subscribe to this perspective, which is often dominated by a concern to explain deviations from the 'standard' European case.

There are some legitimate reasons why these Eurocentric notions developed in the past and for their continued salience. Nonetheless, it is a fundamental problem that such 'false' generalizations and dualistic models of comparison continue to plague both academic and policy discussions, with the result that few concepts and theories generated in the study of non-European regions have been able to influence the study and comparison of regionalism. Not only has this prevented the development of more universal conceptual and theoretical toolboxes, but it also has limited our understanding of European integration itself. Hence, as this book attempts to show, more theory-driven studies of regionalism in the rest of the world will have a positive impact on the study of European integration.

In this context, it also bears mentioning that the policy debate about regionalism in the developing world is plagued to a large extent by 'false universalism' and Europe-centred beliefs about what these regional organizations can and should achieve. For instance, the EC/EU's integration path (and its institutional trajectory) is considered as the most viable route for a wide range of other multipurpose regional organizations such as SADC, ECOWAS, AU, Mercosur and ASEAN. This despite the fact that there are no convincing arguments as to why other regions would (or should) follow the EC/EU's historical path (Katzenstein 2005). In policy-making circles this often leads to the rather naive conclusion that remedying the lack of success and poor implementation of regional organizations in the developing world requires the strengthening of regional organizations to make them more similar to the EC/EU's institutional structure.

If the mainstream literature on regionalism has favoured generalizations from the case of the EU, a more or less reverse tendency is apparent in the more critical scholarship on regionalism in the developing world. Many critical scholars and policy analysts have tried to reject Eurocentrism or tried to avoid it, and numerous innovative attempts to develop a regional approach specifically aimed at the developing world (or particular regions) have evolved from this work (Axline 1994a; Bach 1999a; Bøås et al. 1999). On the one hand, there are good reasons for taking stock of this research on non-European regions and for being cautious regarding the mainstream domination of EU-style institutional perspectives. On the other hand, much of this scholarship and policy tends to mirror the Eurocentric view by taking the EU as an 'anti-model' and by celebrating the differences in theory and practice of regionalism in Europe and in the developing world. This has resulted in a failure to engage European integration theory and practice, while emphasizing that regionalism can be more or less tailor-made to suit specific regional realities and contexts.

At an empirical level, many scholars in the field specialize in a particular region, which quite often is viewed as 'special', even *sui generis* (Söderbaum 2009). Too many scholars offer the mantra-like suggestion that 'my' region is distinct, special or unique and too complex for comparison. When the uniqueness of a given region is emphasized or when other cases are considered to be too different to allow comparison, regional specialization easily becomes parochial. To be fair, some of the best studies in the field of regionalism are case studies. Certainly, detailed case studies are necessary and relevant; they identify historical and contextual specificities and allow for a detailed and intensive analysis of the dynamics and logic of regions and regional organizations (according to mono-, multi-, or interdisciplinary studies). As such, case studies and regional specialization may not necessarily constitute a scientific 'problem'. Yet, too many case studies remain atheoretical, descriptive or, in the worst cases, even parochial, which makes them less relevant for non-specialists of a given region. Despite many good exceptions, there is a strong tendency in the field for regional specialists not to contribute to comparative and general debates (Söderbaum 2009). This book adopts the stance that a more advanced debate about comparative regionalism will not be reached simply by celebrating differences between European integration and regionalism in the rest of the world, or by painting all regions as unique. The proposed way forward for a more integrated debate about regions, regionalism and regional organizations is the integration of the case of Europe within a larger discourse of comparative regionalism, built around general concepts and theories whilst still showing cultural and contextual sensitivity.

The eclectic approach offered in this book is built around the richness of comparative regionalism. Regions and regionalism come in many guises, and there are also many different forms of comparison (in time, across space as well as between different types of organization). Conceptual and methodological pluralism is not necessarily problematic: the fundamental challenge is to be clear about the research questions and what constitutes appropriate case selection, all the while maintaining conceptual clarity and sharpness. The eclectic perspective outlined here charges that it is possible to compare both the comprehensive and multidimensional regions at various scales (such as regions or subregions in Africa, Asia, Americas, Europe, and so forth) and the more distinct types of regions and regionalism (such as trade blocs, security regions, cognitive regions, river basins). As an example, the EU as an object of research can be studied in different ways and its comparability, or not, depends on the issue studied. As all other aspects of the social realm, a case such as the EU has simultaneously both specific features and general characteristics that it shares with other regions and regional political communities. It may also be relevant to compare the EU with federations such as the US or Germany, or even other nation-states around the world.

Rethinking Regions in Global Perspective

Since regions are not formed in a vacuum, the region in itself cannot be the only unit of theory-building. Rethinking regions in global transformation denotes approaching regions from a 'global' perspective. Somehow, a more 'global' approach to the study of regionalism needs to be built. Much effort is being made to do so, but what is lacking still from most approaches is a global perspective that also takes into account regional particularities and contexts.

In the 1950s and 1960s, most classical regional integration theorists (especially the functionalists and neofunctionalists) concentrated mainly on the endogenous processes of region-formation and paid little attention to the external and 'global' environment. Contemporary regionalism from the mid-1980s onwards largely emerged in response to exogenous forces, not the least of which was globalization. There were many studies of regionalism and globalization (between the 1990s and the 2000s) and regionalism and global governance (from the 2000s) but still there remains a deficit of knowledge regarding how regions are made and unmade by forces both external and internal, and also how regions, in fact, are shaping global transformation. This book contends that the external projection of regions and their role in global transformation is tied closely to their manner of social construction by both endogenous and exogenous forces and actors (state as well as non-state). This requires that we rethink the way we study and approach the role of regions in global perspective. In this regard, this book draws particular attention to regions in interregionalism and in global governance.

Increasing contacts between different regions are a logical outcome of increasing regionalism, and these increasingly have become important in recent decades. However, interregionalism is a still poorly understood phenomenon. Scholars and policymakers devote too much attention to institutionalized relations between two regional organizations (so-called 'pure interregionalism'). In contrast, this book 'unpacks' and problematizes the region, the driving actors and institutions that are engaged in interregional relations.

Regionalism and multilateralism are essential ingredients of global governance. At various junctures during the last century, the relationship between regionalism and multilateralism was discussed intensively. The long-standing, prevailing view is that regional institutions should be subordinated to multilateral agencies (such as WTO/GATT or UN Security Council). Yet, linear developments are the least likely outcome, as multilateralism and regionalism produce their own counterforces with mixed results in different regions. Any static dichotomy between multilateralism and regionalism needs unpacking and rethinking. A telling indicator that global governance is not a singular, universal project was the apparent revival, as well as redirection, of regional and interregional projects towards the end of the last century; clearly, alternative reactions and directions were possible. This book underlines that regions are fundamental in this regard. The main point is that contemporary global governance has regions as an essential ingredient, albeit not always the most important one.

The Organization of the Book

Chapter 2 (Learning From History) traces the origins and evolution of regionalism as an object and as a field of study. Progress in the study of regionalism requires a better understanding of the intellectual roots of the field; it also requires that academics acknowledge the fact that there are many types of regions in many different historical contexts, thus rejecting firmly the simple notion that regionalism 'started' in Europe after the end of the Second World War. The chapter describes the historical evolution of the field, identifying four main phases: early regionalism, old regionalism (in both Europe and the developing world), new regionalism, and the current phase of regionalism, referred to as comparative regionalism.

Chapter 3 (Learning From Theory) provides an overview of the most important schools of thought in the field in terms of theoretical and conceptual formulations as well as empirical focus. The review highlights the richness of regionalism theory, spanning a variety of new regionalism and reflectivist approaches along with realist and intergovernmental approaches, functionalism, liberal institutionalism and neoclassical economic integration theory. The chapter pinpoints that different theorists are engaged in different kinds of knowledge production and that they also focus on different research questions, a fact that previous debates tended to overlook, and that has created unnecessary divisions in the field. The chapter concludes by identifying the theories that are most useful for rethinking regionalism along the four lines presented in this book.

Chapter 4 (The Richness of Comparative Regionalism) departs from the fact that comparison often is suggested as a useful point of departure for studying and theorizing regionalism. A fundamental disagreement about how to and what to compare is the problem here, and to a large extent this is related to contestation about European integration theory and practice, as well as the inherent tension in the field between regional specialization and theory-driven comparative research. Rethinking regionalism needs to escape Eurocentrism/anti-Eurocentrism and instead insert European integration theory into a comparative perspective, whilst still maintaining cultural sensitivity.

Chapter 5 (Obviating the Gap Between Formal and Informal Regionalism) begins by clarifying why some theories are so heavily geared towards formal regionalism, while others are much more focused on the formal-informal nexus, or even informal regionalism *per se*. The chapter then describes how the formal-informal nexus is played out in the debates about regionalism in Africa, Asia, Europe and Latin America. This examination of the regional debates illustrates how the dominant emphasis on formal regionalism can be replaced by a perspective that allows that regions are made and unmade by a combination of formal and informal actors and institutions.

Chapter 6 (Organizing Regional Space) reveals the many types of regions and above all, the many ways of organizing regional space. This analysis emphasizes the increasing heterogeneity of contemporary regionalism and the fact that a variety of state, market, civil society and external actors are involved in a series of overlapping, contradictory and sometimes competing organizations, networks and modes of governance, all of which coexist, overlap, intersect and sometimes clash.

Chapter 7 (Multidimensional Regionalism) shows that regionalism has no single cause, but rather emerged under the influence of a number of problems, 'interests', 'ideas' and 'identities', usually varying in importance in different geographical areas and in different policy fields. The chapter illustrates the multidimensionality of contemporary regionalism, in particular focusing on security regionalism, economic and development regionalism, environmental regionalism and social regionalism.

Chapter 8 (Civil Society in Regionalism) seeks to expand how we understand and study civil society actors during the making and unmaking of regions. Civil society somewhat surprisingly is often neglected in the study of regionalism, considering the emphasis it receives in the study of 'national' and 'global' politics. Drawing upon Africa as a 'least-likely case', the chapter argues that regionalization of civil society in Africa is quite vibrant and comes in many different forms. In addition, the chapter reveals that regional civil society contains several internal paradoxes and conflicts, resulting in a variety of complex links between civil society actors and political regimes as well as external powers and donor agencies.

Chapter 9 (External Actors in Regionalism) focuses on the roles of external actors in the making and unmaking of regions. External actors usually interact strongly with state and non-state actors in a range of policy areas and have varied impacts on region-building, both positive and negative. This chapter also draws heavily on the case of Africa, exploring the ways whereby external actors engage in the making and unmaking of regions in the fields of regional market-building, transboundary waters and security regionalism.

Chapter 10 (Regionness: The Solidification of Regions) offers an analytical tool to better grasp the ways by which the many varieties of regionalism and regional agencies consolidate and converge within a particular region. Regionness is designed to capture the fact that when multidimensional regionalism has been set in motion, it appears that different logics begin to develop, resulting in a consolidation and solidification of the region – ranging from regional space, regional complex, regional society, regional community to regional institutionalized polity. Regionness is not intended as a parsimonious theory. It should be understood as a heuristic and conceptual tool for improving our thinking about the ways whereby multidimensional regions are made and unmade by different agents and institutions and processes. Increasing regionness describes the transformation of any region from object to subject, with a certain actor capacity in its external relations. The external dimension is linked to the fourth component of rethinking regionalism.

Chapter 11 (Regions in Interregionalism) shows that as regions consolidate internally, they have increased impact externally. A logical outcome of increasing regionalism is increased inter-regional (region-to-region) relations, which increasingly have become important in recent decades. Nevertheless, most observers misunderstand the logic of interregionalism as well as its significance for global politics. Much of the problem arises because interregionalism is analyzed through the prism of narrow and particular understandings of state-led regional organizations and their secretariats. In contrast, keeping with the approach of this book, the chapter 'unpacks' and problematizes the region, the driving actors and institutions that all are engaged in a multitude of interregional relations: for example Heads of State, Ministerial Councils, Regional Secretariats, Regional Parliaments, Regional Courts of Justice, individual member states as well as a range of economic and social actors. The result is a patchwork of interregional and transregional relations, tied to bilateral, regional and multilateral practices and processes.

Chapter 12 (Regions in Global Governance) deals with the role of regions in global governance through a comparative assessment of the policy fields of security, trade, health and the environment. From a global perspective, there still is a striking 'governance gap', which has to do with the transformation of the Westphalian nation-state and the move in many policy fields and parts of the world from government to governance. Key here is not whether Westphalian bilateralism, regionalism or multilateralism will dominate, but rather an understanding of the essential role of regional governance as one crucial element in the reorganization of multi-layered global governance.

Chapter 13 (Conclusion) presents the main theoretical, methodological, and empirical conclusions of this book. It emphasizes that the four elements of rethinking outlined in this book will help us to a better and more comprehensive understanding of regions and regionalism in today's global politics. By implication there is a need for 'global social theory' that takes regional peculiarities into consideration, since regions cannot be understood merely from the point of view of the single region in question. Global social theory means a comprehensive social science that abandons state-centrism and methodological nationalism in an ontologically fundamental sense, yet one that goes beyond the mystifications of the concept of globalization and global governance. The emerging 'multiplex' world order simultaneously involves a range of actors, institutions and processes interacting at a variety of interconnected levels (global, regional, national and local levels) (Acharya 2014). Even if it is not possible to identify which scale is dominant, because actors and processes at various levels interact and their relative importance changes in time and space, this book makes it clear that regions and regionalism have moved into centre place in international theory.

2
Learning from History

This chapter traces the origins, meanings and evolution of regions as objects and as a field of study. Even with wide use of the distinction between old and new regionalism, history has received muted attention in the general debate. Most scholars claim that regionalism is a post–Second World War phenomenon, which is to ignore the many varieties of regions and regionalisms apparent in different historical periods. A historical perspective implies that regions need to be closely related to the changing historical and political contexts, especially those concerning political organization and world order and, consequently, that new forms of regions may occur in different times. However, throughout history there have also been important continuities between various types of regionalism. It is therefore plausible to distinguish between the intellectual history of regionalism and the 'real world' history of regionalism. This chapter distinguishes between four phases in the historical development of the field: early regionalism, old regionalism, new regionalism and comparative regionalism, which is the most recent phase.

Early Regionalism

Translocal economic, political, social and cultural integration has taken place in many different historical contexts. Premodern exchange systems were often based on symbolic kinship bonds and also contained an important element of diplomacy and the creation of trust between 'isolated' communities. In many premodern communities, outside relations were dispersed, first and foremost through trade and migrations, and did not always have a very strong impact on everyday life and political community. Often geographical and environmental obstacles prevented more organized political interaction with the external world. In order to further regionalize, the potential region ('proto-region') must, necessarily, experience increasing interaction and more frequent contact between human communities. Migratory patterns were particularly important for the creation of new ethnicities, social and cultural structures and spaces, as well as more bureaucratic and organized political entities, compared to the smaller chiefdoms that previously coexisted.

The construction of assorted regions can be traced far back in history, as seen in a rich variety of geographically confined empires, kingdoms, alliances, trade leagues, pacts, unions, and confederations between a range of political units.

Perhaps the most explicit historical trajectories can be identified in Europe, where observers refer to centuries of shared history and political thought, dating back to ancient Greece. The many and diverse 'early' visions and projects for European cooperation and unity were made up of divergent views about the importance of culture and identity, security, political economy, and law. Some ideas about European unity were inward-looking and concerned with intra-European aspects, while others were outward-looking and usually concerned with protecting Europe from the outside world. In contrast to most subsequent theories of the old regionalism phase, these early ideas seldom perceived a competition between the unification of Europe and the strengthening of the nation-state. Jönsson, Tägil and Törnqvist underline the pluralism of perspectives in European region-building:

Hundreds of plans for the peaceful unification of Europe have been presented throughout history. In the sixteenth century, humanists of various nationalities demanded that the European rulers unite, primarily as a response to the then-imminent Turkish threat. In the late seventeenth century, an outline was drawn for a European league of nations. Some hundred years later, the German philosopher Immanuel Kant argued that a lasting peace in Europe required a federation of states based on the principle of international law. In the revolutionary year 1848, the idea of a united Europe gained a broader following. French writer Victor Hugo advocated for the creation of a United States of Europe based on political democracy and respect for the rights of man. The outbreak of a world war in 1914 shattered any such hopes, however. Between the First and the Second World Wars, new plans were drafted for integrating Europe. (Jönsson et al. 2000: 22–3)

There are thus deep roots behind the many plans for European unity and integration that after the end of the Second World War led to the formation of the European Community (EC). At least in the comparative and theoretical discussions, these historical trajectories are often overlooked.

In the last few centuries, most of the European nation-states, especially the powerful ones, were also colonial powers. Colonialism influenced and shaped ideas about region-building and regionalism both in Europe and in the periphery, and these trajectories continue to influence more recent regionalist ideas and projects, not only in the post-colonial world but also in contemporary Europe. European colonial empires were sometimes organized regionally, but anti-colonial struggles also took a regional form.

Africa is a case in point. The 'scramble for Africa' and the attempt to gain control over its mineral resources had strong regional implications, which has continued to influence the theory as well as the practice of African regionalism. Indeed, it is in the colonial quest for mineral exploitation that we find the link between state-building and the temporal 'beginning' of regions in Africa, such as Southern Africa (Niemann 2001: 69). For instance, the Southern African Customs Union (SACU) is the world's oldest, still-functional custom union currently, originating in the Customs Union Convention of 1889 between the British Colony of the Cape of Good Hope and the Orange Free State Boer Republic. Upon the creation of the Union of South Africa in 1910, the agreement was revised and extended to the British High Commission Territories (HCTs) in current Botswana, Lesotho, Namibia, and Swaziland. Even well into the 1990s, Southern African politics was dominated by the struggle between a colonial/apartheid bloc, on the one hand, and anti-colonial/anti-apartheid bloc, on the other hand. The anti-colonial/anti-apartheid bloc gradually strengthened from the 1980s onwards, and gained further strength through what was then the Organization for African Unity (OAU) and the Southern African Development Coordination Conference (SADCC); a legacy that continues to affect the self-image and practice of their predecessors, the African Union (AU) and the Southern African Development Community (SADC; see Söderbaum 2004).

Colonialism shaped the formation of regions in other parts of Africa as well. The 'special' relationship between France and the francophone African colonies/countries, has worked both ways and it has impacted on ideas and practices of regionalism in francophone Africa. On the one hand, the relationship sustained French imperial dreams, and on the other, the former colonies have used their francophone legacy to foster francophone regionalism among themselves, sometimes as a counterweight against the hegemonic aspirations of Nigeria. The CFA Franc Zone (CFA) dates back to 1945 but still impacts on regionalization in contemporary Africa. Other economic integration arrangements still functioning in francophone Africa, such as the West African Economic and Monetary Union (UEMOA) and the Central African Customs and Economic Union (UDEAC) also have imperial and colonial origins.

Latin America provides another example of the deep roots and trajectories of regionalism (Fawcett 2005b). The struggle for independence in Latin America in the early nineteenth century evoked a sense of unity, leading up to pan-Americanism and then also inspiring regionalism throughout the twentieth and twenty-first centuries. Simon Bolívar (1783–1830) played a key role in Latin America's struggle for independence from the Spanish Empire, as well as in the efforts to create a league of American republics, with a common military, a mutual defence pact, and a supranational parliamentary assembly. Bolívar's vision outlined at the Congress of Panama in 1826 never succeeded, particularly due to the growing strength of Latin American military nationalism and national rivalry during much of the nineteenth century. In 1889–90, regional cooperation in the Americas returned to the forefront at the First International Conference of American States held in Washington, DC when 18 nations decided to form the International Union of American Republics (later to become the Pan-American Union), and meet periodically. There is a direct link between these Pan-American Conferences and today's Organization of American States (OAS), which is the oldest still functional regional organization in the world. Hence, regionalism in Latin America has deep roots and many visionaries; politicians and intellectuals in Latin America throughout the post-independence period have considered regionalism a source of strength (Fawcett 2012).

Other pan-continental/regional movements – such as pan-Europeanism, pan-Africanism, pan-Asianisms, and pan-Arabism – also emerged in the late nineteenth and early twentieth centuries (Fawcett 2015). These pan-regional movements were usually motivated by a mixture of geopolitical, socio-economic, cultural (sometimes even racial) and, to some extent, functional beliefs and goals. They were multidimensional and reflected shared ideas and goals of political and intersocietal unity rather than intergovernmental regionalism in a more narrow sense (Acharya 2012: 5). The pan-regionalist movements took somewhat different shapes in different regions, depending on the historical context that included the character of colonialism and external domination, but all of them 'offer vital insights into regionalism's trajectory past and present' (Fawcett 2015: 13).

Old Regionalism

Voluntary and comprehensive regionalism for many scholars is predominantly a post-Second World War phenomenon. It emerged in Western Europe in the late 1940s, subsequently spreading to the developing world. Old regionalism lost much of its dynamism in Europe in the early 1970s and, gradually, also in the developing world. As will become evident below, it is relevant to try separating the European-centred debate from the debate in the developing world.

Regional Integration in Europe and Beyond

The debate about old regionalism in Europe has to be contextualized in relation to the devastating experience of inter-war nationalism and the Second World War. Both policy makers and scholars usually viewed the (Westphalian) nation-state as the problem rather than the solution, and the purpose of 'regional integration' was to avoid war. A series of initiatives were launched, which in 1951 resulted in the European Coal and Steel Community (ECSC). The long-term goal, however, was more ambitious, and the Treaty of Rome in 1958 integrated the European Economic Community (EEC) and the European Atomic Energy Community (EAEC) into the EC.

The most influential theories in the European context were federalism, functionalism, neofunctionalism, transactionalism and intergovernmentalism (Rosamond 2000). Federalism had in many ways inspired the pioneers of European integration, but was less a theory than a political programme; it was sceptical of the nation-state even though its project was in fact to create a new kind of 'state'. Altiero Spinelli and Ernesto Rossi, both Italian anti-fascist communists, drafted the 'Ventotene Manifesto', which later led to the European Federalist Movement. Spinelli continued to be one of the figures of European federalism until his death in 1986, but even so there was no obvious theorist associated with federalism.

Functionalism was primarily a strategy (or a normative method) to build peace, constructed around the proposition that the provision of common needs and functions can unite people across state borders. This school of thought was strongly associated with the works of David Mitrany (1943). In the functionalist view, form was supposed to follow function, whereas for the federalists it was primarily form that mattered (especially a constitution). Ideally, the nation-state would be bypassed, and international cooperation was preferred to regional cooperation. Mitrany criticized both federalism and neofunctionalism on the basis that both were primarily based on territory and form rather than function.

Neofunctionalism enjoyed an enormous reputation during the 1960s. Ernst Haas was the central figure, and he was accompanied by a number of leading or soon-to-be leading political scientists of the time, such as Leon Lindberg, Philippe Schmitter and Joseph Nye, all who contributed a vast number of articles in leading academic journals, especially *International Organization* and the *Journal of Common Market Studies*. Neofunctionalists challenged the functionalists and claimed a greater concern for the centres of power (Haas 1958, 1964). Haas in fact theorized the 'community method' pioneered by Jean Monnet (a French diplomat and considered as one of the chief architects of the EC). Even if the outcome of this method could be a federation, it was not to be constructed through constitutional design.

Much of the debate about the old regionalism in Europe centred around the concept of regional integration. Haas (1958: 16) defined this concept as 'the process whereby political actors in several distinct national settings are persuaded to shift their loyalties, expectations and political activities toward a new centre, whose institutions possess or demand jurisdictions over the pre-existing national states'. Neofunctionalists emphasized the deliberate design of regional institutions, which were seen as the most effective means for solving common problems in strategic economic sectors. These institutions and supranational authorities were to be initiated by states, but then the regional bureaucrats and self-organized interest groups would become important actors in the process, ultimately leading to a redefinition of group identity 'beyond the nation-state' (Hurrell 1995: 59; cf. Haas 1964).

In the late 1960s and early 1970s, the neofunctional description (and prescription) became increasingly remote from the empirical world then dominated by Charles de Gaulle's nationalism. Stanley Hoffman (1966) became the key figure of the intergovernmental approach to regional integration. In contrast to neofunctionalists, Hoffman explained that regional integration would not spread from low politics (economics) to the sphere of high politics (security). Regional integration happened only as long as it coincided with the national interest and 'by taking along the nation with its baggage of memories and problems' (Hoffman 1966: 867). Consequently, the image of the EC began to change.

Karl Deutsch's work on security communities also needs to be mentioned in any discussion about regional integration. Just like Ernst Haas, Karl Deutsch was one of the most highly acclaimed political scientists of his time. Deutsch's main hypothesis was that a sense of community and trust were directly related to the level of transaction and communication between peoples and states (Deutsch et al. 1957). In this sense there was no fundamental difference between a national and a regional community, and Deutsch therefore was somewhat less sceptical of nationalism and the nation-state compared to many other regional integration scholars during the old regionalism period. Although the debates about security and regional integration often referred to Deutsch's approach, it was not at the centre of empirical research.

In the late 1960s and the early 1970s, intellectual controversies were first and foremost conceptual and ontological rather than epistemological. Nye (1968) referred to a fundamental conceptual confusion, whereas Puchala famously used the fable of the elephant and the blind men, complaining that '[m]ore than fifteen years of defining, redefining, refining, modelling and theorizing have failed to generate satisfactory conceptualizations of exactly what it is we are talking about when we refer to "international integration" and exactly what it is we are trying to learn when we study this phenomenon' (Puchala 1971: 267). The conceptual discussions sometimes were framed in terms of finding the 'best' definition for a given phenomenon, especially the dependent variable 'regional integration'. For Caporaso (1971: 228), this lack of agreement on definitions indicated that studies on regional integration were still in the 'pre-paradigm stage' of the development of science. Haas (1970) responded to his critics by labelling the study of regional integration 'pre-theory' because it relied on teleological assumptions of progress and that there was no clear idea about dependent and independent variables. A few years later, Haas referred to the field in terms of 'obsolescence', and concluded that the study of regional integration should cease to be a subject in its own right (Haas 1976). As a result, the study of regional integration was deserted in favour of wider and non-territorial logics and patterns of integration and interdependence.

Many controversies would have been avoided if scholars had appreciated that they were not, to paraphrase Puchala, dealing with the same 'part' of the elephant, or not even with 'the' elephant at all. Some scholars were focused on regional sub-systems, regions or regional cooperation rather than international and regional integration (Thompson 1973: 95). For instance, Binder (1958) used the term 'subordinate international system' to capture the position of the Middle East in the global system. Inspired by the systems approach in the 1960s and 1970s, a series of other scholars tried to develop a more comprehensive framework for comparative analysis, which focused on regions and regional sub-systems. Cantori and Spiegel (1970: 6–7) identified the following characteristics of a region: geographic proximity, common bonds (historical, social, cultural, ethnic and linguistic), a sense of identity, and international interactions (also see Russett 1967). However, neofunctionalists such as Haas (1970: 612) criticized the regional systems approach as merely descriptive and stressed that the concerns of the 'regional integration' scholars were different from those of the regional systems scholars.

The early debate always was centred on Europe (arguably less so for the regional sub-systems approach). Clearly, neofunctionalists, such as Haas and Nye, were conscious of the ambiguous and complex character of the EC and the problem of comparability of the regional integration experiences in other regions. However, they never rejected comparison, which later many scholars of European integration did (see Chapter 4, The Richness of Comparative Regionalism). The problem with neofunctionalist theorizing is that the narrow focus on 'regional integration' was less relevant in the developing world.

Old Regionalism in the Developing World: Development and Nation-Building

There was also an 'old' debate in the developing world, especially in Latin America and Africa, and to some extent in Asia and some other developing regions. This debate was certainly influenced by European integration theory and practice, but rather than regional integration and avoidance of war, the keywords in the developing world were regional cooperation, economic development, and nation-building.

Many of the discussions about regionalism in the developing world, especially in Latin America, were heavily influenced by the structuralist tradition of economic development, pioneered by Gunnar Myrdal, Arthur Lewis, and Raul Prebisch. In the case of Latin America, the structuralist discussion about underdevelopment that took place reflected the specific economic experiences of various countries, particularly terms of trade problems. The economic depression of the 1930s also had severe impact on Latin American development, creating pressure for change. Encouraged by the United Nations Economic Commission for Latin America (ECLA) and its dynamic Executive Secretary, Raul Prebisch, the vision was to create an enlarged economic space in Latin America built on regional rather than international imports. Liberalized intra-regional trade in combination with regional protectionism seemed to offer large economies of scale and wider markets, which could serve as stimulus to industrialization, economic growth and investment (Prebisch 1959).

From this perspective, the rationale of regional cooperation and integration among less developed countries was not found in functional cooperation or marginal economic change within the existing structure as stipulated by neoclassical economics and customs union theory. Instead, it lay in the fostering of 'structural transformation' and the creation of productive capacities (especially industrialization). This school thus shifted focus away from neoclassical trade theory and the European concern with avoidance of war by economic integration towards an approach whereby regional economic cooperation/integration was considered a means for economic development and state-formation. In contrast to the functionalist logic, this required a deliberately political approach to regionalism. Indeed, weak regional political efforts would only result in regional disintegration (Axline 1977). Axline later clarified that the dependent variable as well as the underlying conditions for regionalism were so different that it called for a different theory, according to which Europe and the developing world were not comparable cases (Axline 1994a: 180).

Structuralist ideas about regionalism resulted in the creation of the Latin American Free Trade Association (LAFTA) in Montevideo in 1960. LAFTA was a comprehensive and continental trade project, and included all countries on the South American continent plus Mexico. Despite some early progress and the lively theoretical discussion, the old regionalist projects in Latin America were never implemented on a larger scale and made little economic impact. This limited track-record was due to internal conflicts, a general failure among states to cooperate, and the whole structure of dependence. The member countries of the various partly overlapping regional schemes were politically and/or economically unstable and not willing to or capable of pursuing viable regional cooperation. Furthermore, the smaller member countries claimed that LAFTA benefited mainly the 'Big Three' of Mexico, Argentina and Brazil, and so opted for a more radical and ambitious strategy that focussed on a jointly planned industrialization strategy. This was the basic foundation for the establishment of the Andean Pact in 1969. However, just like in the case of LAFTA, the high ambitions were never achieved. During the 1970s, military dictatorships were established throughout the continent and these regimes proved to be poor partners in regional cooperation schemes. Indeed, the return to democracy in the mid-1980s provided a big boost for the new Latin American regionalism.

In Africa, debates about regionalism must be situated in the post-colonial context of the continent, even if they were also loosely influenced both by the intellectual debates in Latin America as well as by European integration theory and practice. The general ideological foundation of regional cooperation and integration in Africa was first and foremost formulated in the visions and series of treaties developed within what was then the Organization of African Unity (OAU), now the African

Union (AU). In the past, pan-African visions stressed collective self-reliance and introverted and mercantilist strategies based on protectionism as well as planned and import-substitution industrialization in a similar manner to regionalism in Latin America – what Mittelman (2000: 112) refers to as 'autocentric regionalism' (territorially based autarchies).

Following the moves to independence of African states in the 1960s, a large number of varied states-led regional frameworks and organizations were created. As noted in the section on early regionalism, some of these projects had colonial origins, whereas other regional organizations were explicitly designed in order to work against dependence, colonialism and apartheid. Even if the relevance and efficacy of the OAU has been widely discussed, it cannot be denied that the organization was important for coordinating a common African stand against colonialism and apartheid.

The Southern African Development Coordination Conference (SADCC) (the predecessor of today's SADC) was created in 1980 in order to work against apartheid and external dependence. The SADCC approach was loosely influenced by the Latin American tradition and on paper, it favoured a dirigist strategy of import-substitution industrialization coupled with an equitable distribution of costs and benefits. In practice however, SADCC was limited to being a structure for project coordination and implementation, funded mainly by donors from Europe and the Nordics in particular. One of the fundamental problems with the radical and structuralist approach was that it became politically irrelevant due to the increasing importance of structural adjustment and neoliberalism throughout the 1980s.

As far as Asia is concerned, the meaning of regionalism changed in relation to the question of what sub-regions to include and exclude, what dimensions of regionalism to investigate (such as security, economics, politics and culture), and which particular theoretical perspectives to employ. A considerable body of literature was concerned with the study of ASEAN, which was established in 1967. A major reason for this emphasis appears to be that ASEAN was one of the few sustainable regional organizations in the larger East/Southeast Asian region. ASEAN was understood as a joint attempt by a rather narrow but strong political elite to consolidate the nation-states and to enhance stability in recent but shaky state formations. Hence, as with most other regional debates in the then developing world, the primary aims were state-building and nation-building. Even if the treaties did not mention security explicitly, communism was the primary threat, irrespective of whether it was internal or external. In the 1960s, 1970s and 1980s, there were many 'politically steered' policy declarations and attempts to create joint industrial ventures and to achieve preferential trading schemes. For the most part, the development impact of these attempts was low, and during this time the economic development in Southeast Asia can hardly be attributed to the policies of ASEAN as a regional organization. Subsequently, ASEAN has consolidated and to some extent, even flourished as a regional organization, a fact analyzed during the new regionalism.

New Regionalism

Scholars of new regionalism referred to a number of novel trends and developments, such as the rise of a more multidimensional and pluralistic type of regionalism, which was not centred primarily around protectionist trading schemes or security cooperation. These new types of regionalism also had a more varied institutional design and business and civil society actors played a more active role (de Melo and Panagariya 1995; Mansfield and Milner 1997; Schulz et al. 2001). In contrast to the time of Haas, Nye, Deutsch, and the early regional integration scholars, it was evident that there were many regionalisms and many regional agencies.

Most scholars trying to understand the new wave of regionalism emerging from the mid-1980s and picking up speed in the early 1990s realized that the phenomenon needed to be related to the multitude of often inter-related changes of the global system, such as the end of bipolarity, the intensification of (economic) globalization, the recurrent fears over the stability of the multilateral trading order, the restructuring of the nation-state, and to the critique in the developing countries as well as in the post-communist countries of neoliberal economic development and political system.

The increasing multidimensionality of regionalism resulted in an expanded research agenda and a proliferation of theories and perspectives, such as varieties of neorealist and neoliberal institutional theories, new trade theories and new institutionalist theories, multilevel governance approaches, a variety of constructivist and discursive approaches, security complex theory, and assorted critical and new regionalism approaches (Mansfield and Milner 1997; Laursen 2003; Söderbaum and Shaw 2003; Wiener and Diez 2003). This richness of theorizing, both in Europe as well as in the rest of the world, can be seen as intellectual progress. Yet, there also was a significant degree of confusion and rivalry between different theoretical standpoints and regional and thematic specializations.

Clearly, during this period the study of regionalism was dominated by a variety of rationalist theories (assorted types of realist, liberal and liberal institutionalist and liberal intergovernmentalist approaches; see Moravcsik 1993; Mansfield and Milner 1997; Mattli 1999; Laursen 2003). In fact, this is one way to define what is 'mainstream' in the study of regionalism and, from this point of view, the difference between old and new regionalism is less clear. Furthermore, even if rationalists disagreed about power versus the independent effects of institutions, the various rationalist approaches moved closer together during the 1990s than was the case during the old regionalism. Not only do rationalists agree broadly on a common epistemology and a set of core ontological assumptions, they also share a similar research agenda, which is focused on the origins, shape and consequences of assorted regional organizations and arrangements. This agenda circled around questions such as: Why do states choose to enter regional arrangements? Why has integration proceeded more rapidly in some policy domains than it has in others? What institutional forms are most effective? When and why the arrangements deepened, and with what effects on trade, finance, development, security and so on?

Another main characteristic of the field since the 1990s has been the emergence of a multitude of constructivist and reflectivist approaches to regionalism that challenged core rationalist assumptions, such as the separation of subject and object, fact and value, the state-centred ontology of most rationalist approaches as well as the role of norms and identities in the formation of informal and formal regions. Some constructivists first and foremost are engaged in a debate with the rationalists and mainstream discourses (see Katzenstein 1996; Adler 1997a; Acharya 2004), whereas others are engaged with more radical and critical approaches. In the former case, it can be somewhat difficult to draw a line between constructivism and reflectivism (Neumann 1994; Hettne and Söderbaum 2000; Paasi 2001; Söderbaum 2004).

Reflectivist approaches had a particular concern for structural transformation as well as for whom, and for what purpose, regionalism is put into practice. Many critical scholars in the 1990s investigated whether the new regionalism represented the 'return of the political' in the context of economic globalization. Some were sceptical and argued that regionalism primarily was a manifestation of economic globalization and prevailing forms of hegemony (Gamble and Payne 1996a) whereas many others were more optimistic about the effects of regionalism (Hettne et al. 1999).

One major point of contestation during the new regionalism concerned the relative importance of regionalism as a states-led project as opposed to regionalization resulting from 'the growth of societal integration within a region and the often undirected processes of social and economic interaction' (Hurrell 1995: 39). Most scholars clearly emphasized the importance of states-led and formal regionalism, but new regionalism/regionalisms approaches in particular also underlined the importance of non-state actors. As pointed out by Bøås et al. (2003: 201), 'regionalism is clearly a political project, but it is obviously not necessarily state-led, as states are not the only political actor around [...] we clearly believe that, within each regional project (official or not), several competing regionalizing actors with different regional visions and ideas coexist' (see also Schulz et al. 2001; Söderbaum 2004).

Most but not all, rationalist scholars focus on pre-given regional delimitations and regional organizations. Reflectivists and constructivists in contrast, are concerned more with how regions are constituted and constructed (Murphy 1991; Neumann 1994; Hettne and Söderbaum 2000). The new regionalism approach (NRA) is quite influential, claiming that there are no 'natural' regions, but these are made, remade and unmade – intentionally or non-intentionally – in the process of global transformation, by collective human action and identity formation (Söderbaum 2004). Since regions are social constructions, none are 'given', and there are no given regionalist interests either, but instead the interests and identities are shaped in the process of interaction and inter-subjective understanding. Compared to the mainstream and rationalist research agenda, this type of theorizing leads to different answers and methodologies regarding why and how regions are formed and consolidated, by whom and for what purpose.

A final distinction is between structural and macro-oriented approaches compared to the agency- and micro-oriented ones. To some extent, this distinction obviates or at least cuts across the rationalist-reflectivist divide. Some scholars are concerned particularly with historical structures and the construction of world orders, while other analysts are interested more in the particularities of agencies and lived social spaces. How to balance structure and agency (macro versus micro; outside-in versus inside-out), has no need for dogmatism, because to a large extent it is closely related to differences in metatheoretical position as well as the nature of the research question. For instance, structural analysis may be more plausible when the research focus is put on the role of regions in world order transformation, whereas, a stronger emphasis on agency is necessary for a better explanation of agencies and micro-processes on the ground. Here it is important to recognize that different assumptions may be made to illuminate different aspects of regional politics and often, different perspectives and their concomitant narratives tend to be complementary rather than mutually exclusive (Neumann 2003).

Conclusion: Towards Comparative Regionalism

One of the main advantages of a long time perspective is the revelation of intellectual richness; but it also makes it possible to trace the various ways in which earlier ideas about regions and region-building (sometimes) influenced more recent ideas and projects. The fact that others early on elaborated many important ideas and theories of regionalism has been ignored for too long by too many.

The inclusion of the section on early regionalism serves to draw attention to the deep roots of and diverse trajectories of regionalism preceding the era of old regionalism. Among other things, early regionalism underlines the interaction rather than the competition between regionalist and statist ideas, and at least in some respects this resembles more recent debates about multilayered global governance. Early regionalism also draws attention to the various pan-regionalist movements that then developed, usually consisting of a mixture of geopolitical, cultural and functional beliefs. Some of these pan-regionalist ideas continue to influence contemporary regionalist projects, especially in Africa, Europe, Latin America and the Middle East, and to some extent in Asia.

Apart from early regionalism, this chapter identifies three subsequent phases in the scholarly development of the field: old regionalism, new regionalism, and comparative regionalism, which is the current phase. This final section defines the meaning of comparative regionalism by contrasting it to old and new regionalism.

As stated by Hettne (2005), after 2 to 3 decades it is time to move 'beyond the new regionalism'. The fact that something had happened with the nature and study of regionalism since the turn of the millennium or shortly after, is seen in a diverse set of new concepts and labels, such as 'post-hegemonic regionalism' (Riggirozzi and Tussie 2012; Telò 2014), 'post-neoliberal regionalism' (Riggirozzi 2012), 'heterodox regionalism' (Vivares 2013), 'porous regional orders' (Katzenstein 2005), 'regional worlds' (Acharya 2012, 2014), 'converging regions' (Lenze and Schriwer 2014), and 'networking regions' (Baldersheim et al. 2011). These and similar concepts and labels are all signs of the increasing diversity and complexity of regionalism. Even if the new regionalism did emphasize multidimensionality, there are many new ideas about the changing nature of regionalism here that takes us 'beyond' it.

Understanding the changing context of regionalism is one relevant strategy to try and understand the changing character of current regionalism. In contrast to the context of new regionalism, which was dominated by the fall of the Berlin Wall, neoliberalism and economic globalization, current regionalism is shaped by a global order characterized by many diverse and sometimes contradictory trends and processes, such as the War on Terror, the responsibility to intervene and protect, changing understandings of government and governance, a multi-layered or 'multiplex' global order, the rise of the BRICS and emerging powers, recurrent financial crises, and the persistent pattern of overlapping and criss-crossing regional and interregional projects and processes in most parts of the world (Shaw et al. 2011; Acharya 2014; Fioramonti 2012).

Another observation is that in the 1980s and 1990s, both the prevalence and the relevance of regionalism could be questioned.

By contrast, in the new millennium it is difficult to dispute that regionalism now is a structural component of today's global politics. Some of the most influential observers even claim that today's world order is a regional world order. Katzenstein (2005: i), for instance, rejects the 'purportedly stubborn persistence of the nation-state or the inevitable march of globalization', arguing instead that we are approaching a 'world of regions'. Similarly, Acharya emphasizes the 'emerging regional architecture of world politics' (Acharya 2007) and the construction of 'regional worlds' (Acharya 2014). Buzan and Wæver (2003: 20) speak about a 'global order of strong regions' (also see Van Langenhove 2011). The fundamental point is not that regionalism necessarily dominates all aspects of global politics, but rather that 'regions are now everywhere across the globe and are increasingly fundamental to the functioning of all aspects of world affairs from trade to conflict management, and can even be said to now constitute world order' (Fawn 2009: 5).

One important issue discussed throughout the history of regionalism is the relationship between national, regional and global modes of governance. Whereas many old regionalism theorists focused on (and hoped) that regional integration would shift loyalty and decision-making to regional institutions, 'beyond the nation-state', other theorists considered regionalism as a means to strengthen the nation-state and facilitate nation-building. In the next phase, new regionalism scholars focused heavily on the relationship between regionalism and globalization. Even if this issue has not disappeared, the global-regional nexus has changed meaning during the last decade. While much of the previous debate focused heavily on the relationship between globalization and regionalism *per se*, the current debate stresses the complexity of regionalism and the multifold interactions between state and non-state actors, institutions and processes at a variety of interacting levels, that range from the bilateral, to the regional, interregional and global (Shaw et al. 2011; Baert et al. 2014). By recognizing the increasing multidimensionality and multilayeredness of regionalism, contemporary scholars have been able to move beyond binary conceptualizations that dominated the debate during new regionalism, such as formal versus informal regionalism, regionalism versus regionalization and state versus non-state actors. Scholars may continue to disagree about the relative importance of state and non-state actors in specific cases, but it is no longer relevant to question the multiplicities of state and non-state agencies within a variety of modes of regional governance, regional networks and institutional forms that all interact in complex ways within a multilayered structure of global governance (Shaw et al. 2011; Fioramonti 2014). It must also be acknowledged that regionalism is expanding and becoming more important in many more policy fields compared to what was the case during the new regionalism, such as monetary and financial governance, health, gender and social policy, migration, democracy and human rights (Börzel and Risse 2016). Table 2.1 summarizes old, new and comparative regionalism in terms of context, the links between national, regional and global levels, and finally, sectors, actors, and forms of organization.

Theoretical and methodological dialogue is another emerging feature of the most recent phase in the study of regionalism. Whereas the debate about new regionalism was characterized by fragmentation and a series of paradigmatic and methodological rivalries, regionalism now is being consolidated as a field of study. During the new regionalism there often was a lack of dialogue between academic disciplines and regional specializations, as well as between theoretical traditions. Thematic fragmentation was another feature, in the sense that various forms of regionalism, such as economic, security, and environmental regionalism, only rarely were related to one another. Such fragmentation undermined further generation of cumulative knowledge as well as theoretical and methodological innovation. In contrast, today's discussion about regionalism is characterized by a changing intellectual landscape, with increased dialogue and at least to some degree, a greater acceptance of contrasting scientific standpoints and perspectives (see Warleigh-Lack et al. 2011; De Lombaerde and Söderbaum 2013; Telò 2014).

From a methodological point of view, it can be argued furthermore that the consolidation of comparative regionalism constitutes one of the core characteristics of the current phase in the study of regionalism, perhaps its most important one. According to Acharya (2012), comparative regionalism is indeed 'a field whose time has come'. Certainly, even if attention was given to comparison during the new regionalism, many studies were either parallel case studies or rather rigid quantitative studies that usually failed to take history and the regional context into consideration. We now are witnessing an increasing creativity in the

Table 2.1 Old, new and comparative regionalism

	Old regionalism	New regionalism	Comparative regionalism
World order context	• Post–World War II and Cold War context (in Europe) • Bipolarity but also post-colonialism provided context for the developing world	• Post–Cold War context • Globalization and neoliberalism • Unstable multilateralism (e.g. trade, security) • Transformation of the nation-state	• Multipolar and 'multiplex' world order • War on terror • Financial crises • Rise of BRICS and emerging powers
Links between national, regional and global governance	• Regional integration 'beyond the nation-state' (in Europe) and advancing development and nation-building (in the developing world)	• Regionalism seen as resisting, taming or advancing economic globalization	• Regional governance part of multilayered global governance
Sectors, actors & forms of organization	• Sector specific (e.g. trade and security) • Formal and states-led regionalism through regional organizations	• Multisectoral or specialized • State vs. non-state actors • Regionalism vs. regionalization • Formal vs. informal	• State and non-state actors grouped in formal and informal forms of organization in growing number of sectors

way regions are compared across time and space. The increasing cross-fertilization and interaction between students of European integration and regionalism elsewhere is particularly important, not least because this promises to lead to less Eurocentrism in the field. Acharya (2012: 12) is correct in that the 'global heritage' of regionalism needs to be acknowledged: 'ideas and literature that constitute comparative regionalism come from and have been enriched by contributions from many regions, including Latin America, Asia, North America, the Middle East, Africa and of course Europe'. It must also be recognized that our understanding of regions and regionalism has changed during recent decades, which is good news for comparative regionalism as well as for attempts to move away from narrow and conventional understandings of European integration. 'While the contemporary interest in comparing regions and regionalisms may not be completely new, it is different from older approaches. Our understanding of what makes regions has changed with social constructivist and critical theoretical approaches that have led to less behavioural and more nuanced, complex, contested and fluid understandings of regions' (Acharya 2012: 3). This book is a consolidated attempt to show how we can think about regions and regionalism from such a nuanced and complex perspective.

3
Learning from Theory

This chapter underlines the richness of regional theory and reviews a spectrum of partly overlapping and partly competing approaches to regionalism. A thorough theoretical discussion is motivated by the fact that any attempt to rethink regionalism rests, at least partly, on previous and competing theoretical experiences. This type of theoretical reflection takes a step backwards in order to take two forward later on. Since a single theory cannot give a sufficient picture of the multiplicity of regionalism, this book embraces several relatively distinct theories in a broad and eclectic approach (Katzenstein 2005). Clearly, some theories are divergent, with competing meta-theoretical and conceptual points of departures, different ways of producing knowledge and a concern with different research questions. This chapter presupposes that an overview of the theoretical landscape is essential to an understanding of which theoretical elements are compatible and which are not.

There are many interpretations of what constitutes 'theory' – especially 'good theory'. Some theories are strictly causal and 'objective', with a separation of 'facts' and 'theories', while others are built on different meta-theoretical foundations, being normative, constitutive, critical, post-structural or post-modern and so forth. In this regard, the distinction between 'rationalist' and 'reflectivist' approaches to international theory is relevant (Smith 1997). Rationalist theory refers to varieties of realism, liberalism and functionalism and neoclassical economic integration theory, whereas the reflectivist position refers to a more diverse group of theories and approaches, such as critical theory, post-structuralism, post-modernism and new regionalism approaches. Within this array, social constructivism is often portrayed as occupying the 'middle ground' (Adler 1997a; Christiansen et al. 1999).

Neorealist and Intergovernmentalist Approaches

Neorealism is the most influential approach in international relations (IR) as a whole and it analyses the formation of regions from the outside-in. Neorealism views states as unitary and rational egoists, and holds that structural features of the anarchical system make them predisposed towards competition and conflict. This perspective privileges the importance of states and emphasizes sovereignty and power, an emphasis that neorealism shares with the closely related intergovernmental perspective. States are believed to have their own distinctive problems and concerns and so their interests often fail to converge. Consequently, any effort to build a community 'beyond the nation-state' will be very difficult, and may even intensify the differences and conflicts between states (Cini 2003: 95).

Regions and regionalism may develop under particular circumstances and serve as a means for state survival and power maximization. For instance, the distribution of power may open up opportunities for cooperation, for geopolitical reasons, or through the politics of alliance formation, especially in order to counter the power of another state or group of states within or outside the region (Gilpin 1987; Buzan 1991). States and politicians may embody domestic policy preferences, but decisions generally result from intergovernmental bargaining among states at the regional level (Cini 2003: 103).

The neorealist emphasis on the great powers and state-centric utilitarianism has been challenged from many quarters. One criticism is that the power politics of neorealism tends to reproduce itself and reinforce the existing self-help structure as well as the dominance of great powers. Not only is the theory and its particular *problematique* a social construction (Wendt 1992), but it is also designed for someone and for some purpose (Cox 1996). Addressing this, critics have argued that the theory reflects a selective reading of the United States' post-war experience, often in combination with nineteenth-century Britain (Gamble and Payne 1996a).

Responding to the specific critique (mostly from liberal institutionalists) that they do not adequately explain the evolution of cooperation, neorealists and their intergovernmentalist comrades have counter-argued for the continued relevance of state/national interests, power and sovereignty. Although the EU is seen as an interesting polity, these scholars argue that it is shaped by more or less the same intergovernmental politics and bargaining that has determined it from the start: 'There is nothing particularly special about it, other than that it has taken a highly institution-alized form in Western Europe since the 1950s' (Cini 2003: 95). Accordingly, the EU developed and became institutionalized in order to protect national interests. Closely related to this, the bargains and supranational laws of the EU reflect the interests of the most powerful member states, whereas weak states 'band-wagon' or are kept in line through side-payments (Christiansen 2001a: 200).

Moravcsik's (1998) liberal intergovernmentalism has emerged as one of the preeminent theories of European integration and reflects an intense debate between realists/intergovernmental-ists and liberals/institutionalists on the European question. As indicated eponymously, the theory incorporates both intergov-ernmentalist and liberal features in a two-level game. Moravcsik considers the EU as an intergovernmental regime, and empha-sizes the power of states and their preferences. This neorealist/ intergovernmentalist perspective, then, is combined with a lib-eral stance on how domestic national preferences are formed and the underlying societal factors that provoke a demand for cooperation and the regional-level management of economic interdependence.

In another attempt to respond to critics, Grieco (1997: 175–9) argues that a regional hegemon is neither a necessary nor a suf-ficient condition for the development of regional economic insti-tutions. Through his 'relative disparity shift' hypothesis, Grieco argues that when there is relative stability of capabilities, which in part depends on the relative gains from regional cooperation and the expectation of a continuation of such gains, then deeper institutionalization of economic relations is likely. On the other hand, circumstances of instability in relative capabilities will limit the likelihood of regional institutionalization.

Grieco's analysis complements other neorealist studies. For instance, Mansfield and Bronson (1997) claim that economic regionalism may prosper within political-military alliances. They argue that the efficiency gains stemming from trade flows can be used to enhance political-military capacity. This also implies that states may be concerned with absolute and collective power within alliances, but relative power distribution towards outsiders.

Barry Buzan is another prolific theorist who to some extent is associated with realist thought, especially the English School or a specific type of 'liberal realism'. In the development of his security complex theory, Buzan (1991) challenges conventional neorealism, particularly as defined by Waltz, arguing that power theorists underplay the importance of the regional level in international relations. Buzan charged that regional patterns of security since the end of colonialism have become both more autonomous and more important, a tendency further reinforced by the end of the Cold War. Buzan's invention of the regional security complex has had a profound impact on the research field. Originally, it was defined as 'a set of states whose major security perceptions and concerns are so interlinked that their national security problems cannot reasonably be analyzed or resolved apart from one another' (Buzan 1991: 190). Buzan's early definition of the regional security complex is thus state-centric and, in a rather orthodox manner, the states are taken more-or-less as 'given' and as the (only) units in the international system.

In collaboration with Ole Wæver, Buzan went on to examine the interplay both among the global powers and between the powers and all of the security regions that make up the contemporary international system. This resulted in a new definition of security complex as 'a set of units whose major processes of securitization, desecuritization, or both, are so interlinked that their security problems cannot reasonably be analyzed or resolved apart from one another' (Buzan and Wæver 2003: 44). This revision of security complex theory reflects Buzan's and Wæver's attempt to move beyond a state-centric and military-political focus whilst also drawing on processes of securitization/desecuritization and a particular type of constructivism. The units can be states, but also other units can be predominant, and security complexes are not givens but constructed in the process of securitization, which adds some fluidity to the concept. The new definition made the actual delimitation of the unit more nuanced, albeit not easier, since different security sectors (economic, environmental, and societal) may define different regions. Buzan and Wæver argue that the constructivist approach is necessary if one is to keep the concept of security coherent and, to the traditional military and political security sectors, add the new ones of economy, environment and social. Buzan and Wæver claim that the new formulation allows them to move away from some of the most orthodox state-centric assumptions and they also acknowledge that regions are even less 'given'.

Nonetheless, in spite of continuous theoretical innovation, Buzan still shares the conventional neorealist conviction that strong states make strong and mature regions (cooperative anarchies), whereas in their quest for power and security, weak states tend to create (regional) conflicts and immature regions. It follows for Buzan that Western Europe is an example of a mature region, whereas the weak states in Africa create immature or weak regions. Again, neorealism and the security complex theory are based on foundations that make them more applicable to some parts of the world rather than to others, especially those parts where Westphalian state-building prevails.

Functionalist, Liberal and Institutionalist Approaches

This cluster of approaches includes a variety of like-minded functionalist, liberal and institutionalist theories, both 'old' and 'new', which first and foremost analyse regions through the inside-out and with emphasis on institutional and liberal aspects. Notwithstanding important differences, this group of theories shares some common traits, such as actor rationalism (although all frameworks are not 'pure' rational choice theories), pluralist assumptions, a similar liberal view of the state, and the regulating influence of institutional frameworks. Functionalism is one important and early approach to emerge within this cluster of approaches. It is primarily constructed around the proposition that the provision of common needs and functions can unite people across state borders (Mitrany 1943). As noted in the previous chapter, form should follow function, and cooperation should at least initially, concentrate on technical and basic functional programmes and projects within clearly defined sectors, without challenging national sovereignty or existing power structures within each country. Pragmatic cooperation among experts to solve common problems would eventually lead to a shift of loyalties and expectations from the national to international authorities.

Neofunctionalism challenges the functionalist assumption that politics is separable from economics (Haas 1958, 1964). A utilitarian concept of interest politics is introduced, whereby 'function follows interests' and 'ruthless egoism does the trick by itself' (Mattli 1999: 23). Neofunctionalists place emphasis on a particular set of non-state actors, such as the regional secretariat and the interest groups and social movements that are formed at the regional level. States continue to be important but by no means, exclusive actors. Neofunctionalists furthermore emphasize the deliberate design of regional institutions and supranational authorities. These are initiated by states, but then the regional bureaucrats and interest groups and self-organized interests become important actors in the process. In turn, the regional institutions are instrumental for the creation of (functional, political and cultivated) spill-over and, ultimately, this leads to a redefinition of group identity around the regional unit (Haas 1964; Hurrell 1995: 59).

In retrospect, it seems that the neofunctionalists expected too much too quickly. They underestimated the anti-pluralist and nationalist orientations of their time and the theory had little regard for exogenous and extra-regional forces (Breslin and Higgott 2000: 335). Their assumptions proved to be false or at least premature in Europe and even more misleading in other regions. In a similar vein, the same underlying assumptions limit the global applicability of contemporary functionalist and institutionalist theories.

Despite a variety of revitalized and reformulated functionalist and neofunctionalist theories (see special issue of *Journal of European Public Policy*, Vol. 12, No. 2, 2005), neoliberal institutionalism has become the dominant approach within the larger liberal paradigm as far as the study of regionalism is concerned. Just like their neorealist comrades, neoliberal institutionalists share the idea of an anarchical system in which states are the most important actors (Mansfield and Milner 1997). However, their understanding of states' behaviour and motives for engaging in international affairs differ. Neoliberal institutionalists argue that the state will act as negotiator at the intergovernmental and supranational level, limited by national political considerations, firms and pressure groups. Non-state actors first and foremost will influence regional politics from the bottom-up and in relation to their national governments. In this sense, there is a 'thin line' between liberal intergovernmentalists and liberal institutionalists (see Moravcsik 1998). One of the important differences emerges when considering for what purpose regionalism emerges and what variables help us understand the process of institutionalization. According to neoliberal institutionalists, regionalism is primarily motivated by the procurement of public goods, the avoidance of negative externalities from interdependence, and absolute gains. Regionalism is expected to be an incremental problem-solving process, mainly driven by or through formal and informal institutions. In essence, 'institutions matter' and efficient regionalization is expected to become ever-more institutionalized.

The role of regional policy frameworks in the field of trade has received enormous attention for several decades. Generally speaking, liberal theorists tend to be quite optimistic concerning the 'positive' potential of regionalism. Tussie (2003) emphasizes that regional projects can give market access, which the developing world at least wished for but was never able to obtain through multilateralism. However, Tussie nuances the typical liberal institutionalist position, claiming that regionalism has both positive and negative implications for liberalization and for multilateralism, thus implying that the choice between regionalism and international trade is not clear-cut. These issues are discussed further in the section on economic theorizing which follows.

Both the widening and deepening of particular regional organizations and institutional variation undoubtedly are important research topics. Nevertheless, one weakness in this line of thinking is the heavy emphasis on regional policy frameworks, such as the EU, NAFTA, Mercosur and APEC (Fawcett and Hurrell 1995; Mansfield and Milner 1997; Coleman and Underhill 1998). This bias is further accentuated by the fact that regional organizations, especially as apparent in Europe, are presented as the point of reference for understanding the global phenomenon of regionalism (an issue that will be discussed further in the next chapter).

Regional Economic Integration Theory

The study of regionalism in economics overwhelmingly is dominated by what is often labelled the 'Theory' of regional economic integration. Sometimes it also is referred to as 'market integration'. In reality it is a body of theories built around customs union theory and ideas about optimal currency areas. The theory assumes the creation, in linear fashion, of increasingly more 'advanced' stages of regional economic integration, namely: preferential trade area, free trade area, customs union, common market, economic and monetary union, and complete economic integration (Balassa 1961; Robson 1998). Market forces that are set into play in one stage are anticipated to have a spill-over effect in the next, so that implementation of that stage becomes an economic necessity. A related proposition is that because economic market integration has its own costs, resources will be misallocated if a more 'advanced' stage is embarked upon before completion of the preceding stage.

A preferential trade area is the lowest stage of integration, whereby member countries charge each other lower tariffs than those applicable to non-members. The second stage is a free trade area in which tariffs and quotas are eliminated among members, but each country retains its tariffs against imports from non-members. A customs union moves further, and members erect a common external tariff in addition to the free trade area. The common market is a further developed stage of economic integration. It combines the features of the customs union but with the elimination of obstacles for the free movement of labour, capital, services and persons (and entrepreneurship). The next step on the ladder is an economic and monetary union, with a common currency and the harmonization of monetary, fiscal and social policies. Complete economic integration constitutes the ultimate stage of economic integration, presupposing the unification of economic and political policies, as well as the control of economic policy by the central supranational authority that is accountable to a common parliament.

The theory is not concerned with institutional and political dynamics and the choices whereby regions are produced. It focuses solely on welfare effects resulting from economic interaction and policy change, and as such it is not a theory of how regions are made and unmade, and by whom, for whom and what purpose region-builders engage in regionalism. In spite of its rather narrow focus and the fact that it is not the only theory around, regional economic integration theory continues to have an enormous influence on the debate on regional economic integration all over the world, amongst both academics and policy makers (see Cable and Henderson 1994; de Melo and Panagariya 1995).

Regional economic integration theory notes that there are both gains and costs of market integration. The welfare gains emphasized in the theory can be divided into static and dynamic gains

(Robson 1993). Owing to the difficulty of calculating dynamic welfare gains within traditional economic models, it is the static comparative gains that conventionally receive attention, particularly whether the economic scheme is trade creating or trade diverting. Static welfare gains may also arise as a consequence of more efficient allocation of resources, primarily as a result of the free flow of factors of production.

In the last two decades there have been new developments in the field of economic integration theory. Two new lines of thinking that made an inroad into economics and market integration are, on the one hand, open regionalism, and on the other, a relaxed model of economic regionalism that emphasizes a broader set of dynamic economic benefits and is particularly relevant to the developing world (Robson 1993: 330). 'Open regionalism' prescribes that policy should be directed towards eliminating obstacles to trade (and to some extent, also to investment) within a region, while at the same time doing nothing to raise external barriers to the rest of the world (Cable and Henderson 1994: 8). The key question here is whether the regional trading bloc is a 'stumbling block' or 'stepping stone' towards a free and open world economy. This is an old question, but open regionalism provides a new solution: It seeks to synchronize the global and the regional levels, and facilitate increased liberalization of trade and investment. According to open regionalists, there is no need to replicate the EU (which is sometimes seen as protectionist) and there can be different routes to open regionalism in Africa, the Americas and Asia. Open regionalism accepts the fundamentals of orthodox market integration and trade liberalization. While some market integrationists accept certain protectionist measures, such as the protection of infant industry for a limited period of time, open regionalists are closer to laissez faire market fundamentalism and neoliberal thinking, whereby liberalization and opening up is seen as a panacea. This notion makes the formation of customs unions unnecessary, because of the real and potential risks of protectionism and trade diversion inherent in such ventures.

Open regionalism developed mainly in order to integrate the South into the global economy in line with neoliberal assumptions about free trade. In contrast, the relaxed model of economic regionalism emerged as a response to risks in the global economy and as a strategy to achieve a broad set of social-economic and political-economic objectives where old multilateralism no longer worked.

According to Mistry (2003), current multilateralism is dysfunctional because the OECD and G7 governments use it to make it serve their own needs. In addition, the interactions among nation-states are so unequal that they no longer enable multilateralism to function effectively. In contrast to orthodox theorizing, which generally considers multilateral free trade as the so-called 'first-best' solution, regionalism for Mistry is not a second-best solution, but actually a first-best (also see Chapters 7, Multidimensional Regionalism and 12, Regions in Global Governance).

The benefits emphasized in the relaxed economic regionalism model include economies of scale, positive terms-of-trade effects as a result of increased bargaining power, productivity gains, technological development, growth effects, domestic and foreign investment creation, production and employment creation, overcoming the costs of non-integration, the development of infrastructure and other services as well as structural transformation (Robson 1993; Mistry 2003). This revised model relaxes the rather unrealistic assumptions present in the orthodox framework, which do not apply in Europe and are even more irrelevant in most other parts of the world. Still, this line of thinking is consistent with neoclassical economics and should not be confused with *dirigist* or structuralist models of economic integration that developed during the old regionalism (see previous chapter).

Social Constructivist Approaches

Social constructivism is one of the most important theoretical developments in recent decades within the larger field of IR. This perspective has also gained a more prominent place in the study of regionalism, particularly in the study of European integration and of regionalism in Southeast Asia (Acharya 2001; Christiansen et al. 1999).

Social constructivism arose out of a critique both of Waltzian structural realism (structural power balance) and of rationalist theories of cooperation (with their emphasis on fixed and endogenous preferences). Constructivists replace determinism with voluntarism and make room for cultural factors and the pooling or splitting of identities as motives for action. By implication, constructivists challenge the heavy emphasis placed on materialist incentives and instrumental strategies by several of the theoretical perspectives outlined above, and instead point at the importance of inter-subjective aspects of identity, interests, learning, communication, shared knowledge and ideational forces, as well as how cooperation and communities emerge. In this sense, social constructivism 'provides a theoretically rich and promising way of conceptualizing the interaction between material incentives, inter-subjective structures, and the identity and interests of the actors' (Hurrell 1995: 72).

In itself, identity is ambiguous and multiple and it does not explain action. Rather, the point of identity is that it informs and transforms individuals (and their behaviour and their interests) as well as the quality of their interactions. 'Identities are the basis of interests. Actors do not carry around a portfolio of interests independently of their social context; instead they define their interests in the process of defining their situations' (Wendt 1992: 398). As Higgott points out:

> Interests can change as a result of learning, persuasion, knowledge and ideology, a phenomenon that parsimonious rationalist assumptions about utility maximization cannot accommodate. … interest is the outcome of a combination of both power and values. Indeed, interests cannot be conceptualized outside the context of the ideas that constitute them. (Higgott 1998: 45–6)

Constructivists argue that understanding intersubjective structures allows us to trace the ways in which interests and identities change over time and new forms of cooperation and community can emerge. The basic assumption is that there is an inevitable connection between the dynamics of collective action and the social identity by which the individual teams up with others in real or 'imagined communities' (Anderson 1983). It follows that constructivism constitutes a sociological approach to systemic theory, which in turn is based on the recognition that political communities are not structurally or exogenously given, but instead socially constructed by historically contingent interactions (Wendt 1992).

As far as regions are concerned, Murphy (1991: 25) underlines that these must be problematized and related to social processes: 'This in turn requires a social theory in which regional settings are not treated simply as abstractions or as a priori spatial givens, but instead are seen as the results of social processes that reflect and shape particular ideas about how the world is or should be organized' (Murphy 1991: 25). This has led most constructivists to stress the 'porous' and non-deterministic character of regions.

Social constructivism, therefore, has helped to transcend the rather introverted debates between the main rationalist theories referred to above, especially realism/intergovernmentalism and liberalism/institutionalism in the debate about European integration theory. The importance given to the role of ideas, values, norms and identities in the social constructivist framework also helps to draw attention away from the formality and particularities of the EU as an institution, which has important consequences for the potential of comparison. Yet, constructivists studying European integration have been linked to general debates in IR rather than showing interest in other regions.

Social constructivism has also been influential in the study of regionalism in Southeast Asia, claiming that the ASEAN forms the core of an emerging security community and is a facilitator of the 'ASEAN Way' of regionalism (Acharya 2001; for a deeper elaboration, see Chapter 5, Obviating the Gap Between Formal and Informal Regionalism). At least in part, this line of thinking is linked to the work of Karl Deutsch et al. (1957), which is sometimes considered a source of inspiration for constructivists. One of Deutsch's propositions was that cultural interaction and communication can become so intense that a region could become a security community, which is defined as having the shared sense of belonging to a community, a 'we-ness' that includes the development of diplomatic-political-military practices and behaviour that lead to the long-term expectation of peaceful relations among the populations.

Adler revisited Karl Deutsch's famous concept of 'security communities', suggesting that 'cognitive regions' or 'community-regions' are socially constructed by people who, 'imagine that, with respect to their own security and economic well-being, borders run more or less, where shared understandings and common identities end' (Adler 1997b: 250). Even if they owe allegiance to a state, people will sometimes 'take their identity cues from the community region as these communities become more tightly integrated' (Adler 1997b). Adler built further on Deutsch's work in a comprehensive volume co-edited with Michael Barnett, investigating the relationship between international community and the possibilities for peaceful change in a rich variety of cases. Their book *Security Communities* (Adler and Barnett 1998a), concluded that security policies are profoundly shaped by the community of nations, and that those states dwelling within an international community can develop a peaceful disposition.

The diversity of constructivism also needs to be acknowledged. Some scholars claim that social constructivism makes it possible to 'bridge the gap' between rationalist and reflectivist approaches to international theory (Adler 1997a). Smith (1997: 245), however, has most of them 'sitting' on the rationalist side of the fence 'trying to talk to those on the other', whereas others are engaged with more radical and critical reflectivist approaches to regionalism (Neumann 1994; Hettne and Söderbaum 2000; Paasi 2001).

Those constructivists who are closer to the rationalist side of the fence are often concerned with state actions and policies and, to some extent, with institutional design. Morten Bøås (2000: 311), a strong critic, argues that 'middle ground' constructivists are reinforcing a state-centric perspective, embedded in liberalism and idealistic notions about institutions, markets, democracy and peace. He claims that such constructivist frameworks are incapable of questioning 'whose regionalism', and asking 'for what purpose' regionalism emerges (Bøås 2000: 311). These are core questions for critical approaches to regionalism.

Critical Approaches

In the 1990s, a series of critical and neo-Gramscian approaches to regionalism emerged. This type of theorizing is heavily inspired by Robert Cox's distinction between 'problem-solving' and 'critical' theory. The former takes the world as given (and on the whole, as good) and provides guidance to correct dysfunctions or specific problems that arise within this existing order; the latter is concerned with how the existing order came into being and the construction of strategies for structural and social change. The associated Coxian proposition that 'theory is always for someone and for some purpose' – that is, theories are historically and politically based – was also important (Cox 1981: 128).

One prominent approach in the critical school of thought is the 'World Order Approach' (WOA), developed by Andrew Gamble, Anthony Payne and their colleagues at the Universities of Sheffield and of Warwick (see Gamble and Payne 1996a, 2003; Hook and Kearns 1999; Breslin and Hook 2002). The WOA builds on Cox's method of historical structures, defined as configurations of forces that consist of material capabilities, ideas and institutions. The architects of the WOA underlined the need to go beyond materialist definitions of power and to insert ideas into the standard framework. In their view, this makes the framework 'substantially more nuanced than mainstream approaches and enables analysts to catch more of the essence of hegemony' (Payne and Gamble 1996: 9). Following Cox, the proponents of the WOA emphasize that material capabilities, ideas and institutions interact on three interrelated levels: the social forces engendered in production processes; the varying forms of state/society complexes (not just states); and types of world order.

The WOA and similar critical approaches usually argue that the ideological power, or even the 'triumph', of capitalism and the dominance of economic globalization has established a new (neoliberal) context within which regionalism must be rethought. For many critical approaches, the central question is the extent to which states (and particular state/society complexes) respond to economic globalization by building states-led regionalist schemes.

It is also evident that many critical theorists remain sceptical of much of regionalism and the underlying motives of the leading actors. They usually claim that regionalism originates in discussions and negotiations within the policy making elites of the Core countries and that it is part of the hegemonic power of free market capitalism and liberal democracy. Contrary to the realist fears that regionalism leads to a new era of trade wars and even military conflict between the great powers, critical theorists generally claim that current regionalism ties into and reinforces economic globalization and neoliberalism. According to the WOA, 'regionalist projects emerge as a means to help achieve the globalist project in a world where there is no longer a single state with the authority and capacity to impose its leadership' (Gamble and Payne 1996b: 252–3). Hence, 'there is very little evidence to suggest that new identities are challenging old, or that cultural barriers and stereotypes are being broken down' (Kearns and Hook 1999: 250).

Ian Taylor (2003) claims that the ideology of neoliberalism has had profound implications for how regionalism and development are reconfiguring many regions in the developing world. Focusing on Africa, Taylor argues that the continent's elites seek to promote economic integration as a means of latching onto what is perceived as the globalization jugger-naut. Nevertheless, if existing regionalist projects often reflect the impulses of a neoliberal world, there are contesting alter-natives, with continual generation of counter-reactions and the construction of diverse forms of regional connections. In a series of studies with Fredrik Söderbaum, Ian Taylor ana-lysed cross-border regions in Africa (Söderbaum and Taylor 2003, 2008). One article interrogated the role of the state in the Maputo Development Corridor (MDC), drawing on the Coxian distinction between the state as the disciplining spokes-man of transnational capital in contradistinction to the state as a 'buffer' that protects the domestic economy from harm-ful exogenous influences (Söderbaum and Taylor 2001). Their study revealed several flaws in the MDC paradigm, showing that the regionalist project reinforces the role of the state as a transmission belt for transnational capital, rather than as a facilitator for development. The neoliberal market fundamen-talism and 'big-bang' approach inherent in the MDC resulted in 'jobless growth'. Similarly, the notion that 'good governance is less government', implies that in the context of economic glo-balization, the state to a large extent is reduced to an 'invest-ment promotion agency'.

Critical scholarship emphasizes that contemporary region-alism is uneven. Unless questions of inequality and uneven development are addressed, one central claim is that regionalist projects are likely to lead to increasing problems and polariza-tion within as well as between regions (Gamble and Payne 1996b: 258). There is a potential for states-driven regionalist projects to mitigate the negative effects of globalization and contribute to a new era of social regulation and community, especially if man-aged in an enlightened way and if opened up more broadly to the influences and interests of labour and civil society. However, the elites have devised these regionalist projects with little popu-lar involvement or motivation for them. Kearns and Hook argue that regional cooperation 'is fundamentally an elite-led process wherever one looks around the world and, indeed, ... it is often used in its own right to out-manoeuvre and stifle popular oppo-sition to the kind of politics and neo-liberal economy which it itself represents' (Kearns and Hook 1999: 249–50). If regionalism 'continues to use the public face of international cooperation to mask the needs of a few private interests, particularly amongst the elite, then it may well become one of the targets for any future radical challenge to capitalist civilization. There is a way to go yet before today's [...] regionalism can be wholeheartedly welcomed' (Kearns and Hook 1999: 257).

New Regionalism Approach

Under Björn Hettne's leadership, the New Regionalism Approach (NRA) was first developed in the mid-1990s within the UNU/WIDER research project on *The New Regionalism* (Hettne 1994; Hettne et al. 1999, 2000a, 2000b, 2000c, 2001). Subsequently, the approach has been developed and used by numbers of scholars in more or less all regions around the world and in most policy fields (e.g. Hettne and Söderbaum 1998, 2000; Mittelman 2000; Schulz et al. 2001; Grant and Söderbaum 2003; Hentz and Bøås 2003; Hettne 2003, 2005; Söderbaum and Shaw 2003; Söderbaum and Taylor 2003, 2008; Söderbaum 2004, 2007; De Lombaerde et al. 2010; Shaw et al. 2011). The original point of departure of the NRA was dissatisfaction with the theoretical and conceptual understanding of regionalism by the old regionalism and in the context of economic globalization. In this sense, the NRA view of regionalism shares several features with critical approaches, especially the view that globalization is a strong and, in some of its dimensions, irreversible force, with deep implications for regionalism. Indeed, globalization and regionalization are intimately connected and together shape the emerging world order and thus must be understood within the same framework. However, whereas the critical approaches understand regionalism primarily as a manifestation of economic globalization and prevailing forms of hegemony (i.e. as neoliberal open regionalism), the NRA applies a dialectical approach, which is more open to a diversity of outcomes, both positive and negative. Drawing on the works of Karl Polanyi (1944), Hettne argues that the dialectics of market expansion and attempts to intervene politically in defence of civil society constitute the basic forces of societal change. Seen in this perspective, the new regionalism represents the return of 'the political'; that is, interventions in favour of crucial values, the most fundamental of which are development, security and peace,

and ecological sustainability (Hettne 1999: 22). In Polanyian terminology, economic globalization constitutes the first movement
(with open regionalism being part of it), whereas political regionalism represents the second movement, and together they constitute a second great transformation:

> The current phenomenon of regionalism could be seen as
> the manifestation of the second movement, the protection of
> society, on the level of the macroregion, as a political reaction
> against the global market expansion which gained momen-
> tum in the 1980s. Thus we can speak of a 'Second Great
> Transformation'. (Hettne 1997: 86)

Closely related to this is a difference between the NRA and many
critical approaches, especially the WOA, in how to interpret the
state in general as well as regionalist projects. In contrast to the
emphasis on states-led regionalist projects in critical scholarship,
the NRA emphasizes the weakened capacity of the state in a
globalized world. The NRA extends the Polanyian ideas about
the (potential) political role of civil society as a means for the
weak and the poor to protect themselves – i.e. the self-protection
of society (Hettne 2003: 37). Not only economic but also social
and cultural regional networks and projects are anticipated to
develop more quickly than the formal states-led regionalist projects (Hettne 1994: 3). From this perspective, in the context of
globalization it is particularly important to identify and encourage the counterforces and agents of transformation. Mittelman
(2000: 225) refers to this as 'transformative regionalism' – i.e. the
alternative and bottom-up forms of cultural identity and regional
self-organization and self-protection, such as the pro-democracy
forces, the women's movement, the environmentalists and so on.

Even if the NRA highlights the possibility of 'political' regionalism, the state will not necessarily be the main object of political
allegiance. The strength of 'political' regionalism depends on its
ability to protect crucial values, such as economic development,
ecology and peace due to the fact that these values are not necessarily ensured by the state. As a result, regionalism becomes a
political struggle between various social forces over the definition
of the region, how it should be organized politically, and how it
is inserted into the global political economy. Depending on the
quality of the dominant form of regionalism and who sets the

agenda, alternative and counter-hegemonic visions of regionalism may emerge in response. The latter are assumed to increase
when hegemonic regionalism creates and reinforces imbalances
and exclusion.

The NRA suggests that there are many regionalisms within
a given region. It is proposed that an actor's decision to engage
in regionalism will depend not only on fixed material incentives
and resources (including power capability, routine behaviour or
'economic man'), but also on ideas and identities (as pointed
out in the social constructivist perspective). Regionalizing actors
depend on who they are, their worldviews, who other actors are
as well as the quality of their interaction. It follows that in the
NRA, regionalism is considered more complex and sometimes
also more detrimental than simply an instrument to enhance an
ambiguous 'national interest' (realism) or the 'public good' in the
form of trade, development, security and so forth (liberalism).
Regionalism will not necessarily be harmonious or beneficial to
all participants and stakeholders. Some actors will be able to use
regionalism and regional organizations in order to achieve private
goals and promote particular group-specific interests rather than
broader societal and common interests. Under certain circumstances regionalism will be exclusionary, exploitative, or reinforce
asymmetries and imbalances. Understanding such multidimensional regionalism requires a transcendence of state-centrism and
'methodological nationalism'.

'Methodological nationalism' refers to the notion that the
nation-state is the main, if not the only, relevant actor or the main
'container' or unit of social processes (Beck 1997). This methodological perspective results in a series of problems. One is that
states as well as regions (and their so-called 'interests') are usually
'taken for granted'. Another is that these theories are also based
on highly normative assumptions about the state and, therefore,
tend to generate highly normative assumptions about regionalism
and regional organizations. Rejecting 'methodological nationalism' is not equivalent to ignoring the state. On the contrary,
states, 'countries' and interstate organizations are crucial objects
of analysis, though some analysts and approaches still privilege
them more than others. The point certainly is not the irrelevance
of the state, but rather that the political and institutional landscape is being transformed fundamentally. There is a need to transcend the obsession with the state and the national space and start

to think in terms of more complex, multilevel political structures, in which the state is 'unbundled', reorganized and assumes different functions and where non-state actors also contribute at various levels, scales and modes of governance. The methodological issue is thus to transcend the Western conceptions of the (unitary) Westphalian state inherent in mainstream theorizing – be it neo-realism, institutionalism or regional economic integration theory. In doing so, the NRA critically assesses state–society complexes in the formation of regions and opens up a broader understanding of how regions are formed and what characterizes regionalism and regionalization in various parts of the world and in a global perspective.

In contrast with the rationalists' concern with more or less fixed and static definitions of regions and states, the NRA adopts a constructivist and post-structuralist understanding of regions, focusing on the processes by which regions are being made and unmade in various fields of activity and at various levels. The NRA by no means suggests that regions will be unitary, homogeneous or discrete units. Instead, there are many varieties of regions and regional subsystems, with different degrees of 'regionness'. Hence, there are no 'natural' or 'given' regions, but these are made and unmade – intentionally or unintentionally – in the process of global transformation, by collective human action and identity formation. Regionalism is a heterogeneous, comprehensive, multidimensional phenomenon, taking place in several sectors and, at least potentially, 'pushed' by a variety of state and non-state actors, both within and outside formal regional institutional arrangements. Regionalization is likely to occur at various speeds in various sectors and regionalization and de-regionalization may also occur at the same time. Yet, with the intensification and convergence of different processes of regionalization in various fields and at various levels within the same geographical area, the cohesiveness and thereby the distinctiveness of the region-in-the-making increases. It is this process that the NRA describes as 'regionness' (see Chapter 10, Regionness: The Solidification of Regions).

Post-Structural and Post-Modern Approaches

Approaches that we may term 'post-structural' and 'post-modernist' generally reject a one-dimensional and fixed notion of regions and regionalism. Adherents of this perspective criticize mainstream and rationalist theories (at least in IR) for their inability to problematize space. Indeed, at least within IR, many mainstream theories are biased towards two spatial levels, namely the state and the global level. Niemann charges that in the study of global politics, the reasons why regions and regionalism have received so little attention stems from:

> the *systematic* exclusion of spatial analysis from the debate of global politics. … questions related to space usually do not occur in the discourse of IR despite the fact that all global politics clearly takes place in space. … A very specific notion of space, that of space as container, became the unquestioned, commonsense view of space, which informed IR thinking. It is only at this stage of the late twentieth century that this commonsense conception of space is being challenged. (Niemann 2000: 4–5)

The conventional, mainstream preoccupation with the 'national' scale and the space-as-container schema has resulted in at least two misleading representations of space, which prevent a more nuanced understanding of regional space. The first view is apparent in an analogy that has dominated much of the IR discussion in which 'states are treated as if they are the ontological and moral equivalents to individual persons. … This assumption privileges the territorial scale of the state by associating it with the character and moral agency of the individual person, an intellectually powerful feature of Western political theory' (Agnew 1998: 3). The second and often associated metaphor is that of 'states as home'. Both metaphors have deep implications for the understanding of space: 'In fact, it is difficult to think and talk of international relations without using these metaphors. By the same token, they limit our vision' (Jönsson et al. 2000: 15). These metaphors carry with them specific and often misleading understandings of who and what is 'inside' and 'outside', which has become a key concern in post-modern theory.

When the 'taken for granted' national scale is transcended and problematized, then other scales/spaces automatically receive more recognition. A richer and more nuanced conception of context and space sees the state's territory as only one of a number of different territorial scales (Agnew 1998: 2). The same point is made by Jessop (2003), who claims that the increasing salience of regions should be understood in the broader context of a deepening of 'the relativization of scale' that came about since the end of the 1980s and 'the end of the territorial nation-state'. Jessop argues that the proliferation of spatial and temporal horizons linked to the relativization of scale, including different forms and results of globalization, involves very different challenges and threats to economic, political and social forces than those that prevailed when the national scale and territorial statehood were dominant. 'Rather than seek an elusive objective … criterion for defining a region, one should treat regions as emergent, socially constituted phenomena' (Jessop 2003: 183). Different scalar processes and strategies often combine to form more complex networks or strategies as well as tangled hierarchies of regions at a variety of levels. Jessop highlights the many different ways in which cross-border regions have emerged in the new era. There are many regional varieties, some policy-directed, others informal and spontaneous, and hence no single regional strategy is likely to predominate. Instead, there will be a large number of strategies, places, scales and temporalities nested into one another.

Iver B. Neumann's (1994, 2003) region-building approach (RBA) is an example of this broader school of thought. The RBA also rejects fixed and pre-given definitions of regions as well as the territorial trap of the nation-state. According to Neumann (2003: 160), 'the nation-state takes on the hyper-real quality of the simulacrum: the metaphorical family of the nation-state becomes more real than the family itself'. The problem is that the state is seen as the main spatial category and actor in a hostile and anarchical world. Equally important, the metaphor carries with it a specific and often misleading notion of who and what is 'inside' and 'outside'. Neumann's RBA is a tool to address these problems. It is well-suited to unpack the 'unitary state' and problematize the so-called national interest as well as the construction of regions. This can be done

> by asking questions about how and why the existence of a given region was postulated in the first place, who perpetuates its existence with what intentions, and how students of regions, by including and excluding certain areas and peoples from a given region, are putting their knowledge at the service of its perpetuation or transformation. (Neumann 2003: 162)

The RBA thus is based on the notion that region-builders precede the establishment of regions – that is, political actors who see it in their interest to imagine and construct a region as part of some political project. All theories make assumptions about what is a region but, according to Neumann, the mainstream and rationalist studies tend to neglect the 'politics of defining and redefining the region'. The point is that 'this is an inherently political act, and it must therefore be reflectively acknowledged and undertaken as such' (Neumann 2003: 166). The RBA seeks to go to the root of where, by whom and for whom region-building statements and strategies are formulated and made relevant: in other words, whose region is being constructed. These views are similar to those of the critical approaches to regionalism discussed earlier, but the RBA is based mainly on a post-structural and discursive approach, which can be understood as an application of a Self/Other perspective to the political project of building regions. Although Neumann claims that regions can be seen as 'imagined communities', cultural ties and identities are not in and of themselves politically relevant, but are made so by political actors in order to serve some political cause. Challenging the mainstream and rationalist notion that regions can be taken as given and as a feature of objective reality, the RBA stresses that regions are constructed and mediated by discourses and practices, emphasizing the agency of 'region-builders' who may be located both inside and outside the region. Neumann makes the point that it is particularly important to understand the dynamics (especially through discursive practices) whereby region-builders seek to present themselves as the 'imagined centre' of a particular region. Neumann's RBA also fits the post-structuralist and post-modern cluster because in contrast to the accepting attitude inherent in many mainstream approaches, 'it insists on an un-accepting, irreverent and therefore invariance-breaking attitude' (Neumann 2003: 177). Furthermore, it is discursive practices that constitute the ontological primitives in the core post-modern approaches; there, object and subject cannot be separated and causality is merely a chimera.

Bøås et al. (1999, 2003, 2005) are the theorists behind the weave-world/new regionalisms approach. They challenge other approaches, including the NRA *inter alia* because they consider them to be 'singular', too concerned with states and overly optimistic about what can be achieved by regional organizations. What differentiates this approach from the other types of school is its post-modern affinity and a deliberate focus on how nexuses of globalization and regionalization have created diversified patterns of interactions and responses at the local, national and regional level (what is referred to as the 'weave-world'). In response to the deficits of other approaches, Bøås et al. claim that they are developing a more historical, contextual, and agency-oriented approach that is able to provide a more comprehensive understanding of the multiplicities, complexities, contradictions and diversities of regions and regionalization processes, especially in the developing world (Bøås et al. 1999, 2003; Bøås 2003; Shaw et al. 2011). Indeed, 'what we are confronted with are juxtaposition, contradictory processes and simultaneous co-operation and conflict interwoven into streams of ideas, identities and more tangible resources' (Marchand et al. 1999: 1062–3).

Against this background, it is important that the processes of globalization and regionalization are addressed in the plural instead of their singular form in order to reflect their multidimensionality. These terms also should not be pinned onto one specific type of actor (most often the state), and more emphasis needs to be placed on what is broadly referred to as 'informal regionalisms from below', which includes a wide range of non-state actors and informal activities, such as transnational corporations (TNCs), ecologies, ethnicities, civil societies, private armies, maquiladoras, export processing zones, growth triangles, development corridors, diasporas from the South to the North, track two diplomacy, and the informal border politics of small trade, smuggling, mafias and crime (Marchand et al. 1999: 905–6):

> It is only when we make deliberate attempts to connect the two broad processes of formal and informal regionalisms that we can get a clearer picture of the connections between them. … The point is that the outcome of these processes is highly unpredictable, and most often there is more to these issues than meets the eye. (Marchand et al. 1999: 905–6)

Conclusion

This chapter reveals a considerable richness in theorizing about regionalism. In the study of regionalism during the last two to three decades, knowledge has grown considerably, especially regarding aspects of European integration, the institutional design of regional organizations, the role of power in the formation of regions, problems of collective action on the regional level, the dynamic relationship between globalization and regionalism and the numerous ways in which regions are built.

There is no doubt that rationalist theories of regionalism have contributed to the explanation of regionalism. Over time, the different rationalist approaches have moved closer together. Not only do they often share a common epistemology and agree on core assumptions – such as the anarchical system and the dominance of states as self-seeking egoists – they also often focus on the institutionalization of regionalism, addressing questions such as why regional arrangements are formed, why states choose to enter regional arrangements, what institutional forms are most effective, when and why are they deepened, and with what effects on trade, finance, development and so on.

This book proposes that despite the cumulative knowledge gained through mainstream approaches to regionalism, there are still important gaps in the explanation and understanding of regions and regionalism, how regions are socially constructed, what actors and coalitions of actors are 'pushing' the processes, what visions and strategies these actors have, and who the winners and losers are. To a considerable extent, these limitations arise as a consequence of how regionalism is studied. Hence, there are a number of reasons to challenge the rationalist theories. One weakness is related to their positivistic logic of investigation, which results in a concern with the methodology of regionalism rather than a genuine concern with the socio-economic circumstances and historical context in which regionalism occurs. The implication is that there is seldom a questioning or problematization of the concepts and assumptions on which the theories are based. This is significant because the underlying ontological and theoretical assumptions – such as the notion of unitary states, the regulating influence of regional organizations, trade and policy-led economic integration and so on – are more relevant in certain contexts than in others. Thus, the rationalist theories are designed first and foremost for the study of the favourite case of Europe and contexts where state-building is predominant. They are also designed to address a particular set of research questions that are frequently linked to supranational or intergovernmental regional organizations. Again, neither the research questions nor the studies need to be irrelevant or wrong. Simply, the argument raised here is that other theoretical perspectives, located in the constructivist and reflectivist camp, are also justified in order to provide a deeper understanding of regionalism and region-building.

Since the mid-1990s, a series of constructivist and reflectivist approaches to regionalism have developed, to a large extent as a result of the strengthening of this type of scholarship in IR more broadly. These approaches seek to open up regionalism and the way regions are made and unmade to a broad and deep interdisciplinary analysis. In spite of the many varieties of constructivist and reflectivist theory, they are similar in that all challenge core rationalist variables and assumptions, such as the separation of subject and object, fact and value, as well as the way interests, ideas and identities are formed and their influence on region-formation.

This perspective does not mean rejecting the idea that regions can be formed on the basis of 'interests', or that actors do not act rationally. Rationalist approaches are based on rational choice and generally take the interests, ideas and identities of actors (usually nation-states or state actors), as prior and given, whereas reflectivists and constructivists focus on how processes of social interaction transform interests, ideas and identities and their effects on region-building. The two approaches lead to radically different answers and methodologies as to why and how regions are formed and consolidated.

At least from a reflectivist perspective, it is also becoming increasingly evident that 'regional space' is itself becoming more elusive and multifaceted compared to the situation during the era of 'old regionalism'. Of course, one may continue to identify 'regions' defined in advance of research, as done by many mainstream and rationalist thinkers. But as soon as one moves away from pre-given and hermetically sealed conceptualizations of space or the viewing of regions as locations or arenas, then regional space automatically becomes more fluid, porous and pluralistic.

Somewhat related to this, the reflectivist theories reject the conventional claim that (dynamic) regionalism is happening primarily in Europe, the NAFTA and the Asia-Pacific and is mainly driven through formal interstate frameworks and regional organizations.

The NRA specifically, but also some other reflectivist approaches, emphasizes the multidimensional nature of today's regionalism all over the world, whereby a multitude of state and non-state actors interact in an increasing set of formal and informal networks and modes of governance. These issues will be analysed in detail in a number of chapters of this book. Before moving into such analysis, however, there is a need to discuss how regionalism should be compared.

4

The Richness of Comparative Regionalism

Despite a growing number of specific comparisons of selected aspects of regionalism (especially concerning regional institutions and the role of power) in selected areas of the world, there is a weak *systematic* debate on the fundamentals of comparative research in the study of global regionalism. Differences over what to compare, how to compare and even why to compare at all, arise predominantly as a consequence of the tension in the field between regional specialization (i.e. case or area studies) and more general research that is built around European integration theory and practice to a large degree.

Treating European integration as the foundation for conceptual development, theory-building and comparison is the most dominant approach in the field of regionalism. This approach readily becomes 'Eurocentric' – a 'false universalism' whereby European integration in general and the EU in particular becomes the marker, model and paradigm from which to theorize, compare and design institutions as well as policy in the rest of the world.

If European integration theory and practice looms large in mainstream discourses, many scholars of non-European regionalism have deliberately challenged Eurocentrism or developed frameworks specialized for specific regions or the developing world. Efforts to avoid the pitfalls of Eurocentrism are commendable but many of these studies result in either parochialism or anti-Eurocentrism. This chapter seeks to transcend the tension between Eurocentrism and parochialism and move towards a more globally applicable and non-Eurocentric comparative regionalism, which is still culturally sensitive.

The following section describes the negative effects of Eurocentrism (in various guises) on theoretical development, empirical analysis and policy debates about regionalism. The next section deals with the problem of parochialism and area-centricity in the study of regionalism. Then there is a section dealing with the unresolved tension and lack of dialogue between EU studies and comparative regionalism. The final section outlines an eclectic (and pragmatic) perspective on comparative regionalism, which seizes the middle ground between context and general theory and underlines the richness of regional comparison.

Eurocentrism and False Universalism

After the Second World War, the study of regional integration was dominated by an empirical focus on Europe. During this era, European integration theories were developed for and from the European experience and then more or less applied or exported around the world. According to the most prominent neofunctionalist, Ernst Haas:

> Integration among discrete political units is a historical fact in Europe, but disintegration seems to be the dominant *motif* elsewhere. Cannot the example of successful integration in Europe be imitated? Could not the techniques of international and supranational cooperation developed in Luxembourg, Paris, and Brussels be put in use in Accra, Bangkok, and Cairo, as well as on the East River in New York? Or, in a different perspective, will not the progress of unity in Europe inevitably have its integrating repercussions in other regions and at the level of the United Nations even without efforts at conscious imitation? Such a development would be most satisfying. Presumably it would contribute to world peace by creating ever-expanding islands of practical cooperation, eventually spilling over into the controversy-laden fields which threaten us directly with thermonuclear destruction. (Haas 1961: 657)

Even if Haas and other like-minded scholars did clearly reflect upon and question the transferability of the European experience, they mainly searched for those 'background conditions', 'functional equivalents' and 'spill-over' effects that were derived from the study of Europe. All too often (but not always), the European Community was seen and advocated as 'the' model, which has led many scholars to criticize the neofunctionalists for their narrow focus on regional integration as well as for using 'the European experience as a basis for the production of generalizations about the prospects for regional integration elsewhere' (Breslin et al. 2002: 2).

The fundamental problem ever since the old regionalism is that different types of Eurocentric generalizations have continued to influence and shape the research field. In this context, Eurocentrism implies that assumptions and theories developed for the study of Europe crowd-out both more universally applicable frameworks and contextual understandings. Compared to the early debate, Eurocentrism has worsened as a result of the consolidation of the EU and the growth of European integration and European Union studies. European integration in general and today's EU in particular, has become a marker, a model and a paradigm from which to theorize, compare and design institutions as well as policies in most other regions of the world. In the past as now, non-European cases and experiences are usually considered atypical, unique, or not constituting 'the real thing', according to the orthodox definition of 'regional integration' (Schmitter and Kim 2008: 23).

Even if classical theories of regional (European) integration and cooperation such as functionalism and neofunctionalism, appreciated liberal-pluralist assumptions as well as cordial relations between states and non-state actors, these early perspectives were subordinated to the analysis of what 'states' did in the pursuit of their so-called 'interests' as well as the consequences of state–society relations for supranational and intergovernmental regional organizations. For instance, Haas claimed that 'countries dominated by a non-pluralistic social structure are poor candidates for participation in the regional integration process. Even if their governments do partake at the official level, the consequences of their participation are unlikely to be felt elsewhere in the social structure' (Haas 1961: 377). Haas acknowledged that the neofunctionalist approach embodied important faults that reflected its origins in the 1950s, which also cast doubt on its usefulness as a framework for comparative analysis. Yet the usual claim, made here by Nye, was that it could 'be modified so that it is not too Europocentric to be useful as a framework for comparative analysis' (Nye 1970: 797).

There was a rich and sophisticated debate about Eurocentrism and the usefulness of comparison in the late 1960s and early 1970s. In many ways, the debate during this time was more advanced than it was in the 1980s and 1990s (during the era of new regionalism) and it had some similarities with more recent debates since the late 2000s. Even so, a number of more recent realist/intergovernmental and liberal/institutionalist approaches to regionalism continue to favour formal institutionalization along the European path, with the result that many rationalist theories are dominated by a concern with explaining deviations from the 'standard' European case. Indeed, anyone engaging with literature and policy on regional integration will notice that many other cases of regionalisms are compared – implicitly or explicitly – against the backdrop of European theory and practice. Hence, the study of regionalism has been and continues to be plagued by sweeping claims that regionalism in Asia is informal and loose, in Africa is primitive or failed and in the Middle East absent entirely. From the Europe-centred viewpoint, European integration is usually considered multidimensional, sophisticated and highly institutionalized – both a descriptive and prescriptive contention – whereas regionalism/regional integration in the rest of the world is seen as weakly developed and weakly institutionalized, and is usually reduced to either an economic or a security-related phenomenon (Christiansen 2001a: 517). These and similar claims are not only advanced by specialists of European integration but also by those working on non-European regions (Asante 1997; Mistry 2003).

This way of thinking is reflected in the vast number of studies on the EU and other state-led regional frameworks, such as the AU, ASEAN, ECOWAS, NAFTA, SADC and Mercosur. Likewise, the policy debate is also focused heavily on supporting regional organization in Europe's image. Explicitly or implicitly influenced by functionalist and institutionalist theories and perspectives, policy-makers often believe that imitating the EU's institutional structure constitutes a way towards progress. This critique in no way means that scholars or policy-makers should cease focusing on regional organizations and 'institutional design'; the point is that the overwhelming dominance of the Eurocentric focus has prevented alternative answers as to how and why regions are formed and who are the relevant region-builders.

A closely related misunderstanding that follows from the Eurocentric perspective is that regionalism outside Europe has little relevance for comparative regionalism or for theory-building (because the European path is the only 'successful' one). Such prescriptions mean that few concepts and theories generated from the study of non-European regions have influenced comparative regionalism (despite the Southeast Asian experience attracting increasing attention since the new regionalism). Indeed, as Hurrell (2005: 39) asserts, 'the study of comparative regionalism has been hindered by so-called theories of regionalism which turn out to be little more than the translation of a particular set of European experiences into a more abstract theoretical language'. This can be thought of as a 'false universalism' and it tends to show a lack of sensitivity to regionalism in the rest of the world.

Parochialism and Area-Centricity

There is a deep tension between the Europe-centred 'false universalism' and regional specialization. Some of the most informative studies in the field of regionalism are case studies or studies situated in debates within a particular region, such as Europe, East Asia, the Americas, or Africa (Söderbaum 2009). Certainly, detailed case studies of regionalism are necessary; they identify historical and contextual specificities and allow for a detailed and 'intensive' analysis of a single case. Case studies have been important for escaping the pitfalls associated with false universalism and irrelevant general theory. Most importantly, case studies of regions and regionalism help satisfy our need for in-depth knowledge of how actors think of themselves, their motivations, identities and strategies, and how they are influenced by other actors as well as the contextual surroundings. Furthermore, the case-study approach is useful in those cases and situations where it is difficult to separate cause and context. Compared to studies with a larger number of cases, it also enables a deeper cross-fertilization and feed-back between theory and empirical analysis. Hence, in itself, regional specialization is not necessarily a methodological or scientific 'problem'.

Too often however, regional specialization – or what Thompson (1973) refers to as 'area-centricity' – leads scholars to develop conceptual toolboxes and theories without engaging with other cases or competing discourses. Exclusive specialization and myopic case-study based methodologies also often prevent scholars from recognizing that they are dealing with phenomena similar to those encountered by scholars of other regions. In this sense, regional specialization and area-centricity likely constitute the breeding grounds for parochialism (Söderbaum 2013). Of course, case studies can be used for assorted types of theory-testing, but one of the main methodological disadvantages of regional specialization is that a single case constitutes a weak base for a new generalization or invalidating existing generalizations (Axline 1994b: 15).

There are many reasons for the tendency to specialize, some of which are more persuasive than others. One reason is the difficulty in generating competence and detailed knowledge of more than one region and regional context. Another reason is the time and resources needed to carry out intensive and field-based research in many regions (although this constraint mainly concerns qualitative-oriented scholars and not quantitative scholars).

The point made here is not that the specialized discourses and debates around particular regions lack either comparisons or attempts to generalize; the issue is that when comparison is used, it is too often conducted from the perspective of a particular region (regional specialization) or, to a lesser extent, it is based on a Eurocentric perspective. Without entering into the specificities of each debate, it is illuminating to sketch some general patterns of the debates about regionalism in Asia, Africa and the Americas.

For several decades, a large number of scholars have addressed the specificity and distinctiveness of East and Southeast Asian regionalism. Its specificity and uniqueness is then attributed to its open character, the existence of multiple centres of influence, the predominance of *de facto* regional integration driven by sub-state and/or non-state actors, and the relative absence of formal regional institutions, reflected in labels such as the 'ASEAN way' or soft institutionalism (Katzenstein 1996: 2–3, 12; Higgott 1997; Acharya 2001; Pempel 2005). Other features highlighted are the importance of partnerships between the private sector and the state, or 'trans-state development' (Parsonage 1997), and the non-confrontational ways of dealing with differences and conflicts between states based on consensus culture (Goh 2003: 14). Most research concerning East and Southeast Asian regionalism is case-study based rather than comparative, albeit that the number of EU–Asia comparisons has increased rapidly since the 2000s and, as a general approach, constructivism has also influenced research. However, a significant portion of such references or comparisons with Europe have characterized East Asian regionalism as looser, more informal and, sometimes, even as 'underdeveloped' (Choi and Caporaso 2002: 485). Acharya (2006: 312–13) is correct in that, rather than elevating the European model over the Asian experience as a preferred model of regionalism, it is more productive to recognize that regional cooperation is a difficult and contested process that will throw up different outcomes, each equally worthy of analysis. Approached in this way, there is thus room for a more mutually reinforcing cross-fertilization in the study of European, East Asian, and any other regionalisms. For instance, there is no reason to believe that soft institutionalism is a uniquely Asian phenomenon. Equally, comparisons should not be limited to contemporary Asia and Europe, but would benefit from considering regionalisms across various time periods.

Most research on regionalism in Africa is overly 'Africa-focused' and heavily centred on states-led regionalist schemes and organizations. There are both studies of single regional organizations (AU, COMESA, EAC, ECOWAS, IGAD, SACU, SADC) and studies incorporating several schemes. In many ways, the analysis of regionalism in Africa is underdeveloped: too much research consists of synoptic overviews of a number of regional organizations or catalogues of various types of political and economic relationships in a given region (Poku 2001: 6). Only rarely does research involve non-African regions; even if both rationalist theory and so-called pan-African discourses actually tend to emphasize European integration theory and practice. Thus, there is little cross-fertilization and comparison between Africa and regions in other parts of the world. This is unfortunate, since it is unlikely that there is a uniquely 'African' regionalism. Any particularities appear to be related to the nature of African state-society complexes and Africa's insertion in the global order. The area-centricity and even parochial tendencies tend to reflect the patterns in the other regional debates, namely that many scholars tend to use context-specific language to describe rather similar phenomena instead of applying general concepts and developing questions and hypotheses that can be transferred to cross-regional comparisons.

There is a rich base for comparative analysis on the Americas, both in time and space, thanks to the considerable time depth to regional projects. Still, most research continues to be case-study based, or built around parallel case studies. When it comes to cross-regional comparison, the EU is by far the most salient point of reference or model (and to some extent NAFTA or other US-led regionalist projects), particularly when we are dealing with variations on the theme of the common market model rather than the free trade model. This implies that European integration theory and practice strongly influences the debate within Latin America and the comparisons offered, albeit not as much regarding NAFTA, which in itself is usually considered a model rather than simply a deviation from the EU.

This short exposé of debates in Asia, Africa and the Americas leads to three main conclusions. Firstly, area-centricity and regional specialization still dominate at the expense of comparative regional studies. There is little cross-fertilization and comparisons between Africa, Asia and other regions. Attempts to try to generalize are limited, arguably because most scholars are so occupied with their own region that they view it as 'unique', *sui generis*, and as *n=1*. This is problematic because, even if both the contexts and the institutional configurations differ between regions, it is unlikely that regionalism is uniquely European, African, Asian, or American. Too few scholars address the core methodological question of what actually a particular form of regionalism 'is an instance of' (Rosenau 1997). Secondly, when comparisons are undertaken, many of these are made *within* particular regions, thereby reinforcing the problem of area-centricity and the exaggerated claims of regional distinctiveness. Finally, to the extent that other regions are included in the analysis, most comparisons are 'uni-directional' and carry the implication that Europe is considered the comparator, marker or model. This in turn helps to explain how Eurocentrism is built into both case-study based regionalism and comparative regionalism. The main exceptions to this tendency are comparisons of Europe and East/Southeast Asia, and to a lesser extent of Europe and NAFTA.

The view offered here is that a more advanced debate about comparative regionalism will not be reached by simply celebrating differences between European integration and regionalism in the rest of the world. Excluding the case of Europe would be counterproductive. The solution here is to go beyond *certain* constructions and models of European and instead draw attention to aspects that are more widespread and comparable (see Warleigh-Lack and Rosamond 2010). In other words, European integration theory and experience should not be a barrier to achieving a more globally applicable comparative regionalism. Neglecting Europe would be to miss the advantage of the richness of the EU project and laboratory (Rosamond 2000; Wiener and Diez 2003) and so the case of Europe should be *integrated* within a larger discourse on comparative regionalism, built around general concepts and theories but still showing cultural and contextual sensitivity. This brings attention to the relationship between European integration studies and comparative regionalism studies.

Integrating 'Europe' Within Comparative Regionalism

One of the central debates in the study of regionalism has been about the role of the European case and, more specifically, about its uniqueness or *sui generis* character (the so-called '$n=1$' problem). Early neofunctionalists such as Haas, Schmitter and Nye, all were conscious of the ambiguous and complex character of the EU and the problem of comparability of the regional integration experiences in different regions. Even so, they did not reject comparison – which others did later. As noted previously, Haas was concerned that regional processes did not follow the European path of regional integration. This led Nye to develop a revised neofunctionalist model, which *inter alia* could accommodate the higher degree of politicization evident in non-pluralistic/less developed societies such as those in Africa (Nye 1971). For those closer to the regional subsystem approach, Thompson argued that:

> there is an [...] excellent opportunity for gaining further insight through comparative analysis. For how else are we to learn which forms of behavior are 'universally' regional and which are peculiar to specific types of region? In this fashion, it should be possible to avoid area-centricities or at least learn where they are appropriate. (Thompson 1973: 91)

On this note, during the old regionalism there was no sharp distinction between the study of European integration and comparative regional integration: both fields of study were part of the same discourse, at least in Europe and the US. Subsequently, large parts of the more recent community of EU studies came to consider the EU as a nascent, if unconventional, polity in its own right (Keohane and Hoffman 1991; Stone Sweet and Sandholtz 1997; Hooghe and Marks 2001). This perspective did generate useful insights but, as Warleigh-Lack and Rosamond (2010) argue, it reinforced the notion that the EU is *sui generis*, thereby down-playing those aspects where the EU resembles other regionalist projects around the world. This perspective also carried a certain intellectual parochialism and thereby kept us from deepening our understanding of the EU as a political system and as a region (also see Rosamond 2005).

In the mid-1990s the view emerged that the EU should be explicitly compared with federal systems in advanced industrial states, with the US being a prominent candidate (Sbragia 1992; Hix 1994). A corollary of this view was that established tools of political science and comparative politics should be used in EU studies and that international studies and relations were not equipped to deal with the complexity of the modern EU (Hix 1994). This enabled EU scholars to circumvent the $n=1$ *problematique*, but at the same time it favoured a narrow perspective about (comparative and scientific) methods as well as cases, thereby widening the gap between EU studies and regionalisms elsewhere.

A number of prominent EU scholars have argued in favour of a more balanced position that recognizes the specificity of the EU but allows cross-regional comparisons (Caporaso 1997; Marks 1997; Moravcsik 1997). Other scholars have also argued in favour of the re-integration of the EU in comparative regional studies (e.g. Checkel 2007; De Lombaerde et al. 2010; Robinson et al. 2010; Söderbaum and Sbragia 2010; Warleigh-Lack and Rosamond 2010; Warleigh-Lack and Van Langenhove 2010; Warleigh-Lack, Robinson and Rosamond 2011; Telò 2014). And yet others have argued in favour of a dialogue between European integration theory and globalization theory (Rosamond 2005).

Few can dispute that Europe is a diverse region. Indeed, it is positive that there has been an explosion of theorizing on European integration in recent decades. Hence, there is no single EU mode of governance but a series of different interpretations of the EU (see Wiener and Diez 2003). In this regard, European integration and the EU are often (wrongly) considered as synonymous. Europe, however, in many of its sub-regions, ranging from the Nordic countries to Eastern Europe and so on, consists of a number of varied and partly overlapping regional projects of different depths and degrees of institutionalization. At least historically, a number of these projects and frameworks were not based on the common market model. This diversity has begun to have a positive influence on the study of regionalism in general and the debate between European integration and comparative regionalism in particular. Warleigh-Lack and Rosamond (2010) warned that scholars of regions other than the EU cannot afford to lock themselves away from the most advanced instance of regionalism in world politics (i.e. the EU).

EU studies is obviously a very dynamic field of research, in which new theories are developed, tested and debated, both between and within the participating disciplines. Warleigh-Lack and Rosamond (2010: 993) are correct in noting that a 'careful treatment of the accumulated insights from EU studies (including a proper re-inspection of classical integration theory) brings clear methodological and meta-theoretical benefits for the project of comparative regional integration scholarship'. EU studies would also benefit both conceptually and empirically from increased comparison with other regions (i.e. an escape from the $n=1$ problem), although this requires care in deciding what can and what cannot be compared.

The scope for increased dialogue and cross-fertilization between EU and comparative regionalism studies depends heavily on the theoretical perspectives and basic assumptions, especially about globalization as well as the nation-state (Söderbaum and Sbragia 2010). The impact of globalization on regionalism is undeniable, and this has been heavily emphasized by various types of critical and new regionalism approaches. EU studies increasingly take this into account, producing more attempts at cross-fertilization between EU studies and 'new regionalism' studies (Warleigh-Lack and Rosamond 2010; Warleigh-Lack and Van Langenhove 2010; Warleigh-Lack et al. 2011, Shaw et al. 2011; Telò 2014). Nonetheless, it also is true that globalization has different causes and consequences in different parts of the world, and the specific positions (and levels of development) of the various states and regions appear to result in particular types of regionalism. As a consequence, comparisons may best be conducted between states and regions at similar stages of development (Söderbaum and Sbragia 2010).

Basic assumptions about the nation-state clearly affect the nature of the dialogue between EU studies and comparative new regionalism. The assumption of a strong and institutionalized nation-state is central to a large part of EU studies. Liberal and realist theories of regionalism in IR make similar assumptions about the state, but, as elaborated in the previous chapter, they also tend to reinforce Eurocentric assumptions about the state that many of the reflectivist theories of regionalism in the developing world have explicitly tried to avoid. Reflectivist approaches problematize the state–society complex in a different way compared to the rationalists (i.e. questioning the assumption about the strong and institutionalized nation-state). These assumptions often come naturally when focus is placed on post-colonial states in the developing world, but they are also relevant for the study of the European nation-state in the context of recurrent financial crises as well as in the geographic context of Central and Eastern Europe. In other words, the European laboratory is diverse enough to enable cross-fertilization between certain strands of EU studies and new regionalism studies in IR.

Conclusion: An Eclectic Comparativist Perspective

Developing the comparative element is one of the four core elements of this book and it is considered crucial to enhancing cross-fertilization between various theoretical standpoints and regional specializations (Cooper et al. 2008; Söderbaum 2009). As Breslin and Higgott correctly point out, 'when conducted properly, the comparative approach is an excellent tool … it is a key mechanism for bringing area studies and disciplinary studies together, and enhancing both. It provides new ways of thinking about the case studies whilst at the same time allowing for the theories to be tested, adapted and advanced' (Breslin and Higgott 2000: 341).

As noted above, comparative regional frameworks are often Eurocentric or based on a 'false universalism'. As a result, area specialists, post-modernists and others have criticized comparative analysis heavily, emphasizing instead cultural relativism and the importance of a deep multidisciplinary knowledge of various contexts and people. Even so, comparative analysis helps to guard against ethnocentric bias and culture-bound interpretations that may arise in over-contextualized or isolated studies (see Buzan and Wæver 2003: 468).

This book adheres to what has been referred to 'the eclectic centre for comparative studies', which seizes 'a middle ground' between context and case/area studies on the one hand, and on the other 'hard' social science as reflected in the use of 'laborative' comparisons (Kohli et al. 1995). Such a middle ground can help avoid the 'evils' of parochialism on the one hand, and 'false' general theory on the other. Adopting the eclectic centre of comparative studies as a perspective will be inclusive rather than exclusive – even if for some it will be too 'social sciency' and too much like 'storytelling' for others (Kohli et al. 1995). There need not be any opposition between area studies and disciplinary studies/ international studies, or between particularizing and universalizing comparative studies. The preferred version of comparative regionalism is eclectic and inclusive. An eclectic perspective should enable area studies, comparative politics, and international studies to engage in a more fruitful dialogue, and thereby overcome at least some of the remaining fragmentation in the field of regionalism. It should also enable continued cross-fertilization between different regional debates and specializations around the world. In essence, an eclectic perspective will enhance a dialogue about the fundamentals of comparative analysis; for example, what constitutes comparable cases, and what are the many different forms, methods and design of comparative analysis (De Lombaerde et al. 2010; De Lombaerde and Söderbaum 2013; Söderbaum 2009).

One premise of this book is that relevant regionalism theory should be reserved neither for the North nor the South. While there is a need to avoid the culturally skewed 'universalism' of many Eurocentric (and rationalist) perspectives, there is no reason to construct a regionalism theory just for the South, which indeed is the case in some critical and post-modern approaches. Transcending parochialism, Eurocentrism and anti-Eurocentrism are crucial for any rethinking of comparative regionalism. Nonetheless, it is still acceptable to claim that Europe and other regions are not always 'comparable' in all respects. Indeed, comparing the EU with other forms of regionalism highlights the difficulty scholars face when working across the divide separating advanced industrial states from developing countries/emerging economies (Söderbaum and Sbragia 2010). Strong state institutions and structures matter in the shaping of both national and regional governance; and so does national wealth. Regions cannot separate themselves from the wealth and power of their members, which has been one important reason for the distinction between studies of European integration and those elsewhere. Avoiding European integration (anti-Eurocentrism) or emphasizing the uniqueness of a particular region (parochialism) often gives rise to the major meta-theoretical and methodological problem of avoiding reflecting upon the issue of comparability. Sometimes the discussion is influenced by ideology, emotion and lack of interest. As pointed out by Warleigh-Lack and Rosamond (2010), many scholars who want to avoid the case of Europe tend to erect a caricature of the EU or classical regional integration theory, especially of neofunctionalism, so they fail to learn from European integration theory and practice. What results is quite unnecessary fragmentation within the research field. A similar argument could be made regarding the attitude of scholars of European integration to other regions, who often either avoid them or simply believe that they are not comparable.

Comparable Cases

In a deepened discussion around comparative regionalism, one of the core elements concerns the question of what are comparable cases. Indeed, case selection deserves more attention in comparative regionalism. One problem is that many comparisons appear to be based on the rather accidental circumstances and opportunities of individual researchers, the availability of data or the view that intergovernmental regional organizations or regional trading schemes are comparable across-the-board without serious discussion about whether or not this is relevant. Case selection should be more closely connected to the research problem as well as the conceptual and theoretical framework being employed.

Of course, definitions are essential in any discussion about what constitutes comparable cases, since definitions, and the choice of concepts, including the fundamental question of what is a case, will affect the ability to compare and ultimately to generalize. As discussed in previous chapters, in the 1960s and 1970s attempts to define regions 'scientifically' produced few clear results as 'region' is a polysemous concept (Russett 1967; Cantori and Spiegel 1970). In turn, this resulted in the retreat of emphasizing the uniqueness of particular regions ($n=1$ and *sui generis*), which still dominates a great deal of the contemporary thinking about regionalism both in Europe and in other regions.

Conceptual pluralism should not necessarily be problematic from a comparativist viewpoint. The eclectic approach offered here underlines the richness of comparison. Regions can and should be compared in time as well as across space and organizational form. It is possible to compare the comprehensive and multidimensional regions at various scales (Europe, Africa/Southern Africa, East and Southeast Asia) but also to compare more distinct types of regions and regionalism, such as trade blocs, security regions, cognitive regions, river basins, and so forth. For example, as an object of research the EU can be studied in different ways and the choice of comparisons depends on the issue studied.

As with any other aspect of the social realm, the EU simultaneously has both specific features as well as general characteristics that it shares with other regions and regional political communities. One can therefore claim that in some respects the EU will be comparable with many other types of regionalism. For instance, one way of looking at the EU is as one of many regional trade agreements registered with the WTO. From a different perspective, the EU is comparable with a much more limited number of other multipurpose and comprehensive regional organizations, such as the Andean Community, ASEAN, AU, ECOWAS, Mercosur, SADC and so forth. Finally, the EU indeed also has some unique properties (De Lombaerde et al. 2010; Van Langenhove 2011). For these reasons, the eclectic perspective offered here does not reject comparisons between the EU and other federations (US, Germany) or between the EU and older formations such as empires (even if such comparisons are somewhat more complicated). Conceptual pluralism does not equal anarchy. The fundamental point is the need for clarity about the research questions and the case selections, whilst maintaining conceptual clarity.

It is important to understand the link between conceptualization and the problem of comparability in empirical research (De Lombaerde et al. 2010; De Lombaerde 2011). In regional studies, one way forward is to focus on the essential characteristics of the region. An ambitious solution in this regard is to analyse and compare regions through the prism of 'regionhood', according to which regions are treated as non-sovereign governance systems located between the national and global level and having (partial) statehood properties (Van Langenhove 2011). If a link between national and regional governance and rule-making are considered essential characteristics of a macro-region, then, for example, it is reasonable to compare the EU with SADC in order to study how national constitutional courts deal with regional rule-making. However, if the essential characteristic of a region is deemed to be the capacity to influence decision-making in the area of global trade (e.g. within the WTO or on the global arena), then it probably makes more sense to compare the EU with the US or the emerging powers rather than SADC, although in principle regions can be included in the sample. It can be seen here that the identification of relevant comparators follows logically from the research questions under study as well as from conceptualization/ontology.

One can take an analogy from comparative politics and a comparison of national polities. Asking the general question 'Is the US comparable with Pakistan?' then the answer is that 'it depends'. Both are formally sovereign states, so in that respect they are comparable. It is possible to compare directly related issues such as about the drafting of their constitutions, about political participation or how they vote in the UN General Assembly. At the same time, however, the two countries are not usually considered very relevant cases for comparison when it comes to their federal systems, their priorities in space programmes, or the impact of monetary policies on the global economy, etc. Returning to the EU, the question of whether it is comparable with SAARC is similar to the questions about the US and Pakistan. The answer is that it 'depends' on the research question and what aspects of the region one is concerned with. Viewed as regions, both belong to the broad category of macro-regions, if these are defined as non-sovereign governance systems involving territories and actors belonging to a few neighbouring states. From this perspective, the preoccupation with the $n=1$ problem in much of EU studies becomes problematic.

Given this, the approach of this book is to underline the pluralism of comparison. Contemporary regionalism is multidimensional, involving many state and non-state actors in different institutional designs and networks. A rich discussion around comparative regionalism already exists in the field of regional security studies as well as in that of economic integration. In these discussions, Europe is treated as just one case among others, which is positive for comparative regionalism.

Conceptual pluralism is an inevitable argument, especially in the current era of multidimensional and heterogeneous regionalism. Above all, the definition and understanding of the region 'depends' on the research question under study and also on the ontology and conceptualization of the region. It must be emphasized that the choice of the definition (and therefore, the phenomenon to be studied) will have implications for the identification of the cases to be employed in comparative research. Subsequent chapters of this book serve to illustrate further the task of comparing regions under conditions of conceptual pluralism.

5
Obviating the Gap Between Formal and Informal Regionalism

In the study of regionalism too much focus has been placed on issues of sovereignty transfer, political unification and policy making within fixed and inter-state regional organizations and inter-state frameworks. This methodological bias is strongly correlated with the tendency to focus on and explain variations from the 'standard' European case, especially formalistic and EU-style institutionalization. This comparative marker is only one of many interpretations (or one essential characteristic) of European regionalism, and over-emphasizing it is a problem. Rethinking regionalism rests on a broader understanding of regions, reaching beyond hegemonic formal/formalistic and state-centric interpretations of regional institutions. This of course implies that comparison becomes a more pluralistic exercise.

Since the late 1990s, a positive development is the broadening of the research agenda on regionalism globally to include 'informal' dimensions and the involvement of a great variety of market and social actors (Bach 1999a; Acharya 2001; Wiener and Diez 2003; Söderbaum and Taylor 2008). This has spurred a fruitful debate about the various ways in which state, market and civil society actors relate and come together in different 'formal' and 'informal' coalitions, networks and modes of regional and multilevel governance (Katzenstein and Shiraishi 1997; Sandholtz and Stone Sweet 1998; Bøås et al. 1999; Christiansen and Piattoni 2004; Robinson et al. 2010). Nevertheless, most discussions are limited to particular regions, thus reinforcing an exaggerated regional specialization and, to some extent, even parochialism. Some of the differences between debates in Europe, Africa, Asia and other regions can be attributed to contextual and regional variations, but the systematic failure to transcend regional particularism signals the need for deepened comparative studies and more general conceptual and theoretical toolboxes. Any rethinking of regionalism needs to build on the knowledge accumulated in these debates, but it also needs to make progress on how formal and informal regions as well as state and a variety of non-state actors relate to one another both within and between regions.

This chapter provides an overview of the concepts, theories and debates on formal and informal regionalism, and identifies directions for how to transcend the current weaknesses and achieve a more globally applicable comparative regionalism.[1] The following section tries to clarify briefly why some theories are so heavily geared towards formal regionalism, whilst others are focused much more on the formal–informal nexus, or even informal regionalism *per se*. Next are four sections describing the unfolding of more regionally restricted debates around formal–informal regionalism in East and Southeast Asia, Africa, Europe and the Americas respectively. The chapter concludes with a summary of what is needed in order to further illuminate the formal–informal nexus in comparative regionalism.

Debates About Formal and Informal Regionalism

Many scholars studying regionalism have concentrated on determining what types of regions are the most functional, instrumental and efficient to 'rule' or govern. As a result, regions are usually conflated with inter-state or policy-driven frameworks. For instance, neofunctionalism emphasizes the deliberate design of regional institutions, which then are instrumental for problem-solving, sovereignty transfer, and the creation of functional as well as political spillover. Even if non-state and group interests are included in neofunctionalist thought, the main emphasis still is on how state 'interests' change, and the consequences of

---

[1] This chapter builds on Söderbaum (2011).

state–society relations for supranational and intergovernmental regional organizations.

Institutionalism, in its various versions, has become the contemporary form of functionalism and neofunctionalism. Neoliberal institutionalists share with the neo-realists the idea of an anarchical system in which states are largely rational and unitary actors. Non-state actors may pressurize their governments but power is performed within the framework of regional institutions. According to this perspective, state behaviour is constrained and affected by variations in the degree of institutionalization across different issue areas of international and regional politics.

Neo-realists and intergovernmentalists analyse the formation of regions from the outside-in. The structural features of the anarchical system make the states predisposed towards competition and conflict. Regions and regionalism may occur under certain circumstances; for instance, when the distribution of power allows for regional cooperation, either for geopolitical reasons or through the politics of alliance formation (Gilpin 1987). Even if neo-realists and intergovernmentalists are less convinced about the autonomous effects of regional organizations and institutions, regions are usually still defined and understood in terms of formal inter-state frameworks and regional organizations that exist 'out there'.

It is evident from the above that most rationalist theorizing is based on methodological nationalism and a concern with formal regional organizations and inter-state frameworks. Probably the most impressive comparative study of regional international institutions is Acharya and Johnston's (2007a) *Crafting Cooperation*, in which they and a range of well-known scholars study how institutions actually work, and the effect of institutional design. They extended their analysis beyond the conventional rationalist approach to institutional design in order to engage with constructivist and other approaches. Acharya and Johnston ask why different forms of institutionalization develop in different regions, and whether variation in institutional design leads to variation in the nature of cooperation; hence institutional design is analysed both as dependent and independent variable (Acharya and Johnston 2007b: 2, 15). Acharya and Johnston's study has a rather broad understanding of institutional design that includes both formal and informal rules and identity as well as norms (which are seen as the formal as well as informal ideology of the institution).

In this way, their approach is able to account for the so-called 'ASEAN Way', which is based on informality, flexibility, consensus and non-confrontation (Acharya and Johnston 2007c: 245). This approach marks a considerable development in the study of regional organizations and institutions and in the engagement with the formal–informal nexus. Regarding Asian institutions, Acharya and Johnston point out that:

> One of the main lines of difference is between the 'formal' informality of Asian institutions and the 'formal' formality of those in other regions. That is, the ASEAN states, for instance, have deliberately and carefully designed their institutions to be informal. And in other regions the formality of the institutions has been a cover for the informality or the weakly legalised way in which they have functioned. (Acharya and Johnston 2007c: 246)

Even if Acharya and Johnston's approach manages to integrate formality and informality within the same framework, it and other studies in the field of institutional design are nevertheless still geared towards existing state-led frameworks and institutions: their focus is institutional design rather than explaining regions and region-formation.

Other types of constructivist as well as reflectivist scholarship particularly emphasize the view that regions must not be taken for granted, nor be analysed as supra-national or inter-state regional organizations. From this perspective, regions are considered dynamic and heterogeneous settings for social interaction. Emphasis is placed on how (state as well as non-state) political actors perceive and interpret the idea of a region, and on notions of 'regionness', regionality and regional community (Murphy 1991; Hettne and Söderbaum 2000; Jönsson et al. 2000; Paasi 2001). It follows that this kind of scholarship is concerned mainly with the relationship between formal and informal regionalization rather than institutional design *per se*. Needless to say, this more eclectic conceptualization poses certain challenges for systematic comparison.

This short theoretical review is by no means exhaustive but simply serves to show that the debate on formal–informal regionalism is both expanding and vibrant. However, new definitions of formality–informality compete with old definitions, resulting in

a large number of alternative and often conflicting conceptualizations. As discussed below, the different regional debates often
are contextually determined and, to a large extent, isolated from
one another. Even if individual researchers often apply coherent
definitions, as a whole the literature is fragmented, leading to a
lack of general and globally applicable concepts and frameworks.

East and Southeast Asia

No consensus exists for a definition of the Asian region. The
meaning of regionalism has changed in relation to questions of
what sub-regions should be included or excluded, what dimensions of regionalism should be investigated (such as security,
economics, politics and identity) and what particular theoretical
perspectives should be employed. Conventionally, Asia is divided
into Central Asia, Northeast Asia, Southeast Asia and South
Asia, with a blurred border towards the Middle East. Most literature related to regionalism has focused on East Asia; that is,
Northeast Asia and/or Southeast Asia. This situation reveals the
difficulty in taking the region as 'given' and also the limitations of
focusing on one particular regional organization.

Even so, a considerable body of literature on East Asian
regionalism is concerned with the study of ASEAN (see Acharya
2001; Collins 2007; Ba 2009). At least historically, a major reason
for this emphasis is that ASEAN is one of the few sustainable
regional organizations in East and Southeast Asia – and to a large
extent, this reflects a preference for studying state-led regional
organizations instead of broader processes of regionalization
and region-formation. During the Cold War, the core of ASEAN
cooperation lay in its joint effort to consolidate the member
nation-states and to enhance stability. These goals were driven by
a narrow political elite in what, at that time, were relatively fledg-
ling and fragile state formations. Communism was the primary
internal and external threat. The raison d'être of ASEAN – as
a bulwark against communist expansion – is long gone from the
political landscape; the focus has shifted now to increasing economic development and to ensuring security in a new context.

During recent decades an important part of the debate about
regionalism in East Asia has focused on collective identity formation and informal or 'soft' regionalism (Katzenstein 2000;

Acharya 2001). This scholarship seeks to account for the non-legalistic style of decision-making that predominates in this region, and the fact that there has been no transfer of national sovereignty to a supranational authority. It is emphasized that East and Southeast Asian regionalism is characterized by a dense network of informal gatherings, working groups and advisory groups, particularly within ASEAN, but also in ASEAN Plus Three (APT) (ASEAN plus China, Japan and the Republic of Korea), the ASEAN Regional Forum (ARF), APEC, and to some extent the Asia-Europe Meeting (ASEM). This informal style of decision-making incorporates its own innate code of conduct that is often referred to as the 'ASEAN Way' (or 'soft institutionalism'). In contrast to European- and North American-style formal bureaucratic structures and legalistic decision-making procedures, the 'ASEAN Way' is built around discreetness, informality, pragmatism, consensus-building and non-confrontational bargaining styles (Acharya 1997: 329). To some extent, the code of conduct reflects the illiberal underpinnings of the 'Asian values' construct, which stresses a communitarian ethic ('society over the self') (Acharya 2002: 27–8). This means that there is a considerable emphasis on cultural factors when explaining the ASEAN Way and its differences to Europe.

As noted above, there is a vigorous debate about the impact and efficiency of the informal and non-legalistic approach to Asian regionalism (see Acharya and Johnston 2007a). The 1997/98 Asian financial crisis not only underlined the interdependence of Northeast and Southeast Asian countries but also, according to Higgott (2002: 2), 'exposed the weakness of existing regional institutional economic arrangements'. To some observers, the crisis undermined confidence in the soft institutionalism of the ASEAN Way, and underscored the move towards deeper institutionalization and stronger commitments from countries in the region. Following the region's recovery from the 1997/98 financial crises, the East Asian countries moved to institutionalize annual leaders' summits and ministerial dialogues through the APT framework. The most concrete project in this regard is the Chiang Mai Initiative (CMI), which was adopted in May 2000 in order to provide emergency foreign currency liquidity support in the event of a future financial crisis. But broader cooperation also exists in a range of areas, such as small- and medium-scale industrial development, human resource development, agriculture, tourism and information technology (Nesudurai 2005: 167). Since the late 2000s, discussions have intensified regarding the role of India and Australia and New Zealand, especially concerning the establishment of an East Asian Free Trade Area (EAFTA).

The question arises whether the informal nature of East Asian regionalism is having an impact on the study of comparative regionalism more broadly. As indicated in the previous chapter, there are few comparisons of the main regions in the world – the main exception being a fair number between Europe and East/Southeast Asia. That is, a number of studies explicitly or implicitly compare (informal) Asian regionalism with (formal) European integration, although a large portion of these seek to understand how East and Southeast Asian regionalism deviates from the EU (Choi and Caporaso 2002: 485). As noted earlier, regarding EU-style institutionalization as an ideal model for regionalism is deeply problematic. There is no reason why European integration should be a model for Asian regionalism: there can be many pathways to successful and legitimate regionalisms. Indeed, as Acharya and Johnston point out, 'more formally institutionalized regional groups do not necessarily produce more effective cooperation … More informal groups such as ASEAN have had a discernible impact in changing the preferences and norms of their members' (Acharya and Johnston 2007c: 268–9). Their important conclusion is that 'greater formality [e.g. a shift from consensus to majority voting] may actually affect cooperation negatively' (Acharya and Johnston 2007c: 270).

Europe

Europe has a long history of integrative and disintegrative processes. In recent decades, the regionalization process has centred ultimately on the dominant project that has widened and deepened in scope, reach and ambition to a remarkable degree to culminate in what today is the EU. Historically, intense debates swirled around varieties of realist/intergovernmental and functional/liberal/institutional perspectives. Focusing on different aspects of the integration process, these different approaches to a large extent share a main concern with formal and state-steered regional frameworks and institutions. For instance, realists and intergovernmentalists appear to have the most to say about the logic behind large Council meetings and treaty reforms such as Maastricht, Amsterdam, Nice and Lisbon (Grieco 1997; Moravcsik 1998). Meanwhile, the functional/liberal/institutional approaches focus more on economic integration and other areas in which the EU's central institutions such as the Commission and the Court play a more prominent role (Sandholtz and Stone Sweet 1998; Pollack 2003). Liberal perspectives especially do acknowledge the role of non-state actors in regional integration but even so, the main emphasis is placed on the ways these non-state actors affect states-led and policy-driven regionalism.

Other scholars emphasize still other variables, such as the fundamentally changed political landscape in Europe that blurs the distinction between international and domestic politics. One such perspective is 'multilevel governance', which posits that power and decision-making in Europe are not concentrated at one level (national or supranational) but rather are characterized by a complex web of relations between public and private actors who are nested in supranational, national and micro-regional levels (Hooghe and Marks 2001). Even if the multilevel governance approach represents considerable progress and innovation in the study of European integration, its main concern remains with authority and governance structures and the nature of policy- and decision-making, especially at the EU level.

In recent years social constructivism has gained a more prominent place in the study of European integration (Christiansen et al. 1999). This line of thinking entered the discussion on European integration mainly as a spillover from the discipline of IR, and as a means of transcending the rather introverted debates between liberal and realist/intergovernmentalist approaches of European/ EU integration. A social constructivist approach emphasizes the mutual constitutiveness of structure and agency, and pays particular attention to the role of ideas, values, norms and identities in the social construction of Europe (rather than EU *per se*) (Christiansen et al. 1999). As such, it draws attention away from the formality and particularities of the EU and this has important consequences for the potential of comparison. Undoubtedly, social constructivism has revitalized the study of European integration, but it makes comparisons primarily between Europe and *international* regimes rather than between Europe and other *regions*. One rather unintended consequence nevertheless is that it facilitates comparisons and cross-fertilization with other regions around both formal and informal dimensions of regionalism. As one of the key European social constructivists, Jeffrey Checkel, points out: 'If not yet completely gone, then the days of *sui generis* arguments about Europe are numbered, which is very good news indeed' (Checkel 2007: 243). Indeed, there is considerable scope for more comparison with the social construction of other regional spaces and organizations.

As outlined in the previous chapter, recent decades have seen a great diversity of theorizing about regionalism in Europe. First of all, there is a series of different interpretations of the EU, and some more recent theories and approaches tend to obviate the distinctions between formality and informality, and between gendered, poststructuralist and postmodernist approaches (Wiener and Diez 2003). Secondly, Europe is not equivalent to the EU. Europe counts a number of varied and partly overlapping schemes, some of which are weakly formalized, in many of its sub-regions, such as the Nordic countries, Scandinavia, the Baltic Sea Region, Eastern Europe and so on. This diversity is having a positive influence on the study of regionalism overall and in the debate between European integration and comparative regionalism.

Africa

Discussions about regionalism in Africa also focus heavily on formal/formalistic state-led regional integration frameworks. Two partly overlapping schools of thought dominate this debate. The first takes its point of departure in the pan-African visions and series of treaties developed within the framework of the OAU and, more recently, the AU as well as regional organizations such as ECOWAS, SADC, and so forth (Asante 1997; Muchie 2003; Murithi 2005; Taylor 2005). Earlier strategies during the old regionalism from the 1960s through to the 1980s were built around state-led industrialization, import substitution and collective self-reliance. In contrast, since the early and late 1990s the dominant view is that Africa 'must unite' in order to avoid its marginalization in the global economy, and instead it should exploit the opportunities provided by economic globalization. Indeed, an overarching market orientation in combination with EU-style institutionalization is the official strategy adopted by most of the main African regional cooperation and integration schemes, such as AU, COMESA, ECOWAS, SADC, and UEMOA. After the end of the Cold War, security regionalism also achieved a more prominent role in the discussions of African regional organizations, as seen in the debates about the African Peace and Security Architecture (APSA).

The second school of thought is associated with institutionalist and functional-liberal lines of thought, concentrating on formal inter-state frameworks and/or official trade and investment flows. This perspective relies heavily on the EC/EU as a comparative marker or model (Foroutan 1995; Holden 2001; Jenkins and Thomas 2001).

There are important similarities in the two schools. Both are state-centric, and biased in favour of formal regional organizations, while largely neglecting underlying societal logic as well as informal regionalism. And both are optimistic regarding the potential benefits of formal and state-led regional frameworks. They differ nonetheless about the causes of failed implementation. The pan-Africanist school explain the limited achievements and poor implementation apparent in the last five decades of regionalism in Africa by referring to unfavourable external conditions, whilst functionalist/institutionalists find reasons in a lack of institutional capacity to implement agreed policies (either within African organizations or on the national level).

In this context, it is noteworthy that the pan-Africanists take the EC/EU experience as an inspiration, and as a justification for the development of pan-African regionalism. Indeed, despite their foundational differences in terms of ideology and understanding of global capitalism, both strands of thought make implicit or explicit comparisons with the EU and come to similar conclusions that notwithstanding the past 'failure' of regionalism in Africa, there still is great potential to build successful regionalism in the future.

Eurocentrism is a fundamental problem with both perspectives that, furthermore, crowds out less sanguine and less politically correct assessments. There is in fact, a third but smaller group of scholars – mostly associated with assorted types of critical and new regionalism approaches – that is more sceptical about the restructured regional organizations being able to attain their goals of highly developed institutional frameworks with attendant economic and political integration (nearly always modelled on the EC/EU). This scepticism has resulted in a radically different interpretation of regionalism in Africa that in the African context eschews the artificial separation of state and non-state actors and of the formal and the informal that traditional regional approaches hold so dear (Bach 1999a and b; Bøås et al. 1999 and 2003; Grant and Söderbaum 2003; Hentz and Bøås 2003; Söderbaum 2004; Söderbaum and Taylor 2008; Shaw et al 2011). Concentrating solely on the state is to misunderstand the nature of politics and regionalism in Africa. As Clapham points out:

> The model of inter-state integration through formal institutional frameworks, which has hitherto dominated the analysis of integration in Africa and elsewhere, has increasingly been challenged by the declining control of states over their own territories, the proliferation of informal networks, and the incorporation of Africa (on a highly subordinate basis) into the emerging global order. (Clapham 1999: 53)

The particular importance of informal regionalism in the African context relates to both the informal economy and the informal nature of politics. Many parts of Africa are characterized by myriad informal and heterogeneous interactions between and activities by a mosaic of informal workers, self-employed agents, families, business networks, petty traders, migrant labour, refugees, and so forth. In fact, relative to the formal economy, the size of the informal economy in Africa is the highest in the world. And in many parts of Africa informal employment represents up to 75 percent of non-agricultural employment, and in sub-Saharan Africa around half or more of total GDP.

This critical and new regionalism school builds on literature about the 'informal' nature of political power in Africa. In Africa, state power is less about administration over the state and its attendant geographic area, with all the attendant implications regarding the provision of services to the populace, and more about the management of a relatively limited set of resources (in terms of geography and economic embeddedness) that are both the sources of revenue and the foundations for entrenching power through patronage. Indeed, the informal character of politics on the continent inevitably impacts upon the types and varieties of regionalism in Africa.

Shadow regionalism – or what Bach refers to as 'trans-state regionalization'(Bach 1999a, 2005) – is an important ingredient of regionalism as portrayed by the new regionalists. Shadow regionalism suggests that regime actors use their positions of power within the state apparatus in order to erect a form of regionalism that is informal and driven by rent-seeking and personal self-interest. The resulting mode of regionalism can be complex. Control of the state serves the twin purposes of lubricating the patronage network and satisfying the selfish desire of elites to enrich themselves – in many cases, in spectacular fashion. Taking the example of the Great Lakes region, Taylor and Williams argue that the war in this region potentially offers substantial resources to well-placed elites and business people able to exploit them. Soliciting foreign involvement is not just about preserving national security and defeating enemies, but also about securing access to resource-rich areas and establishing privatized accumulation networks that can emerge and prosper under conditions of war and anarchy (Taylor and Williams 2001: 273).

These observations show that regionalism can be more complex (and sometimes also more detrimental) than a simple instrument to enhance an ambiguous 'national interest' (realism) or to procure the 'public good' or 'trade' (liberalism). Potentially, state actors can promote regionalization in order to pursue private goals and promote particular (vested) interests rather than broader societal interests. All too often, the state is much less than what it pretends to be. The so-called 'national interest' simply may be a group-specific interest or even the personal interests of certain political leaders, rather than the public good or national security and development in a broader sense. For instance, Bach claims that regional organizations may constitute a means for 'resource capture' and international patronage (Bach 2005). When this occurs, it results in regionalization without (the implementation of) formal regional integration. As a consequence, informal and formal processes exist in a symbiotic relationship and in studying regionalism they need to be integrated within the same framework.

The type of 'shadow regionalism' addressed here may in itself be a goal, but it also may be closely related to a more formal but symbolic 'regime boosting' regionalism (Söderbaum 2004). This refers to the practice adopted by many ruling regimes and political leaders in Africa of engaging in symbolic and discursive region-building activities – praising the goals of regionalism and regional organizations, signing cooperation treaties and agreements, and taking part in 'summitry regionalism' – whilst remaining uncommitted to or unwilling to implement, jointly agreed policies. Regionalism in such cases is a discursive and image-boosting exercise: leaders demonstrate support and loyalty towards one another in order to raise the status and image and reinforce the formal sovereignty of their often authoritarian regimes, both domestically and internationally (Clapham 1996; Bøås 2003). As Herbst (2007: 144) correctly observes, 'African leaders are extremely enthusiastic about particular types of regional cooperation, especially those that highlight sovereignty, help secure national leaders, and ask little in return'. Little wonder then that African political elites continue to participate in regional organizations that have long records of 'failure'. Those who believe that regional institutions truly exist in order to solve regional and collective problems will not understand this tendency, but it is intelligible from a domestic perspective: 'Regional institutions in Africa usually work when they help African leaders with their domestic problems' (Herbst 2007: 129).

Regionalism in Africa is often seen as weak or 'failed', or it is simply ignored by the dominant theories in the field of comparative regionalism. However, regionalism in Africa undoubtedly is vibrant, but this can only be understood if one moves beyond superficial distinctions of formal–informal. If the intricate relationship between formal and informal regionalism on the African continent is to be understood properly, we need to go beyond the over-emphasis on formal and policy-led regionalism, which to a considerable extent is derived from a particular reading of European integration. For similar reasons, we need to move past the related but false assumption that there is necessarily a conflict between sovereignty and regionalism. As noted above, regionalism in Africa is sometimes used to boost national sovereignty and regime interests as well as more narrow group-specific interests.

African regionalism has an important contribution to make to broader comparative studies of regional dynamics. Informal regionalism is by no means absent from EU studies, but the intense link between formal and informal regionalism/regionalization in the African case represents a contribution to both European and comparative integration studies. As shown by the African case, one can speak, for instance, of relevant and truly regional dynamics and patterns that are not mirrored by formal regional efforts. Furthermore, the African (as well as the Asian) case highlights the importance not only of inquiring into the informality underpinning/accompanying formal regional projects, but also taking a broader perspective on the formal–informal aspects of regionalism/regionalization. Scholarly debate on regional integration has taken steps to compare Europe and Asia (often contrasting the former to the latter in terms of formal vs. informal), but inserting Africa (and other regions) into this discussion is required in order to develop a more genuinely global agenda for comparative regionalism.

Americas

Historically, the Americas have been differentiated as North America, Latin America and the Caribbean. Since the end of the Cold War, this division has become increasingly inadequate for understanding regional processes in the Americas. Strong convergences are evident, both within Latin America and between Latin America and North America. As Phillips (2005: 58) asserts, '(t)he most profitable way of proceeding is therefore to abandon traditional categories in favour of a mode of analysis which seeks to advance an integrated understanding of the Americas *as a region*, the various parts of which are best disaggregated into … distinctive but interlocking subregions' (that is, Andean, Caribbean, Central America, North America and the Southern Cone).

There is a plethora of sub-regional projects across the Americas, but most attention in the debate has focused on NAFTA in the north, on Mercosur in the south and more recently, on a set of more recent regionalist projects such as the Union of South American Nations (UNASUR) and the Bolivarian Alliance for the Americas (ALBA). The origins of NAFTA trace back to the growing concerns of Canada and Mexico that protectionist US policies could potentially devastate their economies (Pastor 2005: 220). NAFTA was preceded by a bilateral free trade agreement between Canada and the USA, and when a similar agreement was proposed between Mexico and the US, Canada sought a tripartite agreement. Mexico's involvement is particularly intriguing. Mexico's tradition of combining nationalism, protectionism, and 'anti-gringoism' is still evident, but the country's oil-based self-reliance is no longer credible. Mexico had earlier harboured the ambition of becoming a regional power but, in joining NAFTA in 1992, it nonetheless was the first Latin American country to conclude that a free trade policy was the path out of stagnation.

The North American integration process is characterized by close cooperation between the US administration and American business interests. The NAFTA proposals were hotly debated in the US, where criticism focused particularly on the issues of migration, the relocation of manufacturing industries to Mexico and, to some extent, environment and labour issues. An important aspect of the transformation of the Americas is linked to the changing strategy of the US and to the consolidation of, as well as resistance towards, neoliberal policies. NAFTA maintains a strong emphasis on trade and market liberalization in combination with a weak institutional structure and weak political ambitions that respects the sovereignty of each member state. This contrasts sharply with the emphasis on deep and institutional integration evident within the EU. Although the NAFTA treaty is binding on its member states and involves certain dispute settlement mechanisms, these are *ad hoc* and NAFTA's objectives are limited to the regulation of trade and investment flows and the protection of property rights. 'The style of NAFTA's governance is *laissez-faire*, reactive, and legalistic: problems are defined by plaintiffs and settled by litigation' (Pastor 2005: 220).

Discussions in Canada and Mexico concerning NAFTA predominantly related to the particular neoliberal character of the agreement and the dominant position of the US. Significantly, opposition to the project by civil society has taken a regional form. According to Marchand (2001: 210), the 'hyperliberal' NAFTA constitutes the 'worst' of the new regionalism in North America, whereas the mobilization of a regionalized civil society and other more bottom-up and spontaneous practices constitute the 'best' (see more in Chapter 8, on Civil Society in Regionalism).

While NAFTA more or less emerged as a consequence of US bilateralism, Mercosur emerged both as a consequence of the democratic and economic reforms in Brazil and Argentina and as a planned and intended regional venture. Initially, Mercosur was described in terms of 'open regionalism' (*regionalismo abierto*) (ECLAC 1994). This points to an outward-oriented regional response to the challenges of economic globalization and to a mechanism for the governments to 'lock in' economic and political reform programmes. In this sense, Mercosur represented a clear shift in the South American integration model away from the inward orientation of the past. According to Alvaro Vasconcelos (2007: 166), the main motivation of Mercosur was a desire to create a common market modelled on the EC/EU. In the 1990s Mercosur was widely considered a 'success' (Malamud 2003), particularly because the participating countries agreed on far-reaching tariff liberalization and there was a significant increase in the level of intra-regional trade, at least by comparison with previous, failed projects such as the Latin American Integration Association (LAIA). Today, Mercosur faces serious problems stemming from a range of tensions and conflicts; for instance, recurrent financial and political crises, the role of Brazil, and merging differences with regard to institutionalization and regionalization strategy, etc.

Mercosur has been a strongly statist project. Its formal institutions are weak and directly dependent on national administrations, which are responsible for the coordination and preparation of negotiations between the member governments. This can be understood either as an intergovernmental negotiating structure, or as 'presidentialism'; according to Malamud (2003: 56), the latter should be seen as a 'functional equivalent' to regional institutions within the EU. The intergovernmental institutions exist alongside an embryonic legal doctrine that covers two areas: common trade regulations and a system for the resolution of disputes. Inevitably, the numbers of issues that require community-level regulation has grown but the key member states (especially Brazil) appear to prefer 'political' and intergovernmental solutions over the 'legal' avenue of the supranational court of justice. Brazil's individualistic strategy implies weak central institutions and trade integration only. Conversely, Brazil favours a strengthened political role for Mercosur in the Americas, as a mechanism to resist the US, including the now abandoned US-led Free Trade of the Americas (FTAA). This emphasis on political counterweight has been strengthened by Venezuela's entry into the organization in 2006. In this sense Mercosur might represent a Latin alternative to 'North Americanization', and somewhat reminiscent of earlier Latin American models of regionalism.

Looking more generally at Latin America, scholars draw attention to the overlap and competition between different commercial, political and trans-societal regional projects. According to Riggirozzi (2012), projects such as UNASUR and ALBA are grounded in different system of rules and represent divergent pathways to region-building and 'regionness' in South America.

Conclusion

Researching regionalism has a long tradition of focusing on formal regional organizations and formal regionalism. This is a consequence of the dominance of theoretical perspectives that place exaggerated emphasis on the role of governments and policy-driven and states-led regional organizations. Since the late 1990s, an increased emphasis on constructivist and reflectivist theorizing has seen the introduction to the debate of notions of soft, informal regionalism as well as alternative (non-state) agents. This is certainly a positive development since all regionalism is simultaneously both formal and informal, and only rarely are regions constructed by state actors alone.

This chapter illustrates the lack in these debates of systematic comparisons. Scholars who manage to transcend orthodox and state-centric analyses of regions, mostly tend to be highly specialized in a particular region and have a primary concern with developing conceptual toolboxes and theories for the analysis of that region instead of for comparative purposes. Consequently, the debate around formal–informal regionalism has a problem with parochialism, which prevents scholars from recognizing that they are often dealing with similar or even the same phenomena, but couched in different theoretical language and conceptualizations.

For instance, there is no reason to believe that soft institutionalism is a uniquely East Asian phenomenon. It remains for systematic research to explore the extent to which soft institutionalism applies beyond East Asia. Similarly, there is nothing to suggest that either regime-boosting or shadow regionalism is uniquely African. The role of procedures, symbols, 'summitry' and other rhetorical and discursive practices highlighted in the debate on African regionalism and regime-boosting also appear strongly in other regions, in both the present and past eras. For example, the Arab League is undoubtedly a project shaped and surrounded by rhetoric, perhaps even more so than many African regional organizations. Likewise, there seems to be a strong sense of regime-boosting within ASEAN (backed by the tradition of non-intervention). Furthermore, the Bolivarian project of regionalism (ALBA), is first and foremost an anti-liberal and anti-American project. Even if there is 'implementation' and achievements in some specific sectors, such as oil, gas and health, the ideological and counter-hegemonic component is clearly its foundation. Likewise, it is difficult to dispute that rhetoric and symbols played an important role in the now defunct Soviet-led Council for Mutual Economic Assistance. And discursive practices and symbolism have certainly also played a role in the EU, as seen in the 'circus' surrounding the summits, the extensive uses of flags, hymns, prizes as well as the many attempts to create a shared political history of EU. All these examples highlight the role of procedures, symbols, 'summitry', and other discursive practices in regionalisms from around the world.

Following from the above, there is a need to penetrate the surface and rhetoric of regionalism. Many scholars are rather idealistic about state-led regional cooperation and regional integration, and therefore often fail to ask critical questions about for whom and for what purpose regional activities are carried out. The concept of 'shadow regionalism' is helpful in that it captures regional dynamics that, while keeping up universalistic appearances, mostly serve to uphold parallel and often informally institutionalized patterns of enrichment of a select group of actors. Certainly, patron–client relationships, corruption and informal politics are not unique to Africa, and this implies that there is considerable scope to take lessons from this kind of research and apply them more generally to comparative research.

Concerning shadow regionalism, it may also be possible to draw the contrasts with the EU in terms of the role of rules for cross-border activity. What is different is that, in the EU case, regional economic interactions have been seen largely as developing the impetus for the expansion of rules, whereas shadow regionalism in Africa suggests that informal trade thrives because 'there are no rules', or at least because of the continued presence of formal border disparities. This raises the possibility of research on the comparative political economy of regional economic activity and the role of rules, particularly given the common assumption within the EU that rules are vital to the flourishing of such activity.

The general conclusion is that within the debate a large number of partly overlapping and partly competing labels have been used in order to capture similar phenomena. From the eclectic comparative perspective represented by this book, the solution is not to abandon context but to think in more general terms, while at the same time developing frameworks and concepts that allow for cultural and contextual sensitivity. This requires an understanding of the potential for cross-fertilization between regional debates and for working with both formal and informal regionalism.

6

Organizing Regional Space

This chapter underlines the increasing heterogeneity of contemporary regionalism and the fact that an array of state, market, civil society and even external actors come together at various scales of action to produce multiple regions and regional collaborative mechanisms. At the start, a distinction is made between different types of regions, such as ecological regions, economic regions and political regions. The second section differentiates different forms of regional collaboration mechanisms in terms of forms of organization and scope of action. The third section highlights the interactions between macro-regionalism and micro-regionalism, with empirical illustrations from Europe, Southeast Asia and Southern Africa. The chapter concludes with a discussion.

Types of Regions

From the previous chapters, it is evident that regions appear in many guises and shapes. It is possible to identify at least six general types of regions, which may interact in various ways and occur at different territorial scales: (i) geographic-ecological regions; (ii) cultural or cognitive regions; (iii) economic regions; (iv) administrative regions; (v) political regions; and (vi) security regions (Keating and Loughlin 1997: 2–5; Jönsson et al. 2000: 139).

Regions may, at least partly, be determined by physical geography and ecology. Throughout history, societies have been linked by lakes, rivers and roads, whereas often they have been separated by mountains and forests. Transportation facilities often influenced earlier settlements and societies, and over the centuries led to systems that shaped patterns of interaction, which in turn led to the construction of regions of different size. The Norwegian fjord valleys, river basins such as the Zambezi and the Mekong, lakes such as the Black Sea, the Great Lakes in Africa and North America, and ecological zones such as the Amazonas and the Sahara all count as physical-geographic regions. Geographical and ecological conditions alone do not produce regions. That requires that the geographic extent be filled with social content.

Cultural or cognitive regions may have their origins in physical-geographic regions, but this is by no means always the case. Regions may endure because of their association with culture, identity, religion and a common history. As Jönsson et al. (2000: 139) point out, 'identity is a dual concept. It connotes remoteness and delimitation as well as commonality and community – external remoteness and internal community'. This means that while cultural regions often build on shared history and cultural similarities and compatibilities they may also be defined by opposition to an external 'Other': for instance, in terms of a security threat, or an external cultural challenge (Hurrell 1995: 41). Another cultural distinction is between multicultural and monocultural regions, which tend to correspond to the distinction between macro-regions and subnational/cross-border micro-regions respectively. Cultural macro-regions are larger 'imagined communities', where identity, culture and history are shared but not monolithic (Europe, Latin America, Africa, the Arab world, South Asia, etc). In this sense, identity and culture have been part of the formation of regions and regionalism since far back in history, as exemplified by empires, civilizations, anti-colonial struggles as well as pan-regionalist movements.

Economic regions come in many varieties. Such regions are often functional and demarcated from the outside world in terms of transportation, contacts and other dependencies and flows that connect peoples and structures (Jönsson et al. 2000: 139). Economic regions may also refer to regional production systems and territories/zones for economic development. They may exist on a variety of scales more or less all over the world, ranging from the EU down to smaller subnational or cross-border micro-regions. Theorists have highlighted 'new' economic micro-regions that arose due to local and endogenous development but which are related to economic globalization, technological changes and shifts in the factors of economic production (Ohmae 1995; Keating and Loughlin 1997: 2).

Administrative/planning regions are essentially functional regions as well, but of a different type than economic regions. They exist for purposes of decision-making, policy-making or simply for the collection and publication of statistics. Many administrative/planning regions have little dynamism in their own right; they may bear no relationship to geography, culture or economics and they may have no political function or directly elected bodies. Examples of this are the administrative regions constructed by the UN Economic Commission for Africa (UNECA) or the Global Environment Facility (GEF), which have no correspondence with existing regional organizations or different types of interdependencies.

Political regions are extremely varied. Having strong supranational powers, the EU is by far the world's most advanced political macro-region. Other regions show varying degrees of political cooperation and unification, but generally their political strength lies in the degree to which member states act collectively and in their institutional strength. Political regions differ from administrative regions by having a much deeper impact on political, economic and social life, by means of executive bodies or more comprehensive mechanisms for decision-making and policy.

Security regions may be closely linked to political regions, perhaps even as a sub-category of them. But they may also be related to cultural regions, arising when a sufficient sense of 'community' has developed among their populations that allows a dependable expectation of peaceful change. The Nordic case illustrates a security community without a comprehensive political framework. A less-demanding definition than a security community suggests that if the security concerns of two or more contiguous states are so intertwined that these states cannot be analysed apart from each other, they then may be grouped within a so-called 'regional security complex' (Buzan 2003).

In the real world these different types of regions tend to intersect. Even if one type dominates in a specific region, different types may still compete, overlap or proceed in parallel. Since the emergence of new regionalism from the mid-1980s, it has become more difficult to draw distinctions between the different forms of region. For instance, it is increasingly difficult to distinguish between political and economic regions and, to some extent, also between economic regions and security regions. Likewise, it is also evident that culture and identity shape and intersect with more functional economic and interest-based type of regions.

Institutions, Organizations and Networks

A significant amount of research shows that 'institutions' indeed act as facilitators of international collaboration and collective action. Few observers dispute that 'institutions matter': they can help states and other agents to negotiate mutually beneficial outcomes, for example, by shaping calculations, expectations and interests; by reducing transaction costs; and by facilitating the development of convergent expectations. In essence, institutions constrain and regulate agency across different policy fields in international and regional politics (Mansfield and Milner 1997; Acharya and Johnston 2007a). In liberal and institutionalist thought, there is a widespread expectation that successful regionalism will become increasingly institutionalized. Many realists even accept this proposition. For many observers, the main question is which institutional design is most 'effective', because there are costs involved and different institutional designs have different strengths and weaknesses. In contrast, from a constructivist-reflectivist perspective the concern is not so much which institutional design is most effective, but rather understanding for whom and for what purpose the different organizational forms and designs relate and interact in the making and unmaking of regions. Indeed, institutions do more than just support economic and political life, they enable and shape it (Duina 2013).

Institutions are often mixed up with more specific organizations and networks. Institutions, or perhaps more precisely, social institutions, imply patterned, predictable behaviour and a system of rules. Organizations and networks on the other hand, may or may not possess these characteristics (Hodgson 1988). Institutions underpin, shape and stabilize social order and facilitate cooperation. Organizations and networks may be created overnight and may not necessarily facilitate cooperation. Sometimes institutions may even be manipulated by specific interests. However, an organization may be more readily held accountable for its actions than will an institution.

Few studies of comparative regionalism uphold a distinction between organizations and networks. An organization is commonly defined as having: (i) specified aims, functions and activities; (ii) a membership and (iii) its own formal, permanent structure to order its responsibilities and carry out its functions (i.e. a constitution, treaty and/or administrative structure) (Archer 1992).

Above all, what differentiates most organizations from more loosely structured and less-hierarchical networks is the third component of a formal and permanent bureaucratic structure, with a minimum degree of autonomy from its members. Compared to the hierarchy in organizations, networks are usually more decentralized and horizontally structured. Networks may also be less formalized than organizations. Networks come in many varieties, with different structures, functions, objectives and types of participants: they may be physical and tangible, institutional and organizational, or socio-cultural (Jönsson et al. 2000: 24). Some networks are not concerned with policy formulation and project implementation, but instead are focused on increasing communication and interaction or getting cooperation started.

In comparison, organizations and networks have different functions and advantages. A formalized, clearly defined administrative and hierarchical organization, for example, may be effective and rational with respect to the implementation of strategies and policies, especially in a stable environment and where the problem to be addressed is clearly defined. By contrast, a more decentralized and flexible network structure may be more adaptable in a turbulent, rapidly changing environment and in situations where progress depends on accommodative, flexible cooperation and more informal and inclusive relationships and communication. A primary importance of social relationships and the ways of forming and maintaining communication, cooperation and trust are the basic characteristics of networks. Social network theory is founded on the fact that there often exists a network-like pattern of mainly voluntary, informal and close relationships and communication channels between peoples, that lack clear, visible boundaries or a formally coordinated 'centre' or mechanism (Thompson et al. 1991; Castells 1996). Network theory helps to move beyond methodological nationalism and the reductionist focus on states-led regional organizations:

As a metaphor of human organization, 'network' transcends territoriality; it substitutes horizontal, decentralized organization for vertical, hierarchical organization; it associates to complex, open-ended systems rather than to simple, closed systems. ... In these senses it challenges the very aspects of states that we have come to take for granted. In fact, it challenges the 'container' schema, which forms the basis of our metaphorical understanding of states. (Jönsson et al. 2000: 15–16)

A network-based social structure usually lacks clear-cut internal divisions, and often people are allowed to join or exit with relative ease. Many networks are open, extroverted and inclusive, capable of expanding without (formal) limitations, and interacting with new 'nodes' and other networks as long as the members are able to communicate among themselves.

Networks and organizations may interact and even merge, for instance through hybrid 'network organizations'. According to Castells (1996), this is the key to why the EU is functioning. Thus, networks and organizations may sometimes overlap in practice: a network may very well be an organization, and sometimes an organization is structured like a network.

Types of Regional Cooperation Mechanisms

There are multiple ways of categorizing the organization of regional cooperation. A relevant distinction is between organizational *form* and organizational *scope* (see Table 6.1). Organizational form refers to whether the regional cooperation mechanism is, in fact, an 'organization' or instead a more loosely structured 'network'. Organizational scope refers to whether cooperation in terms of both aims and activities is single-purpose and specialized, or multipurpose and comprehensive. A single-purpose and limited scope implies that the regional mechanism is concerned either with a particular type of activity, usually within a given sector, such as trade or transport, or with one particular task, such as financing development projects. A multipurpose regional organization or network is focused on a broader scope, spanning two or more themes or sectors. Lenz and colleagues refers to task-specific and general purpose regional organizations (Lenz et al. 2014).

Single-Purpose Regional Organizations

A large number of regional cooperation mechanisms correspond to the category of 'specialized organizations'. Most frequently encountered are *functional and sectoral regional organizations* that operate in most fields of activity, such as transport and

Table 6.1   Types of regional cooperation mechanisms

| | | **Forms of organization** | |
		Organization	*Network*
Scope	*Single-purpose*	• Transport organization • Security organization • Regional development bank • UN Economic Commission • River basin organization	• Research network • Public-private partnership • Business networks • Civil society network • Regional power pool
	Multi-purpose	• Development community • Regional economic community • Economic union • Political union • Federation	• Growth triangle • Development corridor

communications, education, research and health. Examples include the West African Health Organization (WAHO), Caribbean Public Health Agency (CARPHA), Southern African Centre for Cooperation in Agricultural Research (SACCAR), the Zambezi River Basin Commission (ZAMCOM) and the Latin American and Caribbean Air Transport Association (ALTA).

Security organizations and alliances specialize in security and conflict intervention, and examples are the Organization for Security and Cooperation in Europe (OSCE) and the North Atlantic Treaty Organization (NATO). Increasingly, they tend to develop out of or become an integral part of more broadly based, multipurpose regional organizations, as exemplified by the security branches of AU, ECOWAS, the EU and SADC.

There are very many *regional trading agreements* of various types and sizes. These may require only a minimal organizational structure, as is the case of the NAFTA and SACU. Nonetheless, there is tendency to build up a certain organizational and institutional capacity in order to regulate regional relations. Furthermore, compared to what was the case during old regionalism, regional trading arrangements have usually become integral parts of more comprehensive and *multipurpose regional organizations*, such as ASEAN, EEC, ECOWAS, Mercosur and SADC, although these do have different historical trajectories.

Regional development banks such as the Inter-American Development Bank (IADB), the Asian Development Bank (ADB) and the African Development Bank (AfDB) have facilitated regional cooperation on their continents. They seek to fund projects in a wide variety of sectors and fields and, consequently, usually have a broad spread of competences. Their mission, nonetheless, is specialized – and that is to finance and mobilize resources for development projects. In addition, their regionality is somewhat ambiguous due to strong non-regional membership/ ownership, and so they may in fact be understood as multilateral development banks operating in a regional context (Mistry 1999).

The *United Nations Regional Economic Commissions*, such as the UN Economic Commission for Latin America and the Caribbean (ECLAC), the UN Economic and Social Commission for Asia and the Pacific (ESCAP), the UN Economic and Social Commission for Western Asia (ESCWA), the UN Economic Commission for Africa (ECA) and the UN Economic Commission for Europe (UNECE), aim to facilitate concerted action in support of the economic and social development of the continents or countries where they operate. They function within the UN framework and are subject to the general supervision of the UN Economic and Social Council (ECOSOC). Many of their activities are technical or preparatory in nature and are carried out in coordination and collaboration with other regional organizations, national authorities and donors rather than implemented autonomously.

River basin organizations/commissions such as the Mekong River Commission (MRC) or the Nile Basin Initiative (NBI), are a particular type of organization. Several began with a rather specialized focus but over time have added more river basin–related themes such as navigation, flood control, fisheries, agriculture, electric power development and environmental protection and so become more multipurpose in terms of scope. Their institutional structure can vary greatly but two trends are recognizable: they tend to become more organized and institutionalized, transforming from loose committees and agreements to more centralized organizations; and they tend to go from being state-centric to include a host of non-state actors and stakeholders such as civil society groups, donors and local communities (implying that they tend to take on more of a multipurpose and/or network character).

Multipurpose Regional Organizations

Comprehensive and multipurpose regional organizations are an important form of regional cooperation in many parts of the world and have become increasingly so in the last few decades. These regional organizations have a multitude of aims and activities across many sectors in combination with a centralized/comprehensive organizational structure. Multisectoral regional cooperation provides them with opportunities to explore the linkages and spillover effects that exist between various sectors such as security, economics, politics and even culture (Table 6.2).

As noted previously, trading blocs/development communities are increasingly engaging in multi-sectoral cooperation under the same umbrella. During the era of old regionalism, regional cooperation was often specified by or separated into specific sectors, whereas in more recent regionalism, a variety of sectors are grouped under a single comprehensive and multipurpose framework. The EU is perhaps the most obvious example of this. Most of the multipurpose regional organizations in the world have rather similar agendas and, to an increasing extent, have a political content. Membership may vary considerably in number, depending on whether the regional organization is continental (and the size thereof), macro-regional or sub-regional.

Single-Purpose Regional Networks

Many networks operate within a specified sector or are concerned with carrying out a specific task, such as research or training. *Regional research networks* that exist more or less globally are an example. Another, somewhat different example is provided by *regional power markets*, such as the Nordic energy market (Nordpool) and the Southern African Power Pool (SAPP). SAPP consists of national power authorities in Southern Africa, with

Table 6.2   Examples of multipurpose regional organizations

AL	Arab League
AMU	Arab Maghreb Union
ASEAN	Association of Southeast Asian States
AU	African Union
CACM	Central American Common Market
CAN	Andean Community of Nations
CARICOM	Caribbean Community and Common Market
COMESA	Common Market for Eastern and Southern Africa
EAC	East African Community
ECOWAS	Economic Community of West African States
EU	European Union
GCC	Gulf Cooperation Council
IGAD	Intergovernmental Authority on Development
Mercosur	Southern Common Market (Mercado Común del Sur)
OAS	Organization of American States
SAARC	South Asian Association for Regional Cooperation
SADC	Southern African Development Community

associative membership by private energy operators (who are expected to become full members in due course).

Yet other examples include *business* or *civil society networks*, such as the Southern African Chambers of Commerce, Hemispheric Social Alliance in the Americas, the Social Justice Network (in Mercosur), the West African Network for Peace (WANEP) and the Southern African Network of AIDS Service Organizations (SANASO). Some of these tend to develop into more organized regional organizations (see Chapter 8, Civil Society in Regionalism).

Public–private partnerships (PPPs) can also be understood as a particular form of network. These partnerships between public and private actors are often formed for specific purposes, such as building a road or a port, such as the consortium for managing the toll road between Johannesburg and Maputo. The main role of the public actors in PPPs (i.e. often the central or regional government) is to satisfy statutory or other legal requirements, whilst the private actors carry out the actual work and often manage the programme. Sometimes, such a network is temporary in nature and is intended to dissolve after completion of the project.

Multipurpose Regional Networks

To be effective, regional networks often tend to be specialized rather than multipurpose. There are some important exceptions, however, which are often related to different types of *micro-regions*. The Öresund Committee is the political platform for cross-border cooperation in the Öresund Region linking southern Sweden and eastern Denmark. The Committee groups assorted politicians and political representatives from both countries, and it coordinates information about the Öresund Region with respect to investments, the establishment of companies, public sector works and other activities that affect people on either side of the Öresund Strait. The Committee also aims to initiate and coordinate collaboration with other private and public players that network in this micro-region.

Growth triangles are another example of multi-purpose regional networks. Having a limited regional institutional structure, growth triangles utilize the different endowments of the various countries of Southeast Asia, exploiting cooperative trade and development opportunities. As will be elaborated below, in the Southern Growth Triangle (SIJORI) Singapore has concentrated on becoming the network's technology centre, locating labour-intensive operations in low-cost neighbouring Malaysia and Indonesia. The private sector provides capital for investment, while the public sector provides infrastructure, fiscal incentives and the administrative framework to attract industry.

Spatial Development Initiatives (SDIs) and *Development Corridors* in Southern Africa are another distinctive type of micro-regional initiatives (Söderbaum and Taylor 2003, 2008). Some of the best-known examples include the SDIs of Phalaborwa, Platinum and Gariep and the development corridors of Maputo, Nacala, Tazara, Namibe and Beira. These SDIs and development corridors are designed to be short-term, targeted attempts to stimulate economic growth by creating globally competitive regional entities through new investment, infrastructural development and job creation. In view of the fairly concentrated size of the SDI projects, they are weakly institutionalized and the intention is to be informal and non-bureaucratic so as to allow flexibility to private business demands.

Intersecting Regional Spaces

It is more or less generally accepted that we can distinguish between different scales or levels of regionalism, such as macro-regionalism and micro-regionalism (Breslin and Hook 2002; Söderbaum 2005). Nevertheless, there is a strong tendency in the field to make overly sharp distinctions between macro-regions and micro-regions and also to concentrate on one particular scale of regionalism. As a result, both the heterogeneity of regionalism and the linkages between different interacting scales is under-emphasized. The view here is that learning more about these linkages should enhance our understanding of the way regions are made as well as unmade.

As described in the Introduction, macro-regions ('world regions' or 'international regions') are large territorial units or subsystems that exist between the 'state' and the 'global' levels. Sub-regions (or meso-regions) are similar to macro-regions in that they also lie between the global and the national levels, but on a lower level than macro-regions. The Nordic region within Western Europe is an example, as is the Mano River Union (MRU) in West Africa. Previously, these two scales or levels of regions (macro-regions and sub-regions) were the main foci in the field of IR. It is only more recently that micro-regions have become part of the debate in IR.

Historically, micro-regions have been seen purely as spaces within the territorial boundaries of a nation-state (or empire). These micro-regions are often shaped by a relationship between central government and micro-regional administrative or political forces, sometimes with the latter in opposition to the former (Jönsson et al. 2000: 149). Today micro-regionalism usually involves a wide range of different public and private forces at various scales, grouped in more horizontal, and even inter-personal, transnational networks (Perkmann and Sum 2002). Clearly, micro-regions may reflect private sector interests rather than those of either states or civil societies, as is often the case in corridors or growth triangles. If regions are indeed made up by actors other than states alone, and if state boundaries are becoming more fluid, then it becomes more difficult to uphold the old distinctions between macro- and micro-regions (Söderbaum 2005).

A twofold argument is put forward here. Firstly, there is a need for a better understanding of the intersecting scales of regionalism. Secondly, our understanding of the links between the scales of regionalism will be limited by static, pre-given regional delimitations, or by the view that macro- and micro-regions are different phenomena altogether (even if sometimes they are). The multiscalar approach adopted in this book enables us to overcome old dichotomies and recognize that various regional spaces tend to intersect and connect to an increasing extent.

In bridging the gap between macro-regionalism and microregionalism, it is insufficient to characterize them as being either 'from above' (macro) or 'from below' (micro) as was often done in the past. As Mittelman points out, 'globalization has not spawned such ideal types but, rather, a mix of contested ... regional projects: in various degrees spontaneous or deliberate, home-grown or emulated' (Mittelman 2000: 158). Thus, all types of regions may be created both from 'above' and from 'below'.

It also needs saying that not all micro-regions necessarily are 'micro' or small in character. Some are not very large but others are. Often, the size of micro-regions depends on the size of the higher scales of regions as well as the size of the countries involved. As an example, given the comprehensive size of the North American macro-region and its constituent countries, it can be expected that some North American micro-regions are very large. There is in fact a functional unity to the entire US–Mexican *maquiladora* cross-border zone, which can be understood as a rather comprehensive 'Cal-Mex' or 'Tex-Mex' cross-border micro-region. This explains why it is more appropriate to talk about hierarchical sets of scales of regionalism and not necessarily different qualities and sizes of regionalism.

There are a range of ways whereby macro-regionalism and micro-regionalism may interact and intersect. These interactions are illustrated below by empirical case studies from Europe, Southeast Asia and Southern Africa.

Europe

Since the 1960s, micro-regions have become an increasingly important component of the political landscape in Western Europe. Previously, only a few European states, such as Germany, Austria and Switzerland, had strong micro-regions. Some centralized states, such as the UK, Ireland and Greece, have regionalized by setting up administrative/planning regions, whereas Belgium became a fully-fledged federal state, with overlapping political, cultural and economic micro-regions (Keating and Loughlin 1997: 9).

Perhaps the most important explanatory variable behind the rise of micro-regionalism in Europe is the nation-state itself. Most European nation-states have decentralized and supported micro-regions as part of restructuring. At the same time, it is important to acknowledge that the rise of micro-regionalism is related causally to European integration. This process is several decades old and has become increasingly institutionalized over time. In fact, a micro-regional policy was stipulated in the Rome Treaty, but it was the EU's re-launch in the mid-1980s that proved decisive for bringing micro-regionalism and macro-regionalism closer together, both in theory and practice (Bourne 2003: 278). The Single European Act and then the Maastricht Treaty made the EU take micro-regional development more seriously, and thus prompted a significant increase in the structural and community funds for poorer regions in the EU. This made the EU friendlier towards micro-regions at the same time as it turned micro-regional actors into both lobbyists and stakeholders in the EU decision-making process (Bourne 2003: 279).

The EU's micro-regional policy aims to reduce economic disparities within the union. It has several explanations (Bourne 2003: 286–9). Firstly, it is generally accepted that European integration and the single market exacerbates the economic disparities between the centre and the periphery and that the regional policy should distribute resources to and enhance the competitiveness of the poorer micro-regions. Secondly, the deepening of the EU restricts the policy instruments that member states can make use of individually in order to deal with domestic economic disparities and support micro-regional development. Thirdly, it has also been argued that EU regional funds have served as side-payments to gain the consent of poorer states over non-regional issues.

Indeed, the EU's structural funds are comprehensive and necessarily create a logic of their own, and there is evidence that some
countries have 'regionalized' their policy-making and administrative systems 'simply to gain a position of competitive advantage
with regard to access to European structural funds' (Keating and
Loughlin 1997: 9).

Micro-regional actors have become more important in EU
politics during the last two decades. Micro-regions seek to gather
information, take part in decision-making and lobby EU politicians in a variety of different ways: witness that more than
170 micro-regions have information and representation offices
in Brussels and have also formed international micro-regional
associations for managing matters of mutual concern, such as
the Assembly of European Regions (AER) (Bourne 2003: 280).
Since 2012 the AER has turned from the motto 'Europe of the
regions' to one of 'Europe with the regions', thereby trying to
promote itself as a key actor in the construction of the type
of multilevel governance advocated by the Lisbon Treaty. The
Maastricht Treaty stipulated a Committee of the Regions (CoR),
which began operating in 1994 as an advisory body representing
local and regional authorities in the EU member states. By 2015
it had 350 members (and as many alternate members) from all 28
EU countries. The role of the CoR has gradually been strengthened within the EU and after the Lisbon Treaty, the CoR needs
to be consulted on decisions and in the pre-legislative processes
that concern local and regional government in policy areas such
as employment, the environment, education or public health.
Despite being an advisory body with rather weak formal powers,
there is evidence that the Commission is taking the opinions of
CoR seriously. As Bourne points out:

> the very creation of such a body in the EU was a significant
> breakthrough. It recognised regional authorities as legiti-
> mate participants in EU decision making and represented an
> important departure from the hitherto prevalent idea that only
> central governments ought to represent their state in the EU.
> (Bourne 2003: 281)

It is thus necessary to transcend methodological nationalism and
state-centrism. As noted above, micro-regions at state peripheries

are most likely to undergo change and then try to take advantage of the new circumstances of this changed European political landscape (Jönsson et al. 2000: 147). Breslin and Higgott expand on this point:

> Cross-border micro-regionalism in Europe (for example between France and Spain) can be seen as a consequence of higher levels of formal regionalism in the EU. The authority and efficacy of national governments in dealing with transboundary issues has been transformed, some would say undermined, by a dual movement: both 'upwards' and 'downwards' that results in the transfer of national sovereignty to the EU in some issue areas. Institutional changes at the EU level, as well as new communication technologies and the development of transportation, have encouraged the formation of regional networks based on common developmental interests. (Breslin and Higgott 2003: 180)

So micro-regionalism can sometimes be a key strategy to 'bypass' central government or the inefficiencies inherent in national space; at other times, micro-regionalism can be pushed, used and assisted by central governments to develop micro-regional spaces, especially for political/administrative/planning and/or economic purposes.

In summary, there undoubtedly is a micro-regional dimension in the European integration process. But as Bourne (2003: 290–1) correctly points out, this must not be interpreted as the emergence of the idea of the EU as 'Europe of the Regions', whereby micro-regions rather than states constitute the principal units in the policy process. States continue to be important actors in EU politics and will do so for the foreseeable future. Nonetheless, as emphasized by the model of multi-level governance, it is hard to deny that the state has lost some of its monopoly over European-level policy-making. According to Hooghe and Marks (2001), multi-level governance conceptualizes the EU as a polity where decision-making authority is dispersed across multiple territorial levels from the European, to the national and down to the micro-regional. This draws attention not only to the tiers of governance but also to the complex web of actors (state and non-state) who are nested into different scales or levels of governance.

Southeast Asia

Since the 1990s, growth triangles have often been seen as a driving force for economic growth in the Southeast Asian economies. Growth triangles use the different endowments of the participating countries, exploiting cooperative trade for production and development opportunities. These initiatives are constructed around partnerships between the private sector and the state, which explains why they have been referred to as a form of 'trans-state development' (Parsonage 1997). In these partnerships, the private sector provides capital for investment whereas the public sector provides infrastructure, fiscal incentives, and the administrative framework to attract industry and investment.

The Southern Growth Triangle (SIJORI) is probably the best known growth triangle in Southeast Asia. Other examples include southern Thailand-northern Sumatra-northern Malaysia and the ASEAN Growth Triangle covering the Sarawak-Brunei-Sabah area. SIJORI was formed in 1989 and covers a population of more than 8 million people. It is built on a vertical division of labour, whereby Singapore serves as the supplier of advanced electronic infrastructure, technology, financial and insurance services, a comfortable international entrance port, and international know-how. The Batam island (in Riau, Indonesia) supplies low-cost labour and land, whereas Johore (Malaysia) provides semi-skilled labour, industrial sites and competence. The functioning of SIJORI is not without friction, particularly related to the fact that Singapore is seen as the main beneficiary and that the arrangement is seen to cement the vertical division of labour.

Growth triangles are interesting from the perspective of intersecting scales of regionalism, not least since there are a series of interpretations of the nature of these linkages. Öjendal points out the multitude of ways in which the growth triangle strategy has been described: as a response to global political transformation; as a complement to macro-regional economic integration; as paving the way for macro-regionalism; and as a way to achieve regional integration while avoiding time-consuming macro-regional political bureaucracy (Öjendal 2001: 160).

In fact, the linkages between the macro-framework (ASEAN) and micro-regionalism (growth triangles) are not straightforward or easily defined. It should be recognized that ASEAN does not consider lower-scale micro-regionalism as competition. On the contrary, ASEAN has tried to capitalize upon and internalize the momentum around the growth triangles, claiming these as part of the 'ASEAN way'. For instance, in 1992 ASEAN formally adopted the idea of growth triangles, outlined a legal and economic framework for them and also stated that they should be seen as complementary to broader macro-regional economic integration and the ASEAN FTA (Öjendal 2001: 160). Some even suggest that the growth triangles will spur a Southeast Asian identity and enhance the role of ASEAN in the larger East Asian region (Parsonage 1997: 273). Although the relevance of these claims can be discussed, it seems that the two forms of regionalism are complementary rather than competitive, and that growth triangles have enjoyed some stability imparted by the more politically oriented ASEAN framework.

Southern Africa

The African continent is filled with a multitude of cross-border micro-regions, such as the Maputo Development Corridor, the Zambezi Valley region, the Zambia-Malawi-Mozambique Growth Triangle, the Parrott's Beak in the Sierra Leone-Liberia border zone as well as a series of micro-regions in the Great Lakes Region, East Africa and North Africa (Söderbaum and Taylor 2008). It is evident that the African micro-regions are both formal *and* informal, often simultaneously so, with deep implications for the respacing of Africa. In fact, borders either essentially do not 'exist' in the Westphalian sense in a considerable number of spaces in Africa (being ignored by actors such as local populations and refugees), or they are used strategically by (often self-styled) representatives of the state to extract resources and rents. In either case, the notion of fixed boundaries and delineations has little purchase in whole swathes of Africa. Furthermore, what occurs at the micro-regional level is invariably reflective of what is happening at higher levels. In other words, micro-regional processes are not just about micro-regions but they also reflect processes at the macro-level, which perhaps are easiest seen at the micro-level.

As far as Southern Africa is concerned, the SDIs/DCs constitute the most important form of policy-driven micro-regionalism (Söderbaum and Taylor 2003, 2008). The SDIs/DCs purport to be short-term, targeted attempts to stimulate economic 'growth' by creating globally competitive spatial entities through new investment, infrastructural development and job creation. Many, but not all, of the SDIs and DCs are cross-border in nature. The strategy is to implement one or several industrial 'mega-projects' such as the Mozambique Aluminium Smelter (Mozal) in the economic micro-region, which are believed then to enhance different types of spread effects and linkages in the broader regional economy. The SDIs/DCs are governed by a limited group of experts and policy-makers who come together with private investors in small, flexible and rather introverted policy networks, in order to fast-track implementation of bankable investment projects in the micro-region. These networks work rather well for a small group of policy-makers and large companies on the 'inside', but have few links to stakeholders on the 'outside' (Söderbaum and Taylor 2008).

Officially the SDIs/DCs are said to contribute to macroregional economic integration in the SADC region. It is also evident that SADC tries to capitalize on the momentum around the SDIs/DCs. In a similar way to ASEAN and the growth triangles, SADC officials claim that development corridors are part of SADC's way of doing things (Söderbaum and Taylor 2003). Yet there is a rather uneasy relationship between micro-regionalism and macro-regionalism in Southern Africa. As demonstrated by the case of the MDC, micro-regionalism emerges, at least partly, as an alternative construction to the more formal SADC project. It is particularly significant that the promoters of the MDC in South Africa are trying to prevent the micro-regional project from being associated – in their language 'hijacked' – by the ineffectiveness and 'politics' of SADC, as stated by an official in the Foreign Ministry (Söderbaum and Taylor 2003). Even if the Mozambican actors involved in micro-regionalism are not as polemical towards SADC regionalism, linkages rarely extend beyond mere rhetoric.

Conclusion

Rethinking regionalism rests on looking beyond the reductionist focus on a particular set of (formal and states-led) regional organizations. Therefore, this chapter draws attention to an increasing diversity of ways in which state and non-state actors come together to create a range of different organizations and networks at different and intersecting levels.

In terms of effectiveness, specialized cooperation mechanisms (organizations and networks) are usually somewhat easier to assess compared to multipurpose organizations/networks, due to the fact that they are designed to achieve more precise objectives. Specialized and functional organizations are seldom designed for multi-tasking and sometimes they tend to lack political clout, which explains why they increasingly create linkages with multi-purpose regional organizations.

Indeed, multipurpose regional mechanisms are usually designed to mobilize political commitment and enhance trans-national political coordination and inter-sectoral coordination in a different way from specialized organizations and networks. Historical evidence shows that the organizational structure and political frameworks of multipurpose regional organizations gradually deepen and broaden as these take on new tasks and add new members. In this sense, multipurpose regional mechanisms/ networks may maintain a momentum regardless of whether or not agreed policies are implemented. Specialized regional organi-zations, on the other hand, are more vulnerable to underfinancing and failures in implementation.

The EU is the best illustration of this. Although it is the most discussed and analysed regional cooperation mechanism in the world, there is actually little consensus over to what extent the EU is (cost)effective at addressing transnational challenges, and for whom this project is intended. And even when the EU does achieve its goals (in an effective way), there is little agreement about why this was so. But this is quite natural: The EU is a politi-cal project, and any claim of 'effectiveness' depends on theoretical assumption and analytical perspective. Furthermore, multipur-pose regional organizations can be improved through a long-term process of trial and error but it would be hard to say that they have 'failed', and therefore have to be abolished. This is one reason why it is reductionist to make sweeping statements that African or Middle Eastern regionalisms are 'failures'. The point is that these political frameworks provide a political arena that may be relevant for many different purposes (which has to be assessed within its own historical context). In addition, a particular institution may seem premature when founded but be highly relevant when its time comes. The evolution of the EU gives many examples of this.

The chapter also demonstrates a range of ways whereby macro-regionalism and micro-regionalism may interact and intersect. Empirical illustrations from Europe, Southeast Asia and Southern Africa make it clear that (i) macro-regionalism may be complementary to or proceed through micro-regionalism; (ii) macro-regionalism may create 'trust' or institutions that can be used by micro-regionalism; (iii) micro-regionalism may compete with macro-regionalism; and (iv) macro-regionalism and micro-regionalism may be unrelated or proceed in parallel (Perkmann and Sum 2002; Breslin and Higgott 2003: 167–82; Jessop 2003).

7
Multidimensional Regionalism

Global transformations during the last two to three decades have resulted in multidimensional regionalism developing in most policy fields. Regionalism has no single cause but is shaped by a number of problems and interests, as well as cognitive factors and imaginations. This chapter illustrates that regionalism has become a core feature of different policy areas and sectors, spanning a range from security, economy, and social policy to the environment.

Security Regionalism

The idea that conflicts within a region are best dealt with directly by those in the 'region' is not a new one; in fact, it was discussed right when the UN was formed. 'Regions' then were conceived simply as intermediate actors, to which a security task could be delegated from the UN. During the subsequent Cold War, many security issues and conflicts followed the systemic logic of that order and this resulted in weakly organized security regionalism. After the Cold War ended and with the rise of regionalism, most of the comprehensive (multipurpose) regional organizations acquired some type of institutionalized mechanism for conflict management and security. This is seen in Africa, Asia, South America and Europe. These new regional formations and organizations often acquired a degree of legitimacy and actor capacity that was lacking in the regional security organizations during the era of the old regionalism.

'Security regionalism' refers to attempts by states and other actors in a particular geographical area to transform a 'regional security complex' from conflictual interstate and intrastate relations into a security community with cooperative external relations and domestic peace. The routes to this goal may differ and pass through several stages. The concept of security regionalism includes more acute interventions in crises, not least because of the risk of a conflict becoming entrenched within the region; i.e. the regionalization of conflict.

A focus on human rather than state security is significant for understanding the transformation of traditional Westphalian conceptions of peace and security. Ideas of a transnational responsibility for human welfare and the need to protect are implied by concepts such as 'human security', 'human development', 'human emergency' and 'humanitarian intervention'. Even if the discourse on global terrorism has reinforced conventional forms of state security, the 'responsibility to protect' has had a deep impact on regional organizations, not least in Africa. In fact, the Constitutive Act of the AU confers 'the right to intervene' in another AU member state – without endorsement from the UN Security Council – in the event of grave circumstances such as war crimes, genocide and other crimes against humanity. The AU also has strictures against unconstitutional changes of government. Among other things, this shows that the conventional hierarchical relationship between UN-based multilateralism and regionalism is being transformed, sometimes even challenged.

The comparative advantages of multilateral versus regional approaches to security and conflict are heatedly discussed (Söderbaum and Tavares 2009). Regional organizations may have greater success than multilateral initiatives at conflict prevention, as well as post-conflict reconstruction, since they must live with the consequences of unresolved conflict, among other considerations. As explored further in Chapter 12, the rise of regional peacekeeping is related to a weakness of the UN system in coming up with effective solutions.

Security regionalism is particularly striking in the case of Africa. Africa has sadly hosted some of the most challenging conflicts in the world since the end of the Cold War (e.g. those in Burundi, Chad, Darfur, DRC, Liberia, Rwanda, Sierra Leone, Somalia, Uganda). One characteristic of these conflicts and wars is the role of sub-national actors and groups such as rebel movements and mercenaries, who often try to function as if they were recognized members of the international community. These groups have introduced new practices into the conduct of armed conflicts, effectively contesting some standard conceptions of modern warfare, not the least of which is blurring the distinction between combatants and civilians, and also between who is 'good' and who is 'evil', who is 'friend' and who is 'foe'. Secondly, even if most contemporary conflicts in Africa are defined as 'domestic', they are deeply embedded in regional and cross-border contexts. In fact, most conflicts on the African continent spill over into neighbouring countries or draw regional actors into what could be more accurately described as regional war-zones rather than simply 'domestic conflicts'. This pattern, in turn, means that there is a much greater role for action, mediation and intervention at the regional level by affected neighbouring countries and especially by regional organizations than there is at the single state level or for multilateral agencies.

A will to 'tackle African conflicts through African solutions' was one of the main impetuses behind the decision by African heads of state and government to reshape the Organization of African Unity (OAU) into the AU. This vision has been strongly supported by the international community, in particular the Western powers (see Chapter 9, External Actors in Regionalism, for a deeper analysis of external actors). Several of the other major regional organizations in Africa (ECOWAS, IGAD, SADC, etc.) have also developed specific approaches to peace and security. Among the regional organizations, there are fundamental differences of outlook and style that reflect different perceptions of threat, historical experience and cultural background and result in correspondingly different strategies for the maintenance of peace and security and the roles of the UN and regional and sub-regional organizations respectively.

Of course, security regionalism does not mean the absence of strong national and regime interests. For instance, even if the intervention by South Africa and Botswana in Lesotho in 1998 was motivated partly by a concern for stability and peace in line with SADC principles, South Africa was primarily concerned with ensuring political stability in Lesotho in order to promote the security of the Lesotho Highlands Water Project (Schoeman and Muller 2009). Similarly, in the case of West Africa national leaders were concerned that if they allowed rebellions against incumbent governments to succeed, it would serve to encourage groups confronted by authoritarian regimes in other countries to take up arms (Obi 2009).

Furthermore, the personalization of politics and relationships between heads of state in Africa – based on either empathy or enmity – also influenced the nature of security regionalism in Africa. For instance, understanding Angola and Zimbabwe's military deployment in the DRC in the late 1990s would be difficult without accounting for the strong interpersonal bond between Eduardo dos Santos (Angola) and Robert Mugabe (Zimbabwe). The same goes for ties in other regions: between Ibrahim Babangida (Nigeria) and Samuel Doe (Liberia); between Charles Taylor (Liberia) and Muammar Ghaddafi (Libya), Felix Houphouët-Boigny (Côte d'Ivoire) and Blaise Compaoré (Burkina Faso); or Abdou Diouf (Senegal) and Joao Vieira (Guinea Bissau). This type of personalization can hardly be seen as a good basis for regional peace operations. Meyer (2009: 165) contends that 'The instrumentalization of the region and interplay of particular interests among political elites make regionalization in Central Africa considerably vulnerable to deadlocks, as it easily leads to discordance among States'. On the other hand, Obi (2009) claims that in Liberia at least, contingencies and personal relations between ECOWAS leaders and the warlords, rather than any structured plans, led to the end of the war.

Summing up, assuming that an intervention is at all justified (or wise), many regional security interventions are introduced too late or undertaken with the wrong means. Perhaps the most fundamental challenge in consolidating security regionalism in Africa is moving towards a more norm-based and institutionalized approach that transcends the current focus on 'quick-fix' military intervention in favour of conflict prevention and post-conflict peace-building. The AU, ECOWAS, IGAD and SADC must move beyond 'fire brigade' operations and arbitrary military interventions, in which personal relationships and the temper of political leaders are allowed to destroy or manipulate the process. A norm-based culture would also prevent political leaders using regional security organizations as instruments against domestic opposition or for their own personal interests. For this to happen, there needs to be a change of attitude on the part of politicians, national bureaucracies and external actors about how to understand conflict dynamics and peace-building.

Economic and Development Regionalism

Economic regionalism is a large topic and covers issues such as trade regionalism, monetary regionalism and development regionalism. The old regionalism focused on trade blocs and economic communities, although other dimensions were added subsequently. In the 1950s and 1960s, many of the regional trading arrangements were inward-looking and protectionist and, even if today's economists generally regard them as failures, in their time they were usually seen as instruments capable of enhancing industrial production and structural transformation.

Since the mid-1980s there has been a strengthening, deepening and widening of regional trading arrangements and economic communities. Some observers consider the proliferation of trading arrangements to be the main characteristic of the new wave of regionalism (Mansfield and Milner 1997). More or less every country has joined one or several trading regimes and, especially in Africa, Asia and the Americas, there are a multitude of overlapping bilateral, regional and plurilateral trading deals, sometimes referred to as spaghetti bowls or needle bowls (Baldwin and Thornton 2008).

One of the main rationales or drivers of regionalism is that it can overcome market fragmentation, constraints of size, and enhance competition. This was emphasized in classical regional economic integration in the 1960s and 1970s, which emphasized sequential 'stages' of regional economic integration, beginning with a free trade area, then a customs union and on to deeper stages of economic and monetary union (Balassa 1961). The relevance of regional economic integration increased after the end of the Cold War and in the context of economic globalization. Today greater emphasis is placed on regionalism as a means of ensuring a closer integration into the world economy as well as broader growth and developmental benefits. It is believed that the larger regional markets can provide a range of benefits such as economies of scale, wider competition and increased foreign investment, which in turn can accelerate the opening of national economies to the rest of the world and enhance the credibility of national reforms through lock-in policy mechanisms (Robson 1993).

Monetary and financial regionalism may be understood as a subcategory of economic regionalism. Monetary cooperation may have many objectives but one of them is a common currency

(CFA, Eurozone, Rand Monetary Area). Following the failure of the Bretton Woods system (1971), there was a trend toward monetary regionalism. In the case of Europe, increasing economic interdependence led to the need for macro-economic policy. Other motivations were the vulnerability to global financial disturbances and the dependence on US hegemony. A monetary union was also seen as a road towards political union. Monetary regionalism in Europe necessitated a transfer of decision-making powers from the national to the regional (EC) level. Achieving this was a slow and winding process and one full of setbacks. The 'snake' (in the 1970s), the EMS and the EMU (including the euro) constituted successive systems, all with less than full participation by all nations (variable speed). The successive systems show that a monetary union is a political goal rather than a narrow economic solution or the ultimate outcome of economic integration (Tsoukalis 1997: 163).

The problems of the European Stability and Growth Pact (SGP) underlined the dangers of political divergence within a monetary bloc. The crisis in 2008 revealed a serious lack of financial cooperation and led to the first major crisis of the Eurozone, which has since escalated into crises in Greece, Spain, Italy and so on. Monetary regionalism in Europe is by no means a runaway success story, and it has exposed the important need for institutional backing, political commitment and a common approach to economic policy.

Global instruments for managing financial crisis show a bias against the weak, and this has triggered regional cooperation in the developing world. According to Griffith-Jones (2003: 448), regional monetary cooperation is particularly relevant in areas such as surveillance, coordination of macro-economic policies, and in dealing with liquidity provision. Regional cooperation can also strengthen the bargaining position of developing countries.

The Asian Financial Crisis (AFC) in 1997–8 underlined the interdependence within the larger region of Southeast and East Asia, and Western attitudes to the crisis frustrated the afflicted countries. Of particular interest here is the Chiang Mai Initiative (CMI), which was based on bilateral currency swaps to counter speculation. Before the AFC there was little discussion outside of Europe about regional approaches to the management of financial stability. In June 2008, finance ministers from the 'ASEAN Plus Three' (APT) agreed to create a pool of US$80 billion for the protection of regional currencies. This replaced the CMI arrangement and was a step towards a regional equivalent of the IMF. This initiative, albeit largely compatible with liberal globalization, may prove to be an important marker for regional financial cooperation in wider East Asia. Similar intentions are evident in Latin America, such as the signing in 2009 of the founding charter of the Banco del Sur (Bank of the South).

There are many additional benefits of economic regionalism beyond trade and monetary issues. 'Development' is a multidimensional phenomenon, which depends on positive spillover and linkages between different sectors. The broader and more comprehensive strategy of economic regionalism explicitly links trade integration, and the liberalization of labour and capital flows, with regional cooperation in many complementary fields of activity, such as infrastructure, transport, agriculture, health, education, natural resources and energy (Robson 1993; ADB 2008).

A regional economic approach can be both fairer and politically more feasible than is the case with multilateral negotiations, as it is easier to liberalize with neighbours and deal with distribution issues in a regional context. Regional trade clubs furthermore have a tendency to deal more effectively with non-trade economic and political challenges such as environmental protection and migration than multilateral mechanisms. A comprehensive regional development strategy appears to be possible only when managed by multipurpose regional organizations such as the EU, SADC, ASEAN and (increasingly) Mercosur, since these can exploit spillover effects and linkages between trade and non-trade and between economic and political sectors/benefits.

A global strengthening of economic regionalism is not an expression of a single trend towards free trade within the ideology of capitalism. Duina (2005) shows that regional market-building is a *social* process, which occurs within 'thick' institutional and political contexts that both guide and limit what is possible and give rise to remarkably different outcomes around the world. State, business and other societal actors expand their regional programmes and come together in new and heterogeneous ways. As Duina (2005: 5) observes, within one particular regional trading agreement (RTA), it is possible to observe the rise of environmental groups with members from several countries and transnational gols and objectives. In the same RTA, it is possible to recognize that, for instance, computer manufacturers have developed regional production network, while national labour departments participate in regional policy networks. Although similar tendencies and dynamics may be recognized in different RTAs, there may also be differences: 'If, for instance, farmers' lobbying groups emerge at the regional level in two RTAs, their members' profiles and their objectives are likely to vary. Similarly, if textile companies expand internationally in two given RTAs, what exactly they produce are likely to differ' (Duina 2005: 6). Duina's main point is thus to challenge the undifferentiated view of RTAs, and the idea that they can be understood as a single and homogenous trend towards global free trade.

Social Regionalism

Social regionalism is closely linked to comprehensive economic regionalism. Social policy was part of the EU's agenda for several decades, but the Treaty of Lisbon both strengthened and expanded the 'social dimension'. The EU recognizes a range of social principles and rights that are related to employment, workers' rights, social security, social protection and inclusion, child and minority rights as well as health care. Even if social policy remains primarily the responsibility of member states, the EU clearly has a strong regulatory system in place, backed up by the goals of the European Commission and the authority of the Court of the EU and the European Court of Justice.

Social policy rarely attracted much attention in regions outside the EU until the early 2000s. At least partly in response to the detrimental effects of economic globalization and the financial crises, there has been a 'social turn' of regionalism (Deacon et al. 2010). There are now discussions in Africa, Asia, the Caribbean and Latin America about issues such as income distribution, social and labour regulation and protection, health, education, social and individual and gender rights, migration and so forth, although they are not yet as developed as in the EU (Deacon et al. 2010). Such issues are also being built into some interregional partnerships involving the EU and other regional organizations such as ASEAN, ECOWAS, Mercosur, SAARC and SADC.

Health is one of the most widely discussed examples of regional social policy when looking beyond the EU. Just like peace, health demonstrates the inadequacies of the old (Westphalian) states system and the imperative for regional and global cooperation. Quite obviously, diseases do not recognize borders. Management and control of pandemics thus requires transnational and global governance (see Chapter 12, Regions in Global Governance).

Riggirozzi (2014: 435) shows that 'health has become a strategic policy driver redefining the terms of regionalism in South America', and hence new forms of regionalization are unfolding alongside conventional forms of market-led regional integration and even transforming them. These new objectives and practices are resulting in new forms of regional coordination for on-the-ground implementation of regional health programmes. Riggirozzi uses the case of the UNASUR to highlight the transformation:

> These actions create new spaces for policy coordination and collective action where regional institutions become an opportunity for practitioners, academics and policy-makers to collaborate and network in support of better access to healthcare, services and policy-making. For negotiators, UNASUR structures practices to enhance leverage in international negotiations for better access to medicines and research and development funding, as well as better representation of developing countries in international health governance. For advocacy actors, UNASUR represents a new normative platform for claiming and advancing the right to health within the region while at the same time attempting to establish itself as a broker between national needs and global norms, a political pathway that differs from the position held by Latin America in the past. (Riggirozzi 2014: 433)

Environmental Regionalism

Environmental regionalism can take a range of forms. Important examples include the many hundreds of initiatives to govern and manage transboundary water resources. These resources provide food directly, as well as water supply for industry and domestic use, for energy and food production as well as other essential public goods and services. The underlying principle is that transboundary water resources should be seen as single ecological units. Thus, when such resources are transboundary, this requires a certain degree of international cooperation because failing to act collectively is often detrimental to the environment (ITFGPG 2006).

In the field of transboundary water management prevailing wisdom takes the river or lake basin largely as 'given', the main challenge being to solve a range of specific 'problems' – especially environmentally sustainable development, land usage, hydroelectricity, irrigation, fishery – through rational, scientific or functional-technocratic policies and institutions. Without rejecting the attractiveness of ecologically sustainable and basin-wide approaches, it has become increasingly clear that river basins are not simply 'givens'. Instead they are politically and socially constructed by agents that spatially imagine them in different and partly competing ways. A constructivist-reflectivist approach helps to reveal that transboundary river basins may mean different things to different people at different times and in different policy fields. In essence, 'environmentally sound' basin-wide solutions are by no means self-evident (Giordano and Wolf 2003).

An ecologically sustainable and 'cooperative' basin-wide approach is often difficult to pursue because, due to national sovereignty, few stakeholders have either the means or the mandate to operate outside their national contexts. Indeed, in many cases each riparian state monitors, plans, develops, conserves and protects the water resources within its own territory, with too little consultation and cooperation among them. The divergent policies and plans of riparian states are usually not fully compatible, and often upstream/downstream users are not keen to consider the problems of the other (Chiuta 2000: 153). As one national water official in a state along the Zambezi River declared: 'The basin stops at the national border' (quoted in Söderbaum 2015: 5). A statist-nationalist orientation is not necessarily detrimental in every respect, but increasingly results in waste, ecological mismanagement and unrealized potential because it prevents regional cooperation and is ineffective in that it benefits only certain groups in society, typically the ruling elite and acolytes.

Conventional 'problem-solving' approaches to transboundary river management have resulted in a flurry of institutionally weak river basin organizations (RBOs) that too often lack the political clout needed to solve complex and sensitive collective action dilemmas. Designing centralized regional organizations, which subsume national interests under a diffuse supranational interest or the common good, is not the solution. Instead, the challenge is to reconcile national interests/benefits and the common good within a governance framework that is able to generate the necessary political leverage.

It is noteworthy that many river basins are undergoing deep changes in terms of transformed governance mechanisms even if there are no standardized solutions (Söderbaum and Granit 2014). For instance, over 25 regional and subregional organizations have some degree of responsibility for sustainable use of the ocean in the wider Caribbean region. Many of these are brought together under the broad umbrella of the Caribbean Large Marine Ecosystem and Adjacent Areas (CLME) project, funded by the Global Environment Facility (GEF).

Another example of new forms of regional environmental governance that extend beyond particular regional organizations can be found in the Baltic Sea Region. Despite the signing of the Helsinki Convention for the protection of the marine environment of the Baltic Sea in 1974, ensuring deep collaboration has been problematic. In 2010 the Baltic Marine Environment Protection Commission– the Helsinki Commission (HELCOM) reported that 'None of the open basins of the Baltic Sea has an acceptable ecosystem health status'. In response, the European Commission in 2008 and 2009 developed the EU Strategy for the Baltic Sea Region in consultation with the EU member states and Russia. This strategy aims to provide an integrated strategic framework for the wide variety of actors, policies and funding mechanisms active within the region and link it to EU policies. In this way, the Baltic Sea governance framework has moved away from a particular organization rather narrowly focused on environment to a more comprehensive and complex governance mechanism.

Conclusion

Regionalization has no single cause but has been influenced by a number of problems and dimensions that vary in importance in different regions. Any analysis of regionalism must take note of historical changes in context; a context dominated by globalization that has deep implications for national sovereignty, for the opportunities for states-led policy-making and for regional cooperation. As a result, there has been a transformation from 'old' and states-dominated forms of regionalism to 'new' and more multidimensional regionalism, shaped by a multitude of state and non-state actors in an ever-expanding number of policy fields. Governments, multilateral and regional organizations, donors and international financial institutions (IFIs), as well as the private sector and many civil society groups, have raised their expectations about the potential benefits of regionalism.

Peace and security is a field where regionalism has great potential, but has had mixed results. Equally, multilateral undertakings have fared little better, and this proves that the entire approach to conflict resolution and peace-building is misconceived and overly focused on reactive actions and militarized notions of security.

One of the reasons for economic regionalism is to overcome constraints of size and market fragmentation. This was in fact emphasized in classical regional economic integration during the 1960s and 1970s, but this strategy has increased in relevance in the context of economic globalization. Larger regional markets can provide a range of benefits, from economies of scale to increased competition and foreign investment as well as credible political reform. Current strategies of economic regionalism explicitly link outward-oriented forms of market integration with regional cooperation in complementary fields of activity, such as infrastructure, transport, health, environment and, sometimes, security. A need to exploit cross-sectoral linkages in different policy fields has promoted an increased emphasis on multipurpose regional organizations. The EU often serves as an inspiration for such developments.

Emerging patterns of regionalism cannot be captured by simply focusing on specified regional organizations. For instance, we cannot understand regionalism in Africa by studying AU, ECOWAS or SADC alone. Even in Europe, regionalism cannot be understood adequately just through an EU lens. This is evident particularly in the field of environment and security, and perhaps less so in economic regionalism. Many policy fields are witnessing the emergence of governance frameworks and architectures that go beyond specific regional organizations and networks. Generalizations are quite difficult since these regional governance architectures tend to play out differently in different regions. It now is quite clear that region-building is a social process.

It is widely believed that successful regionalism and 'regional integration' require that national sovereignty and national decision-making authority be ceded to supranational institutions. The dichotomy between sovereignty and functioning regional integration, however, is first and foremost a remnant of old regional integration theory in Europe. Regarding national sovereignty as an 'obstacle' to regionalism therefore is to neglect the many ways by which state actors and political leaders are able to use regionalism and regional governance to bolster their regimes as well as their national interest.

In several issue areas, one of the most important issues confronting regionalism is the unequal and uneven distribution of the costs and benefits of regional cooperation. If a regionalist project is not perceived to be equal and just, defections and alternative regionalist projects will tend to emerge, giving rise to heterogeneous patterns of regionalisms. Overlapping regional organizations may thus result from different integration models and policy agendas, historical legacies and characteristics, or institutional deficiencies. Some observers have even reasoned that the overlap and duplication of some regional organizations may be deliberate, especially in cases where policy implementation is not the main concern. This underlines the fact that the design or use of regional frameworks may not necessarily be based on the need to solve collective action dilemmas or to achieve public good.

8

Civil Society in Regionalism

In region-building, placing emphasis upon the many business and societal actors rather than state elites and states-led regional organizations is a recent tendency. As this chapter shows, civil society has emerged as a dynamic force in the re-spatialization of contemporary social life. The analysis is structured in two parts.

First is a section based on the notion that the first step towards a better understanding of the regionalization of civil society is to focus the theoretical and conceptual lenses through which it is viewed. To a large extent, the general neglect of civil society in the literature is a conceptual, theoretical and methodological problem. There is a risk of misunderstanding the diversity and many roles of regional civil societies around the world if the theories and conceptualizations of civil society are rooted solely in Western or European experience.

A second section provides a deeper (empirical) analysis of the pluralism of civil society regionalism. The illustrations are drawn from the case of Africa. Civil societies in Africa are usually considered to be among the weakest in the world, and therefore it can be considered as among the 'least likely cases' of civil society regionalism. Four main roles of regional civil society are identified: as partner, as legitimator, as counter-hegemonic force and as manipulator. Whilst developed for the case of Africa, related research reveals that the categories also appear to be relevant to other regions (Armstrong et al. 2011; Fioramonti 2014).

Debates About Civil Society in Regionalism

Civil society regionalization has begun to receive more attention in the last few years, but most of these studies focus on how civil society actors influence and make their voices heard within state-led regional organizations and policy frameworks, such as the AU, ASEAN, CARICOM, Mercosur, NAFTA, SAARC and SADC (Armstrong et al. 2011). Studies and approaches treating civil societies as subjects rather than passive objects are rare.

Rethinking of regionalism emphasizes the need to transcend state-centric perspectives. Indeed, regionalization must be conceptualized as a multidimensional process, occurring simultaneously in many sectors and on different levels, driven by a variety of state as well as non-state actors. Not just economic but also social and cultural regional networks and projects may precede or develop in response to, or hand-in-hand with, formal states-led regionalist projects. It is plausible to distinguish between different regionalizing actors grouped broadly as either state (government), market (business), civil society or external actor. Yet, these groups often interact and come together in a many different ways and will rarely be autonomous from one another.

Key theorists in the New Regionalism Approach (NRA) camp, such as Björn Hettne and James Mittelman, build on Karl Polanyi's ideas about the political role of civil society as a means for the weak and the poor to protect themselves against often-exploitative market forces in the context of economic globalization. In doing so, they emphasize the counter-hegemonic and transformative role of regional civil society fulfilled by groups such as pro-democracy forces, the women's movement and the environmentalists. As Mittelman (2000: 225) points out: '[A]t the end of the day, the possibilities and limitations of transformative regionalism rest on the strength of its links to civil society'.

This notion of civil society's counter-hegemonic and transformative potential reflects the deep dissatisfaction of these authors with neoliberal globalization and their eagerness to discover an alternative world order. Considerable amounts of research confirm the existence of counter-hegemonic regional civil society in different parts of the word. There is, however, a need for a broader and more open-ended framework, which is able to accommodate a wider set of empirical outcomes. For this purpose, insights can be gained from the general debates about civil society (Söderbaum 2007).

There are many definitions and meanings of 'civil society'. Often, it is defined loosely as the public realm and the associational life existing between the 'state' and the 'private'. From this perspective civil society is seen as the arena where different associations, interest groups and citizens can express their opinions and engage with the state. Although not always conceptualized in this way, civil society is often considered to be distinct from the state. Furthermore, Hegel's nineteenth-century definition included the market, as do some current conceptualizations, but most contemporary notions tend to treat civil society as a non-profit sector (Scholte 2002: 146).

Scholte persuasively defines civil society as 'a political space where voluntary associations deliberately seek to shape the rules that govern one or the other aspect of social life' (Scholte 2002: 146). Viewed from this perspective, civil society includes a rich variety of actors and voluntary associations, such as non-governmental organizations (NGOs), community-based organizations, interests groups, trade unions, social movements, faith-based organizations, academic institutions, clan and kinship circles, lobbies, youth associations, development cooperation initiatives and more. It excludes both political parties, since these seek political power, and profit-seeking actors. Active political goals are an important ingredient in Scholte's definition. Contrary to Scholte, this book holds that voluntary associations that do not attempt to shape policies, norms or structures in society (for instance civil society groups engaged in service delivery) are nonetheless worth including in the study of civil society, since their activities do contribute to the reproduction of the current social system.

Historically, most studies on civil society have been heavily influenced by Western and liberal thinking. This implies focusing on the civility, autonomy and sovereignty of civil society. From this particular perspective, only organizations with a normative potential should be considered part of civil society, ruling out for example certain ethnically and religiously based organizations (Chazan 1999: 111). However, what on the surface appears to be 'civil society' does not necessarily contribute to shaping the rules that govern social life. In other words, civil society is not necessarily homogeneous and harmonious, nor does it automatically contribute to the common good and a democratic order, as is generally promulgated in much of Western thought. That there are also competing interests and conflicts within civil society needs to be recognized: competition for power and control, for achieving status, control, exclusion, personal interest or simply activities explicable mainly by pecuniary gain. Since such motives and underlying interests are hidden, they also are more difficult to detect.

According to liberal thinking, civil society has to be understood, furthermore, in terms of its own qualities and not in relation to the state (Azarya 1994: 83). One reason why civil society outside Europe is often misunderstood by scholars is the dominance of Western (liberal) political thought. This results in the myth of civil society as 'autonomous', but it cannot in fact be seen in isolation from the rest of society. Liberals usually fail to recognize the pluralism of state–society interaction (Mamdani 1995).

The perspective developed here seeks to transcend the conventional conceptualization (especially in Western and liberal thinking) of civil society as open and autonomous and engaging with the state in a constructive dialogue for the benefit of society as a whole. Instead, there is a need to problematize civil society (as well as state action) and embrace a theoretical perspective that allows that civil society may contain internal paradoxes and conflicts, exhibited at various spatial levels. What on the surface may appear as 'egalitarian' civil society behaviour, on deeper analysis may not always prove to be so. Furthermore, civil society actors may be involved in complex, rather than simple and straightforward, relationships with other types of actors and this may complicate the distinctions drawn between the actors from civil society, from the state and the marketplace. Meanwhile, it is evident that external actors play an important role in the promotion of civil society in many developing regions (especially Africa, Asia and Latin America); this is a more powerful role than that observed in Western civil society (Howell 2000).

Another limitation of a conventional understanding (and conceptualization) of civil society is related to the notion that civil society operates and consolidates on a 'national' basis (i.e. state–civil society interaction within the nation-state). Such state-centrism needs to be circumvented to escape the Western bias and provide a perspective beyond the nation-state. As Scholte explains:

In earlier Lockean, Kantian, Hegelian and Gramscian formulations, 'civil society' related to *western* politics in a *national* context. However, talk of civil society today circulates all over the world and is sometimes applied to political practices (like kinship networks in Africa and so-called Civic Fora at the local level in Thailand) that derive largely from non-western traditions. Moreover, in contemporary politics civil society associations often operate in regional and global spheres as well as local and national arenas. Conceptions of 'civil society' need to be recast to reflect these changed circumstances. (Scholte 2002: 146)

In other words, civil society is not hermetically sealed from the external environment. Civil society activities on the 'national' and 'regional' levels tend to be closely linked. For example, many regional civil society organizations support the 'national' work of their members and partners. Having said this, there is indeed a separate regional arena for civil society to act in, but alongside, and not replacing, the national. Of particular importance is how this regional arena manifests itself and how various types of civil society groups use it to further their (local, national and regional) interests. This will become more evident in the discussion below.

The Pluralism of Civil Society Regionalism: Evidence from Africa[1]

Regional cooperation and regional networking among civil society actors exist more or less all over the world and in a wide range of policy fields, such as trade, economic integration and globalization, human rights and democracy, social justice, trade and globalization, health and HIV/Aids, food security, student associations, trade unions and research and education. Civil society regionalism tends to be fluid and heterogeneous, and take many different organizational forms and functions depending on the actors and their capacities and the particular nature of the sector.

Civil societies organize themselves in a variety of ways, ranging from loose and open associations and networks to increasingly more institutionalized and centralized organizations and projects (Armstrong et al. 2011; Godsäter 2013; Fioramonti 2014). Often, loose and open-ended institutional and organizational network structures constitute the starting point for regional cooperation and interaction but, unless a loosely organized 'network' fulfils the needs and demands of participants, generally these become more

---

[1] This part of the chapter draws on research collaboration with Andréas Godsäter (see Godsäter and Söderbaum 2011; also cf. Godsäter 2013; Söderbaum 2004, 2007).

institutionalized and organized if participants reach agreement on a common agenda and cooperation deepens. Some regional civil society networks may bring together an extremely heterogeneous group of members in terms of backgrounds and sectors. As elaborated below, this structure is typical of the resistance or counter-hegemonic movements.

Civil society is multifaceted and serves many functions and interests. Some functions for civil society cooperation are manifest, and relatively easy to grasp, such as creation of knowledge and sharing of information; pooling of resources, capacity-building; and joint advocacy and lobbying. Other goals and interests declared by civil society representatives are more ambiguous, such as adherence to the norms of regionalism and contribution to a 'shared' identity. The assorted roles and functions that civil society plays in regionalism warrant some kind of categorization. A previous study on Africa by the author and Andreas Godsäter identified four partly competing and partly overlapping roles of civil society in regionalism: as partner, as legitimator, as counter-hegemonic force and as manipulator (Godsäter and Söderbaum 2011; also see Godsäter 2013).

Civil Society as Partner

Civil society actors function as partners when they engage with state actors and inter-state frameworks (such as SADC) on a partnership basis, mainly in order to solve mutual problems. Usually, such civil society actors are content with formal and states-led cooperation frameworks even if they believe that some policies and programmes need to be modified and implementation accelerated. Such groups may therefore contribute to improving public policy. Together with governments, they may even take on a direct role in the provision of social and public services, especially in peripheral communities where the government has difficulty reaching.

An example is provided by the Osienala (Friends of Lake Victoria), which is a regional NGO based in Kisumu, Kenya, with 15 partner organizations in Kenya, Tanzania and Uganda. Its main objectives are to capacitate partners and other development-oriented civil society groups around Lake Victoria, to provide various regional services to local communities and to lobby local, national and regional policy-makers. Osienala seeks to educate fishing communities around the lake regarding environmental management via its own radio channel, Radio Lake Victoria. It also functions as a partner in a working relationship with the states-led Lake Victoria Basin Commission (LVBC) and, furthermore, the Kenyan government has assigned it as lead agent in assisting NGOs in environmental impact assessments.

The East African Communities' Organization for Management of Lake Victoria Resources (ECOVIC) is another regional network comprising about 30 civil society groups based in Tanzania, Kenya and Uganda. ECOVIC's activities include service delivery, advocacy, capacity building and enhanced networking and regional integration for the sustainable use of Lake Victoria. Most activities are carried out in close collaboration with national or local authorities, and it is funded largely by Western donors. ECOVIC is also involved in lobbying, for instance at the East African Legislative Assembly (EALA), the independent legislative arm of the EAC with the mandate to oversee EAC's work. To this end, ECOVIC conducts meetings and workshops with members of the EALA and suggest improvements in policy-making consistent with its remit. ECOVIC has also been granted observer status in the EAC Council of Ministers and collaborates with the Lake Victoria Fisheries Organization (LVFO), a regional organization under the EAC responsible for coordinating and managing fisheries resources of Lake Victoria. One important example of joint state–civil society regional governance is the so-called 'co-management initiative': a partnership arrangement in which the local communities, local governments and other stakeholders share the responsibility and authority for the management of the fishery.

Civil Society as Legitimator

Civil society actors usually fill this role when they are allowed to participate 'in existing top-down controlled institutional mechanisms that afford some civil society groups voice and influence, in return for legitimization of otherwise technocratic policy-making processes' (Fioramonti 2014: 6). Some civil society groups involved in this way actively strive to make regional governance more accountable and democratic. But there is also a trend for governments to 'manufacture' civil society groups with the express purpose of legitimizing existing states-led regional governance frameworks (Godsäter 2013; Fioramonti 2014: 6).

The East African Sustainability Watch Network (EASWN) is a loosely organized coalition of national networks in Uganda, Kenya and Tanzania. Its most important project is the East African Civil Society Watchdog Project for Sustainable Development in the Lake Victoria basin. This project seeks to increase citizen participation in reforming policies related to sustainable development and improving networking and information-sharing about sustainable development. During the process of establishing the LVBC, the EASWN managed to lobby government representatives for substantial changes in the set-up of the commission and to ensure more space for citizen participation in the management of the lakes resources.

Another example of civil society as legitimator is the National Association of Professional Environmentalists (NAPE), a national advocacy group on environmental issues based in Uganda but which operates regionally in East Africa. NAPE tries to push the LVBC to adopt a 'bottom-up' approach when coordinating development activities in the region and holds that, whilst LVBC and EAC are crucial for governing the development processes in the region, there is a need for radical improvement in the interaction with local communities and civil society groups. Government officials generally recognize NAPE as an important actor in the process, but NAPE's rather critical approach makes for a contentious relationship with government representatives.

The Southern African Trade Union Coordination Council (SATUCC) is a regional trade union organization based in Botswana, and formed and constituted by national labour unions throughout the region. It coordinates trade union coalitions in the region and serves an advocacy role *vis-à-vis* SADC, trying to influence and reform regional socio-economic policy-making and incorporating labour issues. Together with business and SADC governments, SATUCC is part of a regional tripartite structure responsible for developing important policy documents related to labour, such as the Social Charter harmonizing labour laws in the region.

Another example is Mwelekeo wa NGO (MWENGO), a regional partnership-based NGO based in Zimbabwe, that builds institutional capacity and advocacy skills of Southern African NGOs that deal with social justice issues by way of workshops, networking, training, etc. MWENGO encourages its partner groups to become advocates for more democratic governance in organizations such as SADC. Their prime objective is to enhance the ability of civil society groups to participate at national and regional levels in the policy-making processes related to development and to represent the interests of their constituencies in various governmental institutions. MWENGO directly approaches SADC to try and advocate for fundamental policy reform in areas like debt and trade, but in those cases where its critical standpoints are emphasized, MWENGO often becomes marginalized. This leads to the next type.

Civil Society as Counter-Hegemonic Force

Civil society actors that contest the policy-led and states-led regional projects in favour of a transformative agenda fulfil a 'counter-hegemonic' role. As Fioramonti (2014: 6) points out, 'a truly transformative agenda is therefore only possible when civil society provides a counter-hegemonic challenge to the mainstream regional institutions, especially market-driven regional integration processes'. This puts civil society actors on a collision course not only with national governments and intergovernmental regional organizations but with economic globalization more broadly.

One of the best-known examples in Africa is the Southern African People's Solidarity Network (SAPSN), which was established as one of the key nodes in Southern Africa of the so-called 'anti-globalization movement'. The SAPSN network encompasses a broad range of civil society organizations and institutions, including trade unions, development NGOs, church-based social organizations and community-based movements, all working towards regional development and against economic and 'hyperliberal' globalization. Its immediate aims are to promote pro-people socio-economic policies at national, regional, continental and global levels by sharing experiences and information, capacity building, increasing awareness and the building of mass movements. Notably, SAPSN claims that most Southern African governments primarily engage rhetorically rather than substantively with development cooperation and integration. Various SAPSN statements charge that SADC leaders use the SADC as a self-serving 'old boys' club' for mutual support 'whenever the interests and power of the ruling elites come into conflict with the human rights, and the democratic and development aspirations of their own populations' (SAPSN 2000: 1). In other words, SAPSN emphasizes the deficiencies of state-steered regionalism whilst simultaneously calling for a people-driven type of participatory regionalism. SAPSN regularly holds joint regional workshops on issues related to regional integration hosted by SAPSN member organizations. Some of these workshops have taken the form of People's Summits held in parallel to official SADC meetings.

Another example of civil society resisting states-led regional governance is the Anti-Privatization Forum (APF). It contests the privatization of water, electricity, housing, education and health through direct action. According to one representative of APF, they refuse to join the 'NGO crowd' by participating in states-led regional schemes such as AU and SADC, which they claim bring in civil society just to gain a veneer of public legitimacy. Consequently, the APF is very critical of the SADC NGO Council: 'to be very blunt, we think it is a joke and we don't take it very seriously ... It is a classic example of institutionalized co-option' (APF representative quoted in Godsäter and Söderbaum 2011). Even though it operates primarily on a national level in South Africa, APF is still active on the regional arena: for example, together with SAPSN, it is instrumental in developing the Social Forum process in the region, which brings together national and local civil society groups from all around Southern Africa.

Many civil society groups that resist regional governance have managed to fill a vacuum created by the absence of a real alternative to state-led regionalisms that overwhelmingly embrace neoliberal economic ideals. But in filling this gap, are these agents necessarily 'people-driven'? Frequently proclaimed links to the grassroots and to 'peoples' need to be scrutinized and debated. Sections of counter-hegemonic civil society are elitist-led, and dominated by a relatively small number of NGO representatives and activists. This means they are not necessarily 'positive' forces in society or for democracy. Unlike SATUCC, discussed above, most civil society groups participating in SAPSN are not membership-based. The number of participants and stakeholders involved is steadily increasing, but the agenda and output is dominated by a limited number of vocal activists. Their ability of these activists to deliver their message (their 'voice') and finance their activities is heavily dependent on how successful they are in attracting donor funding or other support from Western NGOs. Regional networking and regional cooperation in particular, are heavily dependent on donor funding. These critical factors are not necessarily problematic but they raise questions about legitimacy, accountability and representation.

Regional Civil Society as Manipulator

Civil society as manipulator occurs when apparent civil society activities are performed with the aim of achieving narrow private economic and political gains, and even to manipulate existing frameworks and organizations. NGOs in Africa (as well as elsewhere) can be staffed by relatives or close associates of the ruling political elites, who then use civil society as a platform to exercise political influence or for rent-seeking. Sometimes such structures may be justified, such as charitable-purpose NGOs. Obviously, then, there is a thin line between these and problem-solving NGOs; the latter are transformed into the former when the prime *raison-d'être* is individual political influence. Rent-seeking NGOs raise serious issues about independence and undue influence on NGOs by governments.

As one well-regarded expert on African politics points out: 'If you or anyone else was to look at an NGO in Botswana, the first thing you need to find out is: who is the head and the leading office-holders in the NGO?' Often 'one man shows', some people in Botswana and elsewhere have nicknamed these NGOs as 'MONGOs' (My Own NGO). Of course, this is not to say that every government-linked NGO is compromised. Despite having strong links with government, NGOs may still demonstrate independence by challenging and criticizing government actions and policies.[2]

Due to the fact that political elites and governments may use and abuse civil society in search of legitimacy for their own shaky regimes, this type of civil society activity may be closely linked to regime-boosting regionalism. Hence, civil society may play the 'political' role of reinforcing and legitimating what are controversial, and sometimes repressive, aspects of regional governance, such as large-scale regional infrastructure projects and state facilitation of the regional operations of large corporations.

---

[2] Thanks to Professor Ian Taylor (University of St Andrews) for highlighting these examples.

Indeed, establishing research institutes, think tanks and NGOs that operate as extended arms of, or fronts for, the government is a common strategy of many governments in Africa. These actors rarely criticize their benefactor governments but instead play roles to legitimize often authoritarian, or even illegal, government activities. One classic example is the NGO set up by Zambia's former president, Frederick Chiluba, to debate his (unconstitutional) third presidential term. Another is Ditshwanelo, a human rights NGO in Botswana that had been publicly critical about the Government's treatment of the minority San people. Then headed by a daughter of the Foreign Minister, Ditshwanelo was conspicuously silent about this issue at the 2001 World Conference on Racism, Racial Discrimination, Xenophobia and Related Intolerance in Durban, South Africa. Opinion in Botswana concluded that Ditshwanelo had been influenced by the familial link to try to minimize international embarrassment for the Botswanan Government.[3]

Interviews with representatives of state and civil society actors in Southern and Eastern Africa often mention that manipulative civil society organizations constitute obstacles for development and regional governance, serving the needs of donors and political and economic elites rather than local communities. According to one commentator, many NGOs in Eastern Africa are formed because 'someone wants to make some quick money somewhere ... or some [donor] agency somewhere have convinced them to form so that ... they can serve as a channel for the agency to do what it wants to do' (quoted in Godsäter and Söderbaum 2011). However, due to the controversial economic and political *raison-d'être* of 'briefcase NGOs' they invest heavily in creating a benevolent (development) façade and are therefore difficult to expose.

The significant inflow of donor money into civil society in Africa and elsewhere in the South has made it 'the place to make money' (Hearn 2007: 1102). In general, the quest for making money has professionalized NGOs and increasingly they are headed by members of the middle class, which reveals a narrow social representation (Hearn 2007). Some African NGOs are seen merely as an extension of the dominant donor aid agenda and,

---

[3] Thanks to Professor Ian Taylor (University of St Andrews) for highlighting these examples.

despite delivering all sorts of social services, as agents of Western interests to divert attention to the root causes of poverty. One commentator concludes that many African NGOs have become 'local managers of foreign aid money, not managers of local African development processes' (Nyang'oro quoted in Hearn 2007: 1107). Briefcase NGOs and many rent-seeking MONGOs are mainly interested in promoting and participating in regional cooperation and governance when it enhances economic or polit-ical gain. In this regard, the function of per diems (daily expense allowances) should not be ignored as regional networking is very much associated with international travel. There is reason to believe that representatives of NGOs sometimes engage in too much travel and networking with too little long-term effect and sustainability.

Conclusion

This chapter broadens our horizons about regionalism by plac-ing emphasis on the role of civil society actors, which hitherto has largely been ignored in the analysis of region-building and region-destruction. This is a somewhat surprising neglect, consid-ering the burgeoning literature on global civil society and global social movements.

The chapter suggests that civil society regionalism is hetero-geneous and contains several internal paradoxes and conflicts. Clearly, there are competing interests and conflicts within civil society, for instance competition for power and control, for achiev-ing status, or the search for pecuniary gain. Since such motives and underlying interests are hidden, they are also more difficult to detect. Indeed, sometimes, what on the surface is claimed to be civil society is in reality more of a business strategy, or an exer-cise to boost the status and personal interests of the individuals involved. Although they are often considered to be part of civil society, these activities do not contribute to the civil society as defined in this chapter (i.e. they do not attempt to shape the rules that govern social life).

One of the main messages of the chapter is that roles and func-tions of civil societies in the region cannot be understood properly without taking into account the complex and sometimes intimate links between civil society actors and political regimes. This suggests that the logic of civil society regionalism must be viewed in the context of the functioning of the African post-colonial political environment, resulting in a variety of patterns of 'inclusion' and 'exclusion' for civil society (Söderbaum 2007).

The varied relationships between states and civil societies arise at least partly because of the rich variation of political systems and governing political ideologies between as well as within different regions. For instance, in the case of Africa many NGOs in countries such as Malawi, Mauritius or Botswana work hand in hand with the state and can be seen almost as the extended arms of the state, while in countries such as South Africa, Kenya and Nigeria there is a more varied relationship between state and civil society. A third example is that civil society groups may often be harassed in more authoritarian countries, such as Lesotho, Swaziland and Zimbabwe, implying that a critical attitude towards the state can be rather dangerous.

Furthermore, some NGOs define their activities and organize themselves in relationship to states-led regional organizations, such as SADC, EAC or ECOWAS, as a way to partner with and lobby their governments and their regional organizations. This means that directly or indirectly they serve as legitimators of states-led regionalism. Those forces in civil society that are 'included' are so intimately related to ruling political regimes that their survival is largely contingent upon them, and this likely compromises their performance as civil society actors and their ability to shape the rules that govern social life. In contrast, the more radical critical forces in civil society that challenge authoritarian, patrimonial or simply liberal-capitalist power often are marginalized at best, or harassed by state and regional political regimes such as SADC. Consequently, critical and counter-hegemonic civil society actors have found it extremely difficult to advocate their positions successfully and lobby for change.

Regardless of type, the great majority of the civil society organizations in Africa depend overwhelmingly on funding from external actors, either government development agencies or northern NGOs. Civil society regionalism in Africa would look very different without such external actors, and be less significant. In the past, many donors worked primarily with the state, but today there is a stronger emphasis on forming 'partnerships' with government, the private sector and civil society. To a limited extent, local NGOs can obtain funding by providing services or from their own governments, but the largest proportion of the funds for civil society activities come from donor agencies or Western NGOs. Donors, it needs be said, are by no means 'neutral' and their interests and ways of operating play a significant role in the social construction of the region. The roles of external actors is the topic of the next chapter.

9

External Actors in Regionalism

Clearly, external actors have not received enough attention in the study of regions and regionalism. Most theories and approaches consider regionalism as a project led by intra-regional actors emerging in response to external forces and pressures, such as globalization and hegemonic international powers (Buzdugan 2013). This chapter rethinks how external actors contribute to and influence the making and unmaking of regions.

In historical perspective, the US has had a strong impact on region-building as well as region-destruction around the world. The US repeatedly has tried to remake regions to suit its own national interest. For instance, the US has tried to reshape, undermine and, sometimes, even destroy regionalist projects in the Caribbean, Central and South America as well as Central and East/Southeast/South Asia. In contrast, the US played a more progressive role in the early stages of European integration right after the end of the Second World War.

In recent decades, the EU has emerged as the world's most influential region-builder, with very comprehensive strategies and funding mechanisms to support regionalism in Africa, Asia, Latin America and to some extent in the Middle East and the Mediterranean. As is explored and detailed in Chapter 11, on interregionalism, there is a comprehensive debate about the EU's role as an external region-builder around the world. However, research on actors other than the US and the EU is fragmented and underdeveloped.

Countries and regions in the developing world are much more susceptible to outside influence, and so it is there that external actors are able to penetrate more deeply. Most external actors declare that they support and fund regionalism in order to help regional actors build their 'own' regions. This chapter shows that this is somewhat disingenuous. External actors simply are not neutral financiers and promoters of endogenous projects; they are engaged actively in the making and unmaking of regions. Given that so little is known about the agency of external actors in regionalism, this chapter draws heavily on the case of Africa, where outside penetration is the most deep and evident. The intent is not to create insights that can be generalized to all corners of the world, but rather to stimulate further thinking and theorizing about this overlooked aspect of regionalism. Three of the most important policy fields for external actors in contemporary Africa serve as the focus: market integration, transboundary waters and security regionalism.

Regional Market-Building from Outside

External pressures and actors are crucial for the creation and deepening of the project of market integration in Africa. Since the late 1980s, many of the most powerful external actors have moved from Cold War interests towards a strategy and agenda for regional market-building built on the principles of trade and market liberalization, good governance and democracy. Most of these actors were fairly sceptical of trade blocs and common markets in Africa in the past because of fear that these projects would be protectionist (see Chapter 7, Multidimensional Regionalism).

A shift of attitude by the World Bank is significant. Previously wary of states-led regionalism in Africa, in recent years the World Bank has become a strong supporter of such processes and between 2008 and 2011 its support of regional integration in sub-Saharan Africa increased around 75 percent, reaching US$3.65 billion in 2011 (World Bank 2011). The Bank's new emphasis is on market integration as a means for achieving economies of scale, wider competition, increased foreign investment, the opening of national economies, ensuring national reform through lock-in policy mechanisms and unity for international negotiations. A considerable part of the Bank's funding is geared towards infra-structural projects and development corridors that are believed to improve the conditions for functional market integration.

Enacted by the United States in 2000, the African Growth and Opportunity Act (AGOA) is an important part of the country's economic policy towards sub-Saharan Africa. AGOA rewards those African states that liberalize, privatize and democratize, by way of debt relief, loan guarantees, business partnerships and, particularly, access to United States' markets. It seeks to expand trade and investment between the US and Africa, stimulate economic growth, and foster regional economic integration in Africa while at the same time facilitating sub-Saharan Africa's integration into the global economy. AGOA is a continental strategy, but the US nonetheless deals with each country on a bilateral basis. The strategy provides reforming African countries with the most liberal access to the US market available to any country or region with which the US does not have a free trade agreement. The eligibility requirements include market-based economies; the rule of law and political pluralism; elimination of barriers to US trade and investment; protection of intellectual property; efforts to combat corruption; policies to reduce poverty, increasing availability of health care and educational opportunities; protection of human rights and worker rights; and elimination of certain child labour practices.

As do most other external actors, the EU supports a similar type of market-led and outward-oriented regionalism. The EU has a very comprehensive regional portfolio (worth several billion euros) to the African Union (AU) and the regional economic communities (RECs), such as the Common Market for Eastern and Southern Africa (COMESA), the East African Development Community (EAC), the Economic Community of West African States (ECOWAS), and the Southern African Development Community (SADC). Somewhat special in the EU case is that it is focused much more deeply on supporting and building stable and adaptable regional institutions:

> successful regional integration requires a market-friendly economic environment, openness towards third countries, institutions which are sufficiently strong and have a clear mandate, adequate resources and political support. A flexible institutional framework, permitting progress at various speeds ('variable geometry'), broad participation by the private sector and civil society, and a set-up where responsibility for dealing with an issue is kept as close as possible to the population

concerned ('subsidiarity'), can also be seen as critical ingredients for success, as the EU experience shows. (European
Commission 1995: iii)

A crucial ingredient for understanding the EU's support of
regionalism in Africa can be found in its self-proclamation as
'world champion' of regionalism. In this context, what is important is the fact that that many EU actors believe the EU model
can be exported to other regions. For instance, in the 1990s the
European Commission confidently pronounced:

> There are a number of lessons that can be drawn from the expe-
> rience of regional integration in various parts of the world.
> Probably the most important lesson can be derived from the
> European experience, not only on account of its long history
> but also because, to a large extent, *it can be considered as the
> only successful example of regional integration so far*. (European
> Commission 1995: 8, emph. added)

This self-image has been sustained: a decade later, President Prodi
of the European Commission (1999–2004) praised the virtues of
the EU model:

> Our European model of integration is the most developed in
> the world. Imperfect though it still is, it nevertheless works on
> a continental scale. Given the necessary institutional reforms,
> it should continue to work well after enlargement, *and I believe
> we can make a convincing case that it would also work globally*.
> (Prodi quoted in Rosamond 2005: 473, emph. added)

Such strong conviction about the relevance of the EU model to
the rest of the world clearly suggests that the EU is by no means
'neutral' in the making of regions in the rest of the world. On the
contrary, EU policies are strongly shaped and determined by its
own identity and self-understanding, especially a particular self-
understanding formed in policy circles in Brussels.

The EU's trade policy towards Africa is very much shaped
by the Union's attempt to establish the much touted Economic
Partnership Agreements (EPAs) with geographically more focused
subgroups of the African, Caribbean and Pacific (ACP). In the
EPA framework, the EU claims to be combining trade and aid

policies in a novel way under the frame of the EPAs. According to the EU's official policy, 'the idea is to help the ACP countries integrate with their regional neighbours as a step towards global integration, and to help them build institutional capacities and apply principles of good governance. At the same time, the EU will continue to open its markets to products from the ACP group, and other developing countries' (European Commission 2004: 10). Clearly, this strategy is considered to bring about mutual benefits for all parties involved. What constitutes 'mutual benefit' is of course at the heart of the matter, and fundamentally this is ambiguous, especially since the initiative undermines African regionalism.

There is significant criticism in academia, among policy-makers and in civil society of the EU's policies about the EPAs. The EU's approach is both contradictory and driven by self-interest. On the one hand, the EU provides economic and political support to regional integration and the creation of viable regional institutions on the African continent. On the other hand, the EU undermines regionalist projects, principally by its insistence on negotiating EPAs with regional groupings (created by the EU) that do not match Africa's existing regional frameworks. The EU's trade strategy is difficult to reconcile with the emphasis on an 'equal' partnership so often referred to in the EU's official policies with Africa. This contradiction is linked closely to the underlying purposes of the EU's approach, and especially individual preferences of certain EU member states. Farrell argues that the EU's partnership strategy and the Cotonou Agreement reflect neoliberal goals as well as the imposition of strong political conditionalities, rather than the normative agenda repeatedly mentioned in the EU's official discourse. According to Farrell, this represents 'a triumph of realism over idealism' (Farrell 2006). Another study referred to this as 'soft imperialism' in contrast with the EU's promoted self-identity as a 'civilian' or 'normative power' (Hettne and Söderbaum 2005a).

Gray (2013) expresses a similarly sceptical view of external actors. Gray conducted what is probably the most comprehensive study available of the role played by external actors in the promotion of regional economic organizations in the developing world. As far as Africa is concerned, Gray claims that regional organizations are rarely built on the interests of their member states but instead those of powerful external actors. This has far-reaching implications for contemporary regionalism in Africa. Outside funding is undoubtedly necessary in Africa, but this analysis helps to explain why so many African regional projects are unstable and not under the control of regional actors. Unlike some proponents of the new regionalism, Gray argues that it is irrelevant to speak about post-hegemonic regionalism: in the developing world, regional economic organizations are influenced heavily by external, strong powers and cannot exist and influence the global power structures on their own terms.

Gray's scepticism is linked to the fact that there is still very limited knowledge available on the development results of external support to regionalism in Africa (as well as other regions). Indeed, apart from a number of usually isolated donor evaluations, there is no *systematic* knowledge production about how external actors and outside funding contribute to economic development and poverty reduction. Combaz (2013: 2–3) pinpoints some of the main weaknesses in study of the external support of regionalism and its effect on poverty reduction: 'no information exists at impact level, only at output and outcome levels'; most data focuses on regional integration instead of poverty reduction; causalities are complex; and, finally, if there are assessments about poverty, these usually focus on macro-level and quantitative indicators, with little attention paid to effects and impacts on the meso- and micro-level (Combaz 2013: 2–3).

Building Ecological Regions from Outside

In more or less every river and lake basin in Africa there are multiple, donor-driven programmes for natural resource management. In theory, the donor-driven paradigm of integrated water resource management (IWRM) is supposed to counteract the fragmentation of water resources and ecological regions created by national borders. In practice, however, the donors support and fund a multitude of overlapping and sometimes competing projects, programmes and regional organizations. This socio-political fragmentation is reinforced further by the fact that many donors prefer bilateral dealings with affected countries instead of dealing with them collectively under the regional frameworks (Nicol et al. 2001; Söderbaum 2015). Lake Victoria provides a pertinent illustration of these problems.

Lake Victoria is the second largest freshwater lake in the world. Both the governments in the basin and donors stress the need for transboundary resource management. Yet, too many isolated and overlapping donor projects and mechanisms have resulted in fragmentation and mismanagement of resources in the Lake Victoria Basin. For instance, the Lake Victoria Environmental Management Project (LVEMP), initiated in 1994, is one of the most comprehensive regional programmes for Lake Victoria. It is implemented by the African governments concerned but with extensive external funding, especially from the World Bank and the Global Environment Facility (GEF). LVEMP has achieved rather modest results, resulting from, among other things, a weak connection between this programme and the many similar initiatives within the Lake Victoria basin and the larger Nile Basin. In an attempt to strengthen the LVEMP, the World Bank and GEF stated that a second phase (launched in 2005) should be integrated further with the World Bank's Nile Basin Initiative (NBI) in order to increase economic transactions and peaceful cooperation among the 10 states situated along the Nile, from Egypt to Burundi. However, reconciling LVEMP II with NBI and other donor-driven projects in the region has been very problematic.

The Lake Victoria Initiative (LVI) funded by Sweden is yet another externally driven programme that suffers from rather weak coordination with other initiatives, despite having a comprehensive agenda for better management of the ecosystem through coordination with other donors. Sweden's national self-image is important for understanding the rationale behind the programme as well as its limitations, which resulted in the closing down of the initiative within a decade of its inception. The LVI was promoted as a 'flagship' of Swedish development policy, and as 'the most important challenge for Sida [the Swedish International Development Cooperation Agency] during the coming 20 years' (Sida 2002). In fact, the LVI was modelled on Sweden's experience from the Baltic Sea Cooperation (BSC), and reflects Sweden's self-image as the key driver of this process. Sida declared that it wanted to export the 'unparalleled success' of the BSC to the Lake Victoria region (Sida 2002). There is no doubt that implementing the LVI has proven problematic and been marked by difficulties in identifying the appropriate regional counterparts in the lacustrine states and in civil society and affected communities. The LVI also experienced problems with connecting to the broader agenda of the EAC, and with uncertainty about how to integrate Swedish bilateral and regional aid initiatives in the three lacustrine states (Söderbaum and Stålgren 2010b).

Summing up, many donors favour a flexible projects-based approach in the field of transboundary water management (Söderbaum 2015). Quite often this results in a series of parallel, or worse, competing initiatives and projects, both external as well as home-grown. A general weakness is that most donors are focused heavily on achieving narrow project 'outputs' in their separate initiatives. Duplication and consequent waste of resources is a clear matter of concern. The tendency to avoid using endogenous regional mechanisms has been shown to be deeply problematic (Söderbaum and Granit 2014).

Constructing and Deconstructing Security Regions from Outside[1]

In the field of peace and security many external actors are focusing on the emerging African Peace and Security Architecture (APSA). The EU is the most important external supporter of the APSA, as well as security regionalism in Africa more broadly. In this field, the peace and security partnership within the Joint Africa–EU Strategy (JAES) provides a general framework for cooperation between EU and Africa. The partnership has three priority actions: (i) to reach common positions on and implement common approaches to peace and security in Africa, Europe and globally; (ii) the full operationalization of APSA; and (iii) reliable funding for Africa-led peace and security operations, especially through the African Peace Facility (European Commission 2005). Most of the funds within the Facility have been used for peace operations, such as the AU Missions in Sudan (AMIS), Somalia (AMISOM), Comoros (AMISEC) and the CEMAC Mission to the Central African Republic (FOMUC).

Nonetheless, the EU's involvement in African security goes beyond APSA. Under the Common Security and Defence Policy (CSDP) the EU has launched a large number of civilian and military operations in Africa, dealing with both national and regional conflicts. As noted earlier, national/domestic conflicts often spill

---

[1] Parts of this section build on research cooperation with Rodrigo Tavares (Söderbaum and Tavares 2008).

over to the region, which emphasizes the importance of security regionalism. Some of the EU's peace operations had limited mandates focusing mainly on stabilizing security and improving the humanitarian situation in geographically confined areas and with a short-term perspective. Examples include the EUFOR Chad/CAR mission in 2006 and Operation Artemis in the DRC in 2003. Both missions are generally regarded as having achieved their objectives. Yet, in view of their limited mandates and short time frame, it is equally clear that these operations had only a marginal impact on the conflicts and security regionalism more broadly (Froitzheim et al. 2011).

The CSDP missions with a more comprehensive mandate and long-term perspective, such as the EUPOL and EUSEC RD Congo, are more problematic. Institutional complexity within the EU is so profound that its role and efficiency are severely constrained by inter-institutional conflict and rivalries: within the Council and between different missions; between the Council and the Commission; and between the EU and the individual interests of the member states (Froitzheim et al. 2011). Weak institutional coherence also affects the EU's relations with African and other external actors. For instance, the EU's official stance is to support a UN-led system and to contribute to 'effective multilateralism'. In most regionalized African conflicts, however, there is a tendency for external powers and donors involved in peace-building to focus systematically on their own 'visibility' by implementing high-profile projects, promising immediate results, rather than following a comprehensive and coordinated – and thus necessarily long-term – strategy. Hence, the external actors rarely support African-led security efforts. The strong emphasis on the visibility of the EU's own efforts may be because of a perceived need to justify the expenditure of resources to domestic constituencies. Hence, the EU's main focus in the Great Lakes region appears to be international and symbolic visibility instead of a clearly defined, committed and credible strategy on how to build peace. An EU representative in the DRC candidly lamented, 'I do not know what I am doing here' and went on to say that 'the EU's involvement is purely political' (quoted in Froitzheim et al. 2011).

Compared to the EU and the EU member countries, US security policy towards Africa, at least partly, is driven by different motivations (Söderbaum and Tavares 2008). Although Africa was never a top priority in US post-Cold War foreign policy strategy, the fixation by the US on security and counter-terrorism post 9/11 has resulted in the militarization of its policy in Africa. The official brief of the US Africa Command (AFRICOM) is to build defence capabilities, respond to crisis, and defeat transnational threats in order to advance US national interests and promote regional security, stability and prosperity in Africa. While there is some support for and collaboration with regional organizations, such as the AU and ECOWAS, the US generally favours collaboration with individual African states. Clearly, the bilateral approach is primarily built on the US security interests rather than by an urge to support APSA and other regional security initiatives in Africa.

For instance, under the Trans-Sahara Counter-Terrorism Initiative (TSCTI), the Pentagon provided aid to increase border security and counter-terrorism capabilities to specific countries such as Mali, Chad, Niger and Mauritania. Similarly, the Africa Contingency Operations Training and Assistance Program (ACOTA) has provided small arms and training for peacekeeping operations to Benin, Botswana, Cote d'Ivoire, Ethiopia, Gabon, Ghana, Kenya, Malawi, Mozambique, Nigeria, Senegal, South Africa, Uganda and Zambia. Furthermore, the US Navy monitors countries from Guinea to Angola and the Defense Department has agreements for access to air bases and ports maintained by local security forces in Gabon, Kenya, Mali, Morocco, Namibia, Sao Tome and Principe, Senegal, Tunisia, Uganda and Zambia. Apart from terrorism and more conventional threats, the US involvement in African security may also be understood in the context of the continent providing the US with an increasing amount of natural resources, such as oil.

Russia's Africa policy is driven mainly by economic links and natural resources. Russia prioritizes bilateral relations in dealing with strategic economic issues and commodities. Apart from periodic diplomatic contacts, marginal support on a project basis and the expression of political support to the formation of the APSA, Russia's financial support to APSA and AU is nominal. That said, Russia's official policy stance is that it wants to develop political dialogue with the AU and the RECs and also contribute to the settlement of military conflicts in Africa. For the time being, Russia's military cooperation with the AU and African countries is confined to the training of African peacekeepers in Russia and to limited participation in UN peacekeeping operations in Africa.

Japan has had little historical experience with Africa and little interest in deepening economic ties with the continent, except for cooperation around raw materials. Since the 1990s, Japan's role in Africa has centred on the Tokyo International Conference on African Development (TICAD), whereby African leaders meet with Japanese officials and leaders. Although TICAD revolves around economic issues, in the 2000s TICAD IV reiterated its support to the APSA. Japan is particularly focused on supporting the AU's efforts in peace and security. For instance, Japan has supported a series of AU initiatives in Darfur and some reintegration projects in the Great Lakes Region (GLR).

China has become one of Africa's important partners for trade, economic cooperation and the exploitation of natural resources. China's policy towards Africa is quite strongly linked to its demand for natural resources and its desire to sell arms. Somewhat similar to the US and several other countries, this has resulted in a Chinese preference for bilateral relations with African countries. For instance, China's voracious demand for energy, oil and natural resources has led it to seek supplies from African countries such as Sudan, Chad, Nigeria, Angola, Algeria, Gabon, Equatorial Guinea, and the Republic of Congo. At the same time, China is a major arms supplier to a range of African governments, such as Sudan, Equatorial Guinea, Ethiopia, Eritrea, Burundi, Tanzania and Zimbabwe. Selling arms to African countries helps China cement relationships with African leaders and offset the costs of buying oil and natural resources from them. Since China does not have the same human rights concerns as the US and the EU member countries, it sells military hardware to more or less any government in Africa. China's relationship with Zimbabwe's Robert Mugabe is a good illustration of this.

China's active exploration of oil and natural resources in Africa has resulted in an increased interest in ensuring security and political stability. To this end, the Chinese military has sent trainers to help its African counterparts. In return, China gains important African allies in the UN – including Sudan, Zimbabwe, and Nigeria – for its political goals, including preventing Taiwanese independence and diverting attention from its own human rights record, and so on. In other words, although the supply of natural resources and access to new markets are key ingredients of China's policy towards Africa, these strategies are intimately intertwined with Chinese geostrategic interests and its quest to bolster its own position in the global arena (Taylor 2008).

Chinese interest and support of regionalism in Africa has increased during the last decade. China appears to acknowledge that African regionalism is conducive to improved political stability (which is in China's interest). Another decisive factor in the recent increased Chinese interest and support of African regionalism seems to be China's willingness to achieve consensus when interacting with the AU or other sub-regional organizations on critical topics (Lammich 2014: 7). Here China recognizes that the AU's efforts to ensure stability and make peace are constrained by a lack of human resources, material supplies and funding. For instance, China consequently provided equipment and material to AMISOM, as well as funding of the new facilities at the AU headquarters in Addis Ababa. All in all, if and when China supports African regionalism, it first and foremost is *ad hoc* and interest-based rather than part of a comprehensive regional strategy.

Conclusion

This chapter broadens the panorama of by whom and for what purpose regions are made and unmade. Previous chapters laid emphasis on state, business and civil society actors from within the region, whereas the present chapter highlights the role of external actors – hitherto largely ignored in comparative regionalism. The study focused on market-building, transboundary waters and security regionalism in Africa, as the fields in which external actors are particularly influential.

As far as trade and market integration is concerned, there has been a shift in regionalist visions and ideas in Africa during recent decades. In contrast to 'old' and inward-oriented projects, a majority of current African regionalist schemes are liberal and market-oriented. Regional market-building projects are supported and shaped strongly from the outside – by the EU, the World Bank, the US and Western donor agencies.

One of the core ideas of the market integration approach is that the rolling back of the state will give private market agents a greater role in the economy and result in a change to the ownership base. This strategy is assumed to serve the public interest. However, the results of barrier-dropping market integration have been much more modest than its advocates claimed. Even the most enthusiastic supporters of this discourse are starting to accept that the desired trickle-down does not work in the absence of functioning political authority. Nevertheless, what many proponents and powerful external actors continue to ignore is the fact that the ideal of an 'open' and 'liberalized' market obscures the real power relations and structural imbalances in these regional and national markets. In addition, these barrier-dropping and market integration projects have few instruments for achieving human development and poverty reduction. As a consequence, the type of economic regionalism resulting from these interventions is both 'thin' and exclusionist, constructed by powerful political elites and capitalist interests, from both within and outside the region. It is a historical irony that this type of economic market integration resembles colonial capitalism, with little or no direct concern for the people on the ground. Given this outcome, future solutions to the development problems in Africa should be grounded better in an understanding of the social, political and economic conditions of the individual countries and the regional political economy as a whole.

Large river and lake systems naturally draw attention to regional settings, as they often straddle human-created boundaries. It is a dominant norm today that river and lake basins should be seen and dealt with as a single ecological unit. Many environmental issues in such systems are transboundary in nature and therefore require some sort of basin-wide solutions. The ecological approach to governance is based on a critique of 'old' solutions, especially the statist-nationalist mode of managing water resources. Attempts to reconstruct the Lake Victoria basin along these new principles are reinforced by the strength of global environmental perspectives, such as 'green lenses', 'the Green Revolution', the Rio Declaration and the Dublin Principles. Donors and powerful environmental civil society organizations in the North embrace these ideals to a considerable extent and, clearly, these external influences and actors give the ecological way of thinking considerable strength.

An ecologically sustainable basin-wide approach is often difficult to pursue because in its current design it lacks internal consistency and can unwittingly legitimate a variety of overlapping and contradictory measures. Importantly, many external donors and agencies design a range of competing regional projects and programmes, all of which are claimed to enhance management of transboundary waters. Many project designers are seemingly free to design intervention strategies without a preferred methodology and in ways that compete with other initiatives and projects, be they home-grown or external (Söderbaum and Granit 2014).

One of the fundamental problems with the prevailing wisdom in transboundary water management is that many river basin organizations and projects lack the necessary political clout. Externally funded transboundary cooperation mechanisms often are unable to assemble the necessary national political commitments or solve the complicated transboundary collective action dilemmas. This results in failures in implementation and agreement on many substantial issues. Given the enormous financial resources pumped into transboundary water management in Africa, the donor community carries a large measure of responsibility for the lack of success.

External geostrategic interests feature strongly in African conflicts and conflict management. Many external powers favour bilateral relations with African countries. Bilateralism is not in itself negative, but as it is currently practised it serves to reinforce existing fragmentation at the expense of more collective security efforts in Africa. Nonetheless, there is growing external support for APSA and the AU's peace operations. One important trend here is strong buy-in by the EU, UN and other countries/agencies to the policy of 'African solutions to African problems'. By following this agenda, external actors are able to downplay their own role and responsibility in complex conflicts and humanitarian emergencies on the African continent. Even if the EU and many other external powers provide substantial funding of security regionalism in Africa, clearly there are not enough resources and capacities available for the strengthening of APSA and for solving the conflicts on the African continent. Much of the outside involvement is indeed selective and sometimes even symbolic, and so effectively side-steps the risk of blame and the shame of failure. It has therefore been argued that the doctrine of 'African solutions to African problems' is serving the interests of external actors as it helps them to *avoid* instead of *share* responsibility for building peace and security in Africa.

10

Regionness: The Solidification of Regions

Most regions of the world contain a multitude of strategies, ideas and identities relating to the region, which meet, merge and compete (Neumann 2003). There is a need to go beyond such diversity and understand the processes by which regions come into existence and are consolidated. When different processes of regionalization playing out in various fields and at various scales, intensify and converge within the same geographical area, this increases the cohesiveness and thereby the distinctiveness of the region in the making. This chapter outlines and advances the 'regionness' framework as a comparative heuristic tool for understanding the construction and solidification of regions in terms of regional coherence and community.[1] It ranges from regional social space, regional social complex, regional society and regional community to regional institutionalized polity. Regionness is also connected to the capacity to act in the outside world. The concept of regional 'actorness' helps us understand a region's ability to influence the external world and its role in global transformation (issues explored in the last parts of this book).

The Essence of Regionness

Even if a continuum or 'stage-theory' approach to understanding region formation may be somewhat theoretically unsatisfying, it is

---

[1] The concept of regionness was coined by Björn Hettne in the 1990s. This chapter draws on our research collaboration, especially (Hettne and Söderbaum 2000).

historically plausible and, as Hurrell (1995: 73) points out, it has a great deal to offer in sharpening our understanding of increasing regionalization in many parts of the world.

The framework of regionness rejects pre-given or pre-scientific regional delimitations. Instead, the focus is on how different actors perceive and interpret the idea of a region and notions of region-ness. Since there are no given regions, there are no given regional-ist interests either, and interests and identities are shaped in the process of interaction and intersubjective understanding. In such a situation, the relevance of 'hard structuralism' is limited. Wendt is correct in that 'structure has no existence or causal power apart from process' (Wendt 1992: 395). To understand structural social change we must move from structure to agency, to actors, to ideas and to identities. It needs noting here that the regionalization pro-cess can be both intentional and unintentional, and may proceed unevenly along the various dimensions of regionalism (i.e. eco-nomics, politics, culture, security, environment, etc.).

Regionness can be understood by analogy to concepts such as 'stateness' and 'nationness'. Just like nation-states, regions are highly subjective phenomena, created and recreated through dis-course, identity and cognitive resources (and to some extent also by our theories). A consolidated region exhibits a similarity to a nation, in that a region too is an 'imagined community' and has a territorial extent (Anderson 1983). But there are also dif-ferences: for instance the greater variety of interests and the more complex problem of coordination within a region compared to a nation-state. External action (but also internal consolidation) depends on 'identity' as an important but hard-to-define com-ponent, and identity is what brings people together to become a 'we'. The regionness framework suggests that regions cannot solidify only on the basis of function and material interests. There is also a need for a 'we' and some type of shared iden-tity. Of course, identity is complex and there are many historical sources of regional identity and belonging. Identity is not simply based on tradition and, in any case, tradition is not reproduced in a simple way. Rather, identity is continuously created and recre-ated by new experiences and challenges of enlarged populations of 'Europeans', 'Africans', Latin Americans' or 'Asians'.

Another central element of the regionness framework is that regions are made and unmade by both state actors and a large variety of non-state actors, such as businesses, transnational corporations, NGOs and various social networks and social movements. Sometimes economic, social and cultural networks can be more active at the regional level than states-led and policy-driven processes. We therefore need detailed comparative studies on the strength of and relationships between various types of state-, market- and civil society–induced processes of regionalization throughout the various phases of regionness. A relevant comparative question is whether there are typical sequences (or 'spillovers') in these regionalization processes. Similarly, since regionalization may often be a response to specific internal or external challenges, the driving factors may differ depending on the precise encounters between various social forces at different points in time. Thus, if trade agreements and market harmonization represent the major task in one case, regional conflict resolution or ecological crisis management may be the predominant issue in others. Even though there are many regional pathways it is relevant to conceptualize and try to understand how regions consolidate and become more coherent.

Regions are political and social projects, devised by human state and non-state actors, in order to protect or transform existing structures. This means that both construction and deconstruction need to be integrated in a single analytical framework. Another central element in the regionness framework is that regions can be disrupted from both within and without as well as ideationally and materially (Adler and Barnett 1998a: 58). Regionness can both increase and decrease as a consequence. Integration and disintegration go hand in hand (albeit at different levels) and at each stage there is the possibility of spill-back. Seen from this perspective, a decline would mean fragmentation and decreasing regionness as well as a dilution of identity. For instance, the failure of the Commonwealth of Independent States (CIS) to keep the post-Soviet space together is an example of such a fragmentary process, even if that region-building now appears to be superseded by a project to establish a different Eurasian region.

Regional Social Space: The 'Proto-Region'

Geographical contiguity should not be exaggerated in importance but it is true that a functioning society cannot exist without territory. That is, a region is rooted in territorial space: a group of people living in a geographically bounded community, controlling a set of natural resources, and united by a set of values and common bonds of social order forged by history.

One can identify a potential region as primarily a geographical unit, delimited more or less by natural physical barriers and marked by ecological characteristics: 'Europe from the Atlantic to the Urals', North America, the Southern cone of South America, 'sub-Saharan Africa', Central Asia or 'the Indian subcontinent'. In the earliest history of each area, people often lived in rather isolated communities with little systematic political interaction. This first level of regionness can therefore be referred to as a 'proto-region', or a 'pre-regional zone', as there is no organized international/world society in this situation.

However, some translocal relations are bound to have developed rather early on. Premodern exchange systems were often based on symbolic kinship bonds rather than expectations associated with market behaviour. Premarket transactions, which Karl Polanyi referred to as 'embedded', contained an important element of diplomacy and the creation of trust between isolated communities experiencing occasional 'encounters' (Polanyi 1944). In order to regionalize further, a particular territory must necessarily experience increasing interaction and more frequent contact between human communities, which after living in separate and distinct political communities are moving towards some kind of translocal relationship, giving rise to a regional social system or what will be called below a 'regional social complex'.

Regional Social Complex

Increased social contacts and transactions between previously more isolated and autochthonous groups – the creation of a social system – facilitates some sort of regionness, albeit on a low level. The creation of Latin Christendom between 800 and 1200, which also implied the 'birth' of a European identity, is a case in point (Bartlett 1993). Such early relations of interdependence also constitute a regional social complex and indicate the real starting point for the regionalization process in Europe.

The emergence of a regional social complex thus implies ever-widening translocal relations – positive and/or negative – between human groups and influences between cultures ('little traditions') and political communities. A longer historical perspective is necessary than simply the Westphalian nation-building period. This is of particular importance in the developing world where the nation-state system is much more recent, and often remains feeble and even quite artificial (see Chapter 2, Learning from History).

State-formation and nation-building leads to a consolidation of what are to become national territories and, for a time, this implies more inward-orientation and usually a temporary decline in the level of regionness. This was evident in the postcolonial creation of states in Latin America during the nineteenth century and in Asia and Africa after the Second World War (although pan-regionalism movements were also formed and active at various junctures). The collective memory of a more disparate identity, albeit confined to a relatively small (national) elite, then dissipates. By definition, the territorial states monopolize all external relations and decide who is friend or foe, which implies a discouragement of whatever regional consciousness there might be. Where a nation-state system exists, the prevailing social relations may very well be hostile and completely lacking in cooperation. According to the dominant theory in IR (realism) this is, in fact, a defining feature of a nation-state system. Citizens of the separate nation-states are not likely to have much mutual trust in or even knowledge of each other, much less a shared identity. However, when the states relax their 'inward-orientedness' and become more open to external relations, the degree of transnational contact may increase dramatically, which may trigger a process of further regionalization and region-building.

In security terms, a region at this level of formation is understood best as a 'conflict formation' or a 'regional security complex', in which the constituent units depend on each other as well as on the overall stability of the regional system for their own security (Buzan 1991). Just like the larger international system of which it forms part, a region at this level of regionness can be described as 'anarchic', with territorial states as the only relevant actors. Europe in the nineteenth century is the classic case of such a regional order. At this low level of regionness, a balance of power, or some kind of 'concert', is the sole security guarantee for the states constituting the system. This is a rather primitive security mechanism. We can therefore talk of a 'primitive' region, exemplified today by the Balkans and, as far as political security is concerned (in spite of a relatively high degree of economic regionalization), by Northeast East Asia.

As with security matters, the political economy of development can be understood as 'anarchic' because of the absence of a transnational welfare mechanism that can ensure a functioning regional economic system. In Europe, this was the legacy of the mercantilism associated with nation-building, which has its counterpart in the Third World in the dependency/economic nationalism syndrome. The patterns of regional economic interdependencies tend to be exploitative rather than cooperative and mutually reinforcing, often resulting in hostile protectionism, trade wars, beggar-thy-neighbour policies and relative gain-seeking. Various strategies are employed to isolate the 'national' economies from the negative effects of the larger regional (and of course global) economic system they form part of, whilst simultaneously trying to exploit the opportunities of the same system(s). The actors may also look mostly towards the larger external system rather than the region. There is no shared sense of 'sitting in the same boat': exchanges and economic interactions are unstable, short-sighted and based solely on self-interest rather than expectations of economic reciprocity, social communication and mutual trust. This economic behaviour is inherent in the ideology of globalism as opposed to regionalism.

Regional Society

The third level of regionness is where the crucial regionalization process develops and intensifies, in the sense that apart from the states, a number of different actors appear on different societal levels and make use of a cooperative and more ordered pattern of relations to begin the move towards transcending national space. At this stage, the dynamics imply the emergence and solidification of a variety of processes of communication and interaction between a multitude of state and non-state actors and along several economic, political and cultural dimensions, i.e. multidimensional regionalism. This rise in intensity, scope and width of regionalization may come about through formalized and policy-led regional cooperation or it may happen more spontaneously. In the case of more formally organized cooperation, the members of the states-led regional organization in question define the region. As discussed in Chapter 5, Obviating the Gap Between Formal and Informal Regionalism, of this book, most conventional and rationalist studies focus on regions of this kind. In order to assess the relevance and potential of a particular regional organization, one has to relate the 'formal region' to the 'real region' or informal region, the latter being defined in terms of potentialities, *de facto* regionalization, convergences and other, less precise criteria (Mittelman 1999).

This level of regionness can be referred to as a regional form of the 'international society' of cooperating states, as used in the English School. The major difference is that the 'regional society' is not confined simply to relations between nation-states (Bull 1977). At lower degrees of regionness, the regional dynamics are often dominated by a state-centric logic, but typically there is increasing interdependence and a relaxed inward-orientation that gives rise to complex interactions between diverse actors. These will include a wide range of non-state, transnational actors: private businesses and firms, transnational corporations (TNCs), NGOs, social movements and other types of social networks formed on the basis of professional, ideological, ethnic or religious ties, which contribute to the formation of a transnational regional economy and regional civil society (see Chapters 5–9 in this book).

Relationships and strengths of the 'formal' and the 'real' (or 'informal') region, between state and non-state actors, differ in time and space, and it is important to acknowledge this. The crucial point is understanding how the region is made and unmade through the interplay between the state, market, civil society and even external actors, and through the interplay between formal and informal processes and mechanisms. Increasing regionness does not mean that the nation-states are becoming obsolete or disappearing, but rather that they are regionalizing as a consequence of major restructuring in the context of global transformation and the interplay of state-market-society relations. Increasing regionalization means that nation-states end up as semi-independent parts of larger regional and supranational political societies. One helpful way of conceiving the ongoing restructuring of the nation-state and the new transnational governance structures that emerge is to understand the Westphalian state as a 'bundle' of functions, loyalties and identities, some of which are becoming delinked from the state level in the new global situation and associated with other political levels. This results in a transscalar political landscape in which actors other than the state also gain strength (Ruggie 1998).

As seen in Chapter 6, micro-regions in the world today come in many forms. Examples such as the Euro-regions are well-known, and must be understood in their particular European context. As illustrated by concepts such as growth polygons, growth triangles, development corridors (DCs), spatial development initiatives (SDIs) and cross-border regions, most micro-regions in other parts of the world are state-assisted and have weak institution-alization whilst being private sector-led and market-driven (see Chapter 6, Organizing Regional Space).

For further regionalization to occur, the processes at various scales (i.e. macro/meso/micro) and sectors must become mutually reinforcing and evolve further in a complementary and mutually reinforcing way rather than a competitive and diverging direction. Increasing and widening relationships between the 'formal' and the 'real' region will lead to an institutionalization of cognitive structures and a gradual deepening of mutual trust and respon-siveness. In this process, formal or social institutions play a crucial role in providing a lead towards community- and region-building.

Regional Community

The fourth level of regionness refers to the process by which the region increasingly turns into an active subject with a distinct identity, with institutionalized and/or informal actor capability, with legitimacy in the eyes of a responsive regional civil society. All this implies an increasing convergence and compatibility of ideas, institutions and processes within a particular region. At this point, the old nation-state borders are gradually transcended. Clashing (national) interests and identities will prevent states and other actors from building regional communities.

To continue this line of discussion, in security terms the refer-ence now is to 'security community' (Deutsch et al. 1957; Adler and Barnett 1998a). This implies that the achieved level of region-ness makes the solution of conflicts (between as well as within states) by violent means inconceivable. With regard to develop-ment, the regional sphere is not reduced merely to a 'market', as regional mechanisms will be employed to offset the polarization effects inherent in the market and ensure social security, regional balance and welfare with similar, albeit still embryonic, functions to those of the old nation-states.

A regional community is characterized by a mutually reinforcing relationship between the 'formal region' as defined by
the community of states, and the 'real region'. A transnational-
ized regional civil society has a role to play in the 'real region'
and may emerge spontaneously from 'below' but ultimately is
dependent on those enduring (formal and informal) institutions
and 'regimes' throughout the region that facilitate and promote
security, welfare, social communication and the convergence of
values, norms, identities and actions.

Micro-regions do not 'disappear' at this stage of regionness. On
the contrary, they often become a permanent feature of the larger
macro-region, thus contributing to the diversity and increasing
the level of cross-border relations within the macro-region. In
particular, at such high levels of regionness, the micro-regions will
not have different visions than the larger macro-region, but relate
with it in a mutually reinforcing manner. As discussed in Chapter
6, Organizing Regional Space, within the EU there is a strong
compatibility between macro-regions and micro-regions, whereas
in Southern Africa these have largely been in competition.

With increasing sentiments of regional community, the often
artificial dividing lines between the separate national communities
within the region gradually disappear. The region can in this sense
be the organizing basis for both internal and external relationships
and identities (Hurrell 1995), i.e. increasing actorsness. This implies
a radical shift away from the organization of the world during the
Westphalian era. Just like nation-states, all regions to a certain
extent are 'imagined', subjectively defined and cognitively constructed. For success, regionalization necessitates a certain degree
of compatibility of culture, identity and fundamental values.

Within a functioning regional community, a regional collective identity has emerged and the relations are characterized by
mutual trust driven by social learning. As Adler and Barnett
observe: 'Learning increases the knowledge that individuals in
states have not just about each others' purposes and intentions
but also of each other's interpretations of society, politics, economics, and culture; to the extent that these interpretations are
increasingly shared and disseminated across national borders, the
stage has been laid for the development of a regional collective
identity' (Adler and Barnett 1998b: 54).

A shared cultural tradition may also be important. Culture, it
must be remembered, is not given, but continuously created and

recreated. Culture and identity may also be manipulated for more detrimental purposes. The defining element of rising regionalization is rather the multidimensional and voluntary quality of regional interaction, and the societal characteristics indicating an emerging regional community. Some examples are the Nordic group of countries and perhaps even North America (gradually including Mexico). On their way are the Southern Cone of South America and (at least the original) members of ASEAN. The community spirit established in these ways may be affected negatively by opportunistic and politically motivated inclusion of new, unprepared members, such as the co-option of the Democratic Republic of Congo (DRC) into SADC. In such cases, the 'formal' region acts without regard for the 'real' region, and this may in fact hamper the regionalization process.

Regional Institutionalized Polity

In the fifth level of regionness, the processes shaping the 'formal' and 'real' region are similar to but by no means identical with state-formation and nation-building. The outcome is a regional institutionalized polity, which in terms of scope and cultural heterogeneity can be compared to the classical empires. Such a regional polity must be distinguished from a nation-state in the Westphalian sense, because it will never aspire to the degree of homogeneity and sovereignty as can a Westphalian type of state. Just as there are many types of nation-states, there will also be different types of regionalized institutionalized polities, even if at the moment there are few historical examples of such high levels of regionness. At this stage, the political logic of regionalization is somewhat different compared to a nation-state. Homogenization within a region cannot imply cultural standardization in accordance with one specific ethnic model as it may in the nation-state, but rather compatibility between differences within a pluralist culture. World regions are by definition multicultural, heterogeneous and porous (Katzenstein 2005; Acharya 2014). By consequence, regionalized institutionalized polities cannot be based on force, as in the old empires (and in many nation-states). This implies that sooner or later they explode from within, as illustrated by the Soviet empire in more recent history.

In terms of political order, an institutionally regionalized polity constitutes a voluntary evolution of a group of formerly sovereign political communities into a new form of political entity, where sovereignty is pooled in the interests of all, and which is also more democratic than other 'international' polities. However, authority and decision-making are not centralized but layered and spread beyond the macro-regional (supranational) to the local, micro-regional and national levels. This is basically the idea of the EU as outlined in the Maastricht and the Lisbon Treaties, which cover the essential functions of an organized regionalized institutionalized polity. For regions other than Europe this may lie far in the future, but should by no means be ruled out. Historically, stranger things have happened. Importantly, this does not imply an expectation that the European path would be followed, simply that the transformation of nation-state capacity will give room for a multilayered governance structure, in which regional governance will play a significant role for historical and pragmatic reasons. The emphasis on governance draws attention away from traditional government. 'Unlike government, governance is not wedded to the state; it provides a framework for comparing institutional settings, in which state and non-state actors at the global, regional, national and subnational level coordinate their actions in multilevel formal and informal networks' (Börzel 2016: 19). The case of the EU suggests that the emergence of a regional institutionalized polity depends on some kind of equilibrium between the levels of governance.

Regional Actorness

The concept of regional 'actorness' adds an additional analytical dimension to the 'regionness concept that helps us to understand a region's ability to influence the external world and its role in global transformation. It has become clear that external action depends on internal cohesiveness and identity (i.e. regionness), meaning that if there is a consolidated internal actor identity, some sort of external actorness may follow.

On the global scene, the EU is the most discussed example of a regional actor (Bretherton and Vogler 1999; Söderbaum and Stålgren 2010a). Europe as an external actor is more than the EU's foreign policy and more even than the aggregate of the EU's policies in all areas of its activity. Simply by existing, and due to its relative weight (demographically, economically, militarily and ideologically), the EU has an impact on the rest of the world. Its footprints are seen in most parts of the world. The concept of presence is often used to signify this phenomenon, constituting the bridge between endogenous and exogenous factors. A stronger presence means more repercussions and reactions and therefore a pressure to act. In the absence of such action, presence itself will diminish.

Actorness suggests a growing capacity to act that follows from the strengthened presence of the regional unit in different contexts. Thus, there is an intricate relationship between internal cohesion and the capacity to act externally. Yet expectations and reactions of external actors *vis-à-vis* the region also impact on regional identity and regional consciousness. By implication, regional actorness shifts over time, between policy areas and between counterparts. This has to do with the specificities of each region as well as their interactions on the global scene. Hence, regional actorness is not specifically related to the EU as a global actor. Regions in the developing world obviously have more limited presence compared to the EU. But the need for regional agency also stems from global challenges, as most nation-states are unable to manage global problems on their own (Wunderlich 2012; Hettne 2014).

Regional actorness is meant to include subjective, institutional, historical and structural dimensions in order to distinguish it from the actorness related to nation-states. The unique feature of regional actorness is that it must be created by voluntary processes and, therefore, it depends on dialogue and consensus within the emerging region. Regional agency thus is distinct from state action, which operates according to a different logic, particularly in the case of a centralized or hegemonic/imperialist state.

Conclusion

It can safely be said that regions are here to stay. Few areas of the world are not organized into regions. Many scholars nonetheless underline the porous and pluralistic nature of contemporary regionalism. Many regionalization processes and experiments are initiated from quite different starting points in terms of regionness. Globalization and regionalization processes are closely related and interact under different conditions, creating a variety of pathways of regionalization, and by implication also leading to many, partly overlapping, varieties of regionalization.

As a concept, regionness seeks to capture the fact that when multidimensional regionalization has been set in motion, different logics appear to develop that may lead to the consolidation and solidification of the region. In explaining the development of regionness, it was argued that the early *regional social space* is more of a pre-regional zone. This level is nevertheless important since it draws attention to the fact that regions are rooted in territory. Ever-increasing social contacts and transactions, the creation of a *regional social complex*, serve as the actual starting point of a great variety of parallel processes of communication, cooperation and interaction between a multitude of actors. Further intensification and spread in the scope and the width of social relations in several dimensions (economic, political, cultural, etc.) lead gradually to the establishment of a *regional society.* Meanwhile, the convergence and mutually reinforcing character of these relations reflect the emergence of a *regional community*. Finally the *regional institutionalized polity* indicates the rise of a new multicultural, multilayered and more dynamic political entity.

Regionness is a heuristic comparative tool, not a parsimonious theory, for sharpening our understanding of the processes whereby regions solidify and converge. Between regionness and theory there is a need for more comparative research, which can further illustrate the different regional pathways around the world (Riggirozzi 2012; Emerson 2014). Certainly, there is no single (or pre-defined) path that is applicable to all regions and that must be passed through successively in order to attain higher levels of regionness. Since regionalism is a political project, created by human actors, it may move in different directions. Indeed, it may also fail.

Finally, a region's ability to influence the external world (actorness) depends at least partly on internal cohesiveness and identity (i.e. regionness). But the capacity to shape outcomes in the external world depends too on international presence (territorial and population size, economic strength, diplomacy, military power, etc.). The question is to what extent a region's regionness and presence is actually transformed into a purposive capacity to shape the external environment by influencing other actors and ultimately the external world. This issue will be further explored in the next two chapters, which respectively deal with regions in interregionalism and in global governance.

11
Regions in Interregionalism

A great deal of discussion on interregionalism has centred on the EU's past and present interregional relations. For instance, there is a long history of loose region-to-region relations between the EU and the ACP group of countries, which the new Cotonou Agreement and other EU–Africa frameworks have revised and developed. There is also a long history of interregional cooperation between the EU and ASEAN since the early 1970s. And from the 1990s onwards the EU further developed interregional cooperation as a key feature of external relations, albeit not always with a consistent formulation (Söderbaum and Stålgren 2010a; Baert et al. 2014).

Most literature on the topic from the 1990s assumed that interregionalism was an integrative process promoting cosmopolitan values and, as such, constituted a building block of a single multilayered global governance architecture (Baert et al. 2014). Since then, a growing number of observers have claimed that interregionalism peaked in the 1990s and early 2000s, and is now receding or being replaced by other forms of activity. Thus, many have talked about the rise and fall of interregionalism (Robles 2008; Hardacre 2010). Camroux has fundamentally questioned the significance and relevance of interregionalism, claiming that the 'imagined alchemy denoted as interregionalism [is not] an appropriate and useful analytical category' (Camroux 2010: 57).

Interregionalism is conceptually and theoretically underdeveloped as a subject and this goes a long way in explaining the misinterpretation that interregionalism has a decreasing significance in global politics. Some political issues certainly involve less interregional cooperation than others, but this chapter will draw attention to the diversity of contemporary interregionalism, and to the

'nesting' of interregional relations with other forms of cooperation in a multilayered governance framework.

Interregionalism involves at least two partner regions, and very
often at least one of them will be from the non-Western world,
but the 'other' in the partnership often seems to be forgotten in
interregionalism studies. In that regard, the empirical illustrations
in this chapter often involve the EU and in fact may be criticized
for being somewhat EU-centred. However, there is a difference between Eurocentrism and having the EU as an object of
analysis. In this chapter the EU is selected as the best and 'most
likely case' in order to 'unpack' the region and provide detailed
evidence about regional agencies and the pluralism of intersecting interregionalisms (also see Söderbaum and Stålgren 2010a;
Baert et al 2014).

The chapter has the following structure. The next section conceptualizes interregionalism in terms of pure interregionalism,
transregionalism and quasi-interregionalism, as well as mega-
regions. A snapshot of the diversity of EU interregional relations
with Africa, Asia and Latin America then follows. The fourth section unpacks the region and the interests and strategies of various regional actors in the case of the EU (such as, the European
Commission, the Council, the EU member states, the European
Parliament and the Court of Justice), and to some extent the
interests and the actorness of its counterparts. The final section
draws conclusions and also situates interregionalism within the
broader context of global governance.

Conceptualizing Interregionalism

Interregionalism is a multidimensional phenomenon and, to some
extent, even a moving target. There is considerable disagreement
about conceptualizing interregionalism. In a generic sense, interregionalism can be defined as a situation or a process whereby two
(or more) regions interact. Often it is also specified as *institutionalized* interregional relations (Hänggi et al. 2006: 3). This is a very
broad definition of the general phenomenon and cannot be used
for operational purposes.

There are a very large number of more specific concepts and
distinctions (Hänggi et al. 2006). One distinction is temporal
and differentiates, for instance, between the actor-centred 'old

interregionalism' of the early years and the more pluralistic and
system-centred 'new interregionalism' of the post-Cold War
period (see Hänggi 2006; Rüland 2014 Doidge 2014). In this
regard, some have referred to the Asia–Europe Meeting (ASEM),
which is sometimes considered as a prototype for new interregionalism (Steiner 2000). Furthermore, Holland makes a distinction
between EU–ACP relations in the classical Lomé period (1975–
2000) and the contemporary Cotonou period (2000–20) (Holland
2006: 254–5). The temporal distinction is useful as a way of distinguishing 'old' and 'new' features, but most scholars agree that
there are many continuities as well, which makes the distinction
less useful as an operational construct.

'Pure interregionalism' is the classical and most often referred
to form of interregionalism. It develops between two clearly identifiable regional organizations within an institutional framework.
Many refer to the ASEAN–EC dialogue in 1972 as the first example
of pure interregionalism (Regelsberger 1990). Pure interregionalism, however, only captures a certain part of contemporary institutionalized interregional relations. It does not feature strongly in
South–South relations (Hänggi 2006: 54). Furthermore, although
EU policy-makers placed heavy emphasis on pure interregionalism in the 1990s, interregional relations involving the EU and
non-EU regions have since become increasingly diverse and pluralistic. The limitation of pure interregionalism derives from the
fact that many regions are dispersed and porous: they lack clearly
identifiable borders and reveal only a low level of regional actorness. In essence, there is both weak regionness and actorness.
Consequently, there is a need for a broader conceptual toolbox
for understanding the emergence and the many varieties of interregionalism in today's global politics. The tendency to exaggerate
pure interregionalism appears to be related to the same bias as
apparent in the literature on regionalism, which is heavily geared
towards the study of regional organizations as 'visible' and
'formal' interstate frameworks.

First steps in unravelling these confusions might lie in unpacking the concept of region and problematizing the dominating
actors involved in an interregional relationship. Santander (2014)
is correct that regions can be understood as 'composite international actors' or dispersed actors rather than as monolithic actors
(the latter tending to be exaggerated in pure interregionalism). This
requires recognizing the intricacies of regions and regional agency.

Hänggi (2006) demonstrates, in a most thorough exercise in conceptualizing and typologizing, a need to distinguish regional groups from regional organizations. In addition to pure inter-regionalism relations between two regional organizations, there are two other types of institutionalized interregional relations: between a regional organization (often the EU) and a regional group, or between two regional groups. All three types may be referred to as 'bilateral interregionalism' (or bi-regionalism), which allows for an increasing diversity of interregional rela-tions. This is closely connected to the concept of transregion-alism and, to a lesser extent, quasi-interregionalism or hybrid interregionalism.

As a concept, 'transregionalism' seeks to go beyond the narrow interaction within a formal and mainly intergovernmental frame-work that occurs between two institutionalized regions (Aggarwal and Fogarty 2004: 5ff). Transregionalism refers to interregional relations in circumstances where two or more regions are dis-persed and have weak actorness and where none of the regions negotiates as a regional organization or group. There can be several aspects to transregionalism. According to Rüland, it can be defined as a 'dialogue process with a more diffuse member-ship which does not necessarily coincide with regional organisa-tions, and which may include member states from more than two regions' (Rüland 2006: 296). Usually member states would also act in their individual national capacities. There is considerable disagreement in the field on how to conceptualize ASEM, but for Rüland, it fits the transregionalist category since its membership cannot be referred to as two distinct regions in accordance with bilateral interregionalism (bi-regionalism in EU terminology).

Transregionalism has also been used to cover so-called trans-national (non-state) relations – including transnational net-works of corporate production or of civil society groups – again for the purpose of moving beyond conventional state-centrism and pure interregionalism (Aggarwal and Fogarty 2004: 5). Transregionalism draws attention to a more flexible under-standing and conceptualization of region/regional organization (Doidge 2011).

Hybrid or quasi-interregionalism is yet another type. Aggarwal and Fogarty (2004: 5) define 'hybrid interregionalism' as when one organized region (for example, the EU) negotiates with a group of countries from another unorganized or dispersed region, for example, the Euro–Mediterranean Partnership. The Lomé Agreement may be taken as a similar example of interregionalism, where the EU has trade relations with a large number of countries that do not have a customs union or free trade agreement. Aggarwal and Fogarty (2004: 5) refer to this as hybrid interregionalism (whereas others have labelled it transregionalism). Formally, these types of relations can be thought of as region-to-state relationships and some scholars do not accept quasi-interregionalism as an instance of interregionalism at all but rather as bilateralism. To some extent, quasi-interregionalism has also been used as a residual category and has covered a wide variety of relationships, such as the continental Europe–Africa process and instances of 'imagined interregionalism' and 'interregionalism without regions', such as the India, Brazil, South Africa cooperation (Rüland 2006). Nevertheless, such marginal status is inherent in the very term, and relevance and utility are of greater importance.

There is a need to avoid conceptual overstretch, but nonetheless, Hänggi (2006: 41ff) is correct about the relevance of quasi-interregionalism. Most importantly, such relationships may be an essential component of the relations between two 'regions' (even though these regions are differently shaped). Furthermore, quasi-interregionalism can be understood as a particular type of 'interregionalism' (in the widest sense) in cases where a single state is included because it plays a particular role in the counterpart region. The EU for instance, designed strategic partnerships with important powers, such as Brazil, South Africa, India and China. Needless to say, such region-to-state relations are not unambiguous and under certain conditions they may prevent the development of a more comprehensive interregionalism, but this simply underlines the hybridity.

Finally, 'megaregion' refers to cases where two or more component regions are linked into a very large region. Similar to quasi-interregionalism, it is also a borderline case. Hänggi is correct in that megaregion 'institutions such as APEC play an interregional role regardless of their conceptions' (Hänggi 2006: 42).

Diversity of the EU's Interregional Relations

This section outlines the diversity of EU interregionalism with a range of counterpart regions around the world, but specifically focusing on Africa, Asia and Latin America and how these have changed. Given that this book strives to escape Eurocentrism, the focus on the EU may invite some criticism. As noted in the introduction to this chapter, however, one should distinguish between Eurocentrism and using the EU as a case analysed through a general framework. Selection of the EU as a 'most likely' case is deliberate – it is the region with the deepest engagement in global interregional relations and has the most diverse involvement of regional actors and institutional strategies. It is intended that this kind of analysis may be replicated in other cases, both North–South and South–South interregionalism. Indeed, it would be erroneous to believe that other regions do not present a similar pluralism, albeit with different institutional configurations.

Historically, the European Communities (EC) had an external orientation that was limited in scope to relations with former European colonies and external trade. A common commercial policy began to develop with the emergence of the EC as a customs union. Today, the EU is a major economic power, and the instruments at its disposal include trade, cooperation and association agreements. It has aid and development policies that include financial, trade, technical and humanitarian components. Its capabilities in diplomacy and security issues are also growing.

Interregional relations occupy a rather strong position among the foreign policy tools employed by the EU, especially in far-away regions of Africa, Asia and Latin America (Hardacre 2010; Söderbaum and Stålgren 2010a; Doidge 2011; Baert et al. 2014). There is debate about how best to categorize the EU's relationships and policies with Central and Eastern Europe, Eurasia and the Mediterranean. Sometimes, they are described as part of the European integration process or enlarged regionalism; sometimes the key emphasis is on 'bilateral' policies between the EU and individual countries; and sometimes they are understood in terms of interregionalism (Söderbaum and Van Langenhove 2006).

Group-to-group relationships have played an important role in EU's relationship with Africa. The former colonies and dependent territories of EC members were incorporated in a dense institutionalized relationship beginning with the Yaoundé convention (1963, 1969). The Lomé agreements (1975, 1979, 1984, 1995) and more recently the Cotonou agreements (2000, 2005), broadened its geographic scope and firmly cemented relations between the EU and the ACP states. Whereas the EU–ACP relationship was originally a highly asymmetrical relationship between donor and recipient states, today it is often described as a 'partnership', at least in the EU's discourse. The ACP Partnership Agreement (signed in 2000) embodies a comprehensive relationship based on political dialogue, preferential trade relations and support for development and economic cooperation. However, EU policy towards Africa is rather diverse. Sometimes, interregional policies are oriented towards 'Africa' as a whole, as in the Africa/AU–EU relationships. At other times they are directed towards regional organizations at various levels (ECOWAS, SADC, EAC) or at countries organized in looser 'regional' frameworks and groups, or even at individual countries.

In this context, it is significant that the EU differentiates among ACP countries, and is establishing Economic Partnership Agreements (EPAs) with geographically more focused sub-regions of Africa, the Caribbean and the Pacific. This is not only a strengthening of formal interregionalism, but is even a novel and contested form. In some instances, the EU undermines existing regional organizations: SADC is the most prominent example in this regard, since the EU negotiates with ESA and SADC8, both groups within SADC. It also is abundantly evident that the EU-driven EPA projects are not motivated solely by the ideal and norm-laden values so favoured by political leaders and policy-makers in the EU's official discourse, but also serve as a means for the EU to establish 'hegemonic control' (Farrell 2010) – what Söderbaum and Hettne defined earlier as 'soft imperialism' (2005a).

EU relations with Latin America date back to the 1980s and the San José Dialogue process. There are interregional partnerships with most relevant sub-regions in Latin America, such as the Andean region, Central America, and above all Mercosur. The EU–Mercosur partnership is the most developed. Trade relations served as the origins of the EU–Mercosur partnership and this aspect remains particularly strong, with an interregional free trade agreement that tolerates quotas only in agriculture and some other sensitive goods. Gradually, this interregional cooperation has spread to embrace other sectors, such as economic cooperation, development cooperation and political dialogue and common 'values'. Concerning trade, Santander (2010) reveals a picture of the EU–Mercosur partnership similar to that of EU–African relations. There is an emphasis on free interregional trade as a value-laden instance of win-win cooperation, together with the economically self-interested objective of bolstering the EU's presence and access to fast growing economies. The EU's aim is not only to conquer new markets for European business, but also to build the EU's strength as a global actor.

Santander (2010) notes that whilst the official rhetoric of the EU is highly committed to free trade, it nonetheless maintains high non-tariff barriers for agricultural products, an area where the weaker partners would otherwise have the most to gain. By this account, the EU–Mercosur cooperation is an interregional relationship built primarily on the interests of the strongest. Barriers to strengthening EU–Mercosur interregionalism lie not only in the economic and trade issues at stake, but also in the strong vested interests within EU member states and a lack of coordination within the EU.

Relations between the EU and East Asia can be traced to the 1970s and the emergence of the EC–ASEAN dialogue. There are at least three phases of the EU's relations with East and Southeast Asia (Grimm 2010). A first phase (1967–80) was informal and loosely structured around ASEAN. A second phase (1980–94) was driven largely by geo-politics, and aid relations with Southeast Asia increased rapidly during these years. Internal and external events in the early 1990s again changed the relationship between the EU and Southeast Asia and produced the third phase marked by the EU's Asia strategy in 1994, and the establishment of the ASEM framework a few years later. The EU's first Asia strategy from 1994 was a late reaction to the rise of Asia. Similarly, ASEM was a consequence of the economic rise of post-Maastricht Europe. Changing geopolitical perspectives were clearly involved here. Notably, one of the reasons behind ASEM was that the EU was denied association status to APEC.

Two great and rival powers dominate 'larger East Asia' in the form of China and Japan, with both of whom the EU maintains 'bilateral' strategic partnerships. But the EU's relations with Japan and China are at the same time integrated into the ASEM framework. As with EU–African relations, EU–Asia interregionalism is comprehensive and multisectoral, spanning trade and investments, politics, security and anti-terrorism, culture, technology and science, drug trafficking, environmental protection and so on. ASEM, involving the EU and 'ASEAN Plus Three' (China, Japan and South Korea), represents a 'new' type of interregionalism, combining classic interregionalism, bilateralism, transregionalism and quasi/hybrid interregionalism. An impressive variety of issues are included within the ASEM framework, but the agenda tends to be *ad hoc*. In reality, much of ASEM's comprehensive agenda remains unfulfilled and of the three pillars – economic, political and cultural relations – just the economic (especially trade and investment) has been in focus.

The ASEM process shows that the institutionalization of interregional relations is very slow, and is susceptible to sudden changes in the geopolitical environment. Indeed, interregionalism itself aims to make this environment more stable and predictable but the institutionalization cannot go deeper than the Asian model of informal consensus building and 'soft institutionalism' allows. The EU's Asia Strategy states that 'there is no single "European model" of social governance' (European Commission 2001: 17). One interpretation of this is that the EU places considerably less emphasis on good governance and human rights in its relations with Asia than it does in the case of Africa. The EU apparently accepts different Asian views about the freeing up of markets and trade. This again contrasts sharply with the EU–Africa relationship, where the EU emphasizes both economic and market-based liberalization as well as political conditionality.

This suggests that, while much of the EU's interregional relations are conducted under the pretext of mutual benefit, the distribution of these benefits appears to be a function of the relative strength of the participants. With weaker 'partners', the EU dictates far more of the conditions for interregional cooperation. The relatively stronger East Asian region benefits from access to European markets and the regional organizations are generally invited to participate in equal or symmetric partnerships with the EU. There is little conditionality attached to East Asian cooperation, which reflects the EU's response to an increasingly powerful region. In contrast, the EU in its dealings with Africa attaches economic, trade and political conditions. In the case of Latin America, the EU's dealings appear to lie somewhere between those with Asia and Africa respectively (Hettne and Söderbaum 2005a; Söderbaum and Stålgren 2010a).

This review shows that the EU is advancing a comprehensive but flexible set of interregional processes and policies. Due to the sheer variety in type, participation and scope of the interregional relations, any simple characterization of EU interregionalism is difficult. EU interregional relations can be bilateral ('biregional' according to EU terminology) or more diverse; they can be issue-specific or multipurpose; and they can involve particular states or link to global governance and multilateral structures. This picture is further complicated by the division of external competencies within the EU between different EU institutions and member states. Far from being anchored to a specific foreign policy doctrine – such as interregionalism – the EU uses whatever type of policy seems appropriate for a given objective and it is difficult to discern a common rationale underlying the various interregional contacts. Based on different foundations, they reflect the nature of the regional states or groupings involved.

Since the late 2000s, a growing number of observers have claimed that EU-driven interregionalism peaked in the 1990s and early 2000s and is now receding and being replaced by other forms of activity, especially bilateralism (Grevi 2010). No doubt there is an emerging 'new bilateralism' in international politics and economic relations, and under certain circumstances it may compete with interregionalism (Heydon and Woolcock 2009). The EU supports setting up relations with new actors such as the BRICS and other strong powers, resulting in the so-called Strategic Partnerships with 'the special 10': Brazil, Canada, China, India, Japan, Mexico, Russia, South Africa, South Korea and the United States (Gratius 2011). However, it is rather misleading to conclude that interregionalism is giving way to bilateralism. This is for two main reasons.

Firstly, bilateralism is not necessarily autonomous from or competing with interregionalism and often both need to be understood within the same broader framework. These strategic partnerships have been a clear feature of EU foreign policy of the last decade, but most of the counterparts play a crucial role within their own regions, in which they are often deeply embedded. As noted in the section above on 'Conceptualizing Interregionalism', these types of relationships have been referred to as transregionalism or hybrid/quasi-interregionalism (Hänggi 2006; Baert et al. 2014).

Secondly, new interregional initiatives are emerging. To name a few, the EU started the EPAs with the six regions of the ACP, revitalized its relationship with its own neighbourhood through the launch of the Union for the Mediterranean, and began projects covering the African Union, Central Asia, the Arctic, Pacific,

Sahel and Horn of Africa. Some of these interregional projects also received the label of 'strategic' and often there is also some type of bilateral process included in these larger frameworks. It seems, then, that far from receding interregionalism remains in play and has an intricate relationship with bilateralism as well as regionalism.

Unpacking Regional Institutions and Agencies

This chapter promotes the view that it is necessary to go beyond a narrow definition of interregionalism to include transregionalism and quasi-interregionalism as well as a broad set of regional actors and strategies. The rethinking offered here suggests that regions may be understood best as composite actors rather than as monolithic and unitary actors. In any case, this requires recognizing the intricacies of the region and the intersecting agencies of interregionalism.

Regional actors usually hold a multitude of ideas about a particular region. This plurality affects external behaviour and so it is important to 'unpack the region' and analyse how different regional actors engage in interregional activities with their counterparts in other regions.

The complexity of the EU's institutional structure has only recently come to the fore in the literature on the EU's global role and in interregionalism. Rather than being designed consciously, the foreign policy machinery of the EU has emerged historically and reactively and there are several EU institutions with different mandates and views on interregionalism. Thus, the EU is by no means a monolithic entity, as it consists of many different actors and institutions – e.g. the Council, the Commission, the European Parliament, the Court of Justice and the individual EU member states. All have powers to engage in various types of interregional activities, although all are inter-connected. In addition, a large number of special agencies and policy instruments are at play in various issue areas. This results in a patchwork of intersecting interregionalisms, which are interlinked with multilateralism, bilateralism and regionalism; what Hardacre and Smith refer to as 'complex interregionalism' – the changing interlinkages of bilateral, regional, interregional and transregional relations developed between the EU and regions around the globe (Hardacre and Smith 2009, 2014).

Hardacre and Smith address the key institutional drivers of the complex interregionalism of the EU (the Commission, the Council, the member states and, more recently, the European Parliament) and analyse the implications of the differing interests in interregionalism. There are inherent tensions between the focus and interests of different institutions within the EU, notably the Commission and the Council, as well as between EU central institutions and the member states. Other literature has also identified various and similar inconsistencies in EU foreign policies (Christiansen 2001b). This is an issue that goes to the heart of regions being actors in interregionalism and in global politics more generally.

Trade

As elaborated earlier in this chapter, much of the EU's relationship with Africa in the field of trade is shaped by efforts to establish the EPAs. EPAs were designed to stimulate regional integration in Africa but also to further the integration between Africa and the EU as well as the rest of the world. In its official rhetoric and also by having one 'common' trade policy, the EU appears highly committed to free trade but there is a rich literature on the diverging preferences of various EU member states. A basic and much referred to distinction is between liberal and protectionist countries. In general, member states such as Denmark, Finland, the Netherlands, Sweden, and the UK belong to the former category, whereas the Mediterranean countries tend to belong to the latter. There are also other divergences within the EU in the case of the EPA negotiations. Another line of division goes between free trade-oriented position of the DG Trade and the EU member states who argue that free trade is the best strategy for growth and development, and the more 'development-friendly' EU member states who insist that the special needs of the least developed countries must be taken into account (Elgström 2009: 452). Given that the Nordic countries belong to the 'development-friendly' group, the divergences cannot be categorized simply along the liberal–protectionist axis. In the case of the EPA negotiations, however, it appears that the free trade position was dominant throughout.

Earlier research on the functioning of the EU suggests that that philosophical and policy differences between EU member states may not only impact negatively on the Council but also may make the Commission weak, as proposals must be reduced to the lowest common denominator to have any hope of passing. Elgström and Larsén (2008: 3–4), however, show that differing preferences among member states in the EPA negotiations resulted in the Commission having significant autonomy *vis-à-vis* the Council. The Commission's autonomy was reinforced further 'due to its informational and procedural advantages given by its institutional position as sole negotiator' (Elgström and Larsén 2008: 3).

Previous research in the field further suggests that internal fragmentation within the Commission may affect its effectiveness and assertiveness negatively with relation to member states and regional counterparts such as the AU and SADC (Carbone 2013). Tensions between DG Trade and DG Development/DG Agriculture during the early phases of the EPA negotiations are well known. Nevertheless, the unity of the Commission increased gradually and DG Trade consolidated its leadership (Elgström and Larsén 2008: 20), so that the new internal coherence enabled the Commission to play a dominant role in relation to the EU member states and the Council.

Development Cooperation

There are important differences in EU behaviour between different issue areas, and to a large extent this variation depends on the EU's institutional configuration. Whereas the EU often speaks with one voice, for instance in trade policy, EU policies tend to be more ambiguous and pluralistic in other areas such as development cooperation and security, where decision-making is either 'shared' between EU institutions and EU member states, or based on national and intergovernmental policies. Indeed, sometimes there appears to be little by way of an articulated policy, and the member states pursue their own national policies outside of the EU framework. This has very important effects on the pattern of interregionalism.

More specifically, with the adoption of the Maastricht Treaty in 1993, development policy was formally introduced as an area of (shared) EU competence. Yet, the institutions of the EU (the Council, the Commission, and the Parliament) have been largely unsuccessful in developing a common EU development policy that also guides the member states. The European Consensus on

Development is very thin and from within the EU there still is very little coordination of development policies on the ground (despite the proud policy declarations coming from Brussels and the European capitals). Instead, 'real' donor coordination is carried out under non-EU coordination mechanisms, and the Commission basically is seen as 'just another donor' or the EU's 29th member state (Söderbaum and Stålgren 2010b; Delputte and Söderbaum 2012). Since aid and development policy is one of the areas of EU action subject to shared competence, individual EU member states may, and do, continue to conduct international development policy according to their own priorities and preferences. For many EU member states, a complete communitarization of international development cooperation is not politically desirable and presumably would be of questionable value for developing countries. It is at least in part the EU's institutional configuration that helps to explain the lack of interregionalism in the field of development cooperation but why it is so important in the field of trade.

Furthermore, the EU's general failure to act as 'one' in development cooperation is at least partly related to competing 'identity claims' in the donor community. Development cooperation remains an arena for the manifestation of international identities, not only for the European Commission but also for individual EU member states. Attempts to centralize and develop a common European development policy with the Commission in the driver's seat compete with the identity-driven ambitions of bilateral donors, such as France and the UK, but also with several other large EU donors such as Sweden, Denmark, the Netherlands which are generally considered as role models in the field. To the extent that development policy is driven by the ambition to project one donor identity, that effort threatens other donors' identities and limits their visibility. As one donor official put it 'A donor who does not give is not a donor' (quoted in Söderbaum and Stålgren 2010b).

Under particular circumstances, however, common aid under the banner of the European Commission is not problematic for individual EU member states. For instance, in Latin America the role of the European Commission has gradually been consolidated by involvement in a series of interregional relationships with various regional and sub-regional organizations and often involving a range of civil society actors (Söderbaum and Stålgren 2010b).

At the same time, the EU has engaged in country-level relationships through a variety of quasi- and transregional arrangements, as well as through classical bilateralism. The important point here is that, with some exceptions, most EU countries have shown limited interest in the region and, increasingly, the Commission has stepped in to act on behalf of members. On occasion, the Commission has been a broker between competing national interests. By sustaining various forms of interregionalism in Latin America and facilitating coordination within Europe since the early 1990s, the EU has thus strengthened the perception of its actorness.

Parliaments and Courts

Hardacre and Smith (2014) discuss the effects on EU inter-regionalism of some of the institutional changes that have taken place since the Treaty of Lisbon entered into force: the creation of the European External Action Service (EEAS), the reinvigorated position of the High Representative on Common Foreign and Security Policy (CFSP), the creation of the President of the Council and the increased powers of the European Parliament. The EEAS was created in order to establish an 'EU diplomatic corps' in response to demands for increased coherence and consistency. There were high expectations of the EEAS, but after a year observers were disappointed to note an increase rather than decrease in institutional complexity (Reynaert 2012). This is problematic since it reinforces negative perceptions in partner regions of the EU's complex institutional set-up.

Usually, the European Parliament (EP) is not recognized as an important actor in interregional dialogues. For many reasons, however, it plays an important role in EU contacts with other regional organizations and their regional parliaments. In the 1970s and 1980s, external relations were a substitute for the weakness of the EP's legislative powers and thus were an important concern for the Members of the European Parliament (MEPs). Furthermore, MEPs have proved to be prone to export the principle of 'political' regional integration to other continents for ideological reasons and as a means to support human rights and democracy. Promoting a proto-federal form of integration was also a way to legitimize the EP's own pretension of playing a central role in the European integration process. Consequently, the

EP has been very active in supporting the development of other regional organizations and the formalization of an interregional dialogue with them, as seen in the Asia–Europe Parliamentary Partnership, the ACP–EU Joint Parliamentary Assembly or the Euro–Latin American Parliamentary Assembly.

In pursuing internal and external legitimacy, initiatives by MEPs to promote regional integration were particularly marked in the Latin American case (Costa and Dri 2014). Indeed, the EP was the first European institution to establish regular contacts with Latin America, at a time when the Commission and the Council of the European Union were mainly absorbed with former colonies in Africa. The recent parliamentarization process in Mercosur resulted partially from these institutionalized relations between Members of Parliament from both regions. As promoted by the EP, regionalism is understood as a means of maximizing the EU's position in the world and affirming itself both externally and internally as a parliamentary institution (Costa and Dri 2014). If the EP gets to promote regional organizations as the key actors of international relations, both goals can be reached. In this case, by its involvement in strengthening a weaker regional integration arrangement, the EP has contributed to the EU's 'capacity building interregionalism' (Doidge 2007: 242).

Hardacre and Smith acknowledge the role of the EP in interregionalism but, unlike Costa and Dri, they are more sceptical about its independent role in interregionalism:

> [T]he European Parliament has not had a major influence over the strategy, or the implementation, of complex interregionalism given its limited role in external relations. The Parliament has evidently played a role in sanctioning EU funding for regional integration in the budget procedure and it has also, on occasion, had an impact on the broad climate of relations between the EU and its key regional partners. For example, the Parliament's championing of human rights in respect of Myanmar has at times had an important influence on relations with ASEAN. Beyond this, the Parliament has largely been supportive of the Commission's strategy and positions, in particular as they have represented a contribution to the building of a distinct 'European identity' in external relations. (Hardacre and Smith 2014: 99)

Largely ignored in the research field, the Court of Justice of the European Union (CJEU) is in fact also involved in inter-regional relations (Smis and Kingah 2014). For instance, initiatives include the strengthening of regional courts of the East African Community, ECOWAS, the Andean Community and the Caribbean Community, the Caribbean Court of Justice, the SADC Tribunal and the African Court on Human and People's Rights. Conventional wisdom has it that the Andean Community has little prospect as a regional organization. Surprisingly then, the Andean Tribunal of Justice, the court of the Andean Community, is one of the more successful regional courts in the world. After the European Court of Human Rights and the European Court of Justice, it is the third most active international court in the world, far more so than the WTO dispute settlement system and the International Court of Justice (Alter and Helfer 2010: 564). Very clearly, the role of regional courts and their interaction with other regional courts deserves further attention.

Conclusion

Although a growing number of scholars now accept the concept of transregionalism, there still are many who hold 'pure interregionalism' as the benchmark. This chapter shows the relevance of incorporating not just pure interregionalism but also transregionalism and quasi-interregionalism into a single framework. Many in the field stress that in the post-Cold War era interregionalism refers to a systemic international phenomenon, namely links between regions in general (Hänggi 2006). But it is not necessary for interregionalism to take a single form, as this also hampers attempts to arrive at clear and unambiguous definitions.

An analysis of the EU's interregional cooperation with world regions (Africa, Asia and Latin America in particular) reveals a great variation in the way the EU conducts its foreign policies towards different regions and in relation to different policy areas (Söderbaum and Stålgren 2010a; Baert et al. 2014). Interregional policy thus is not fixed but subject to adaptation. This chapter also underlines that the EU's interregional cooperation may vary depending on the counterpart region; this in turn raises questions about relevance, power and regional actorness. EU–Asia collaboration differs in the degree of institutionalization as well as in the nature of the issues it covers. Interregionalism in Asia is affected by the fact that ASEAN is more or less the only viable counterpart regional organization. The particular design of ASEM results from this fact.

The interregional model is perhaps most developed in the EU's relationship with Africa, as interregional cooperation and partnerships exist in most issue areas and for Africa as a whole as well as for all of its regional organizations. Yet, it is clear that the EU dominates EU–Africa interregional cooperation and it serves mainly the EU's interests. Such asymmetry derives from Africa's weak actorness; but this is not to say that asymmetric interregionalism is necessarily a bad thing.

Even if the EU does not dictate the agenda, there is strong evidence that that the EU shapes EU–Africa relationships according to its own interests, despite the official rhetoric of civilian or ethical foreign policy. Critical inquiry thus has the potential to balance the current idealism dominating the field and help improve our understanding of the asymmetric relationships that often characterize interregional relations, not just those involving the EU but other interregionalisms beyond the EU as well. Like the EU strategic partnerships, interregionalism is not purely normative or 'good'.

Distinguishing between regionalism and interregionalism opens up an opportunity for research into how regionalism and interregionalism relate and impact on one another. A rather uncontroversial proposition is that regionalism will give rise to interregionalism. But interregionalism may also reinforce regionalism. Engaging in interregionalism creates a need for regions to consolidate further. There is evidence that interregionalism between the EU and Mercosur has impacted on the Mercosur project itself. In the case of ASEM, the need to provide a collective response to interactions with the EU reinforced the regionalizing efforts of the Asian counterpart. Indeed, ASEM provides a mechanism for institutionalizing not only a partnership but also the partner *per se* (Gilson 2006: 74). There is thus a close link between interregionalism and region-building, and a feedback mechanism from interregionalism to regions. Gilson argues that regions act themselves into being, among other things by acting *vis-à-vis* what they perceive to be other regions (Ibid). In this sense, interregionalism creates a public reality, which not only structures interregional relations but also has a constitutive role in the formation of regions. Clearly, relationships between region-alism and interregionalism deserve further exploration.

Some observers claim that bilateralism competes with inter-regionalism, leading them to conclude that interregionalism rose and then declined. This idea of a shift from interregional-ism to bilateralism is believed to be inspired, *inter alia*, by the geopolitical shift from a unipolar to a multipolar world (Conley 2011). No doubt, the new geopolitical environment has brought changes that are associated with bilateralism. In the economic field, we see new powerful actors such as China, India or Brazil penetrat-ing regions like the Middle East, Africa or Latin America, which traditionally were seen as Western 'profit markets' (Cheru and Obi 2010). Indeed, bilateral trade agreements did return to favour – the so-called 'new bilateralism' (Ravenhill 2003; Heydon and Woolcock 2009). However, as this chapter has illustrated, it would be misleading to conclude that interregionalism is giving way to bilateralism.

Hardacre and Smith's (2014) framework of 'complex inter-regionalism' is useful for conceptualizing the fluctuations in EU external relations between transregional, pure interregional and bilateral forms as well as discerning the reasons and driving actors behind them. Complex and intersecting interregionalism gener-ates pertinent questions about the implementation of EU interre-gional relationships and about inter-institutional tensions within the EU, particularly between the Commission and the Council. Indeed, the Commission designs and delivers the strategies, which may contain powerful normative as well as material elements, and it also negotiates with key regional partners; the Council on the other hand, ultimately authorizes these activities by signing Association and Free Trade Agreements, and by approving spe-cific institutional arrangements. With new institutional arrange-ments for the conduct of the EU's external policies, the Lisbon Treaty put these tensions in a new context, but to what extent this actually reshapes EU interregionalism remains to be seen.

Furthermore, complex interregionalism reveals that bilateral-ism is not necessarily autonomous from or competing with inter-regionalism, and often the two need to be understood within the same broad framework. The strategic partnerships with the 'special 10' is a clear feature of EU foreign policy in the last dec-ade, but most of these counterpart powers play a crucial role within their own regions. Santander, for instance, points out that Brussels considers Brazil to be a crucial partner that 'needs external political support in order to counterbalance Venezuela's regional ambitions and the spread of political radicalism in LA [Latin America]' (Santander 2014). Clearly, the partnership with Brazil is seen to be an important way for the EU to strengthen its relations with South America and, although this partnership tends to undermine EU–Mercosur interregionalism, it illustrates a complex relationship between pure interregionalism, quasi-interregionalism, as well as bilateralism with Spain and Portugal as significant players.

By implication, interregionalism may provide a useful forum and framework for enhancing cooperation at other scales of action and governance, including multilateral and global governance. A multilateralism based on regions – a 'regional multilateralism' or 'multi-regionalism' – yields a different kind of multilateralism and type of global governance than that provided by conventional Westphalian relationships (Hettne 2014). The new patterns of global governance are elaborated further in the next chapter.

12

Regions in Global Governance

This chapter deals with the role of regions in global governance. First, governance is conceptualized in light of the transformation of the Westphalian approach (government) and the increased importance of governance, especially at the global and regional level. From this perspective, the key question then is how to understand and conceptualize the relationship between different modes of governance (subnational, national, regional and global) that are nested within a multilayered global governance structure. The remainder of the chapter illustrates the rising strength of the regional dimension of global governance in three rather different policy fields: security, trade and health.

Conceptualizing Regional and Global Governance

In recent decades IR theorists have quarrelled about what implications the transformation of the old Westphalian nation-state model had for governance and government. The Westphalian order gradually emerged after the Peace of Westphalia in 1648 that ended the 30 Years' War and the war between Spain and the Netherlands. The Westphalian logic implies an interstate system made up of sovereign territorial states. Within each set of borders live citizens, whose obligations and rights are defined by citizenship and their allegiance to the state. Outside, in the so-called 'anarchical world', these rights and obligations do not apply. It is taken for granted that the security of citizens and the security of the nation-state are identical.

The Westphalian nation-state order faces many, complex and interrelated problems. Some are external, deriving from the global system or the macro-region; others are internal, emerging from various movements that question the territorial integrity, sovereignty and legitimacy of the nation-state. Many observers acknowledge that the (introverted) Westphalian modes of regulatory authority are insufficient and likely to be more so in the future. Some even refer to the Westphalian system as the 'Westfailure system' (Strange 1999). This implies a rejection of 'methodological nationalism' and other forms of state-centric analysis. Yet, it is not equivalent to rejecting the nation-state, as some observers do (Ohmae 1995).

The transformation and even deterioration of national government does not necessarily imply the deterioration of governance. The view that authority and governance simply 'disappear' or are weakened by the weakening, 'failure' or collapse of states (especially in the South) also needs rejecting. A preferred conceptualization is that authority rarely disappears (when national government is eroding) but rather 'travels' up or down to other levels in the system, and often into new and complex forms. With the political and institutional landscape in transformation, there is a need to think in terms of a more complex, multiscalar approach to government and governance, in which the state is reorganized and assumes different functions and where non-state actors also contribute.

From a global governance perspective, there still is a striking 'governance gap'. Even if the conventional Westphalian model of government is obsolete, global governance is not functioning either, which means that regional governance emerges as a feasible mid-level management strategy – a compromise between the Westphalian and the post-Westphalian logic. Katzenstein (2005: i) underlines that regions have become critical to the functioning of contemporary global politics and may provide 'solutions to the contradictions between states and markets, security and insecurity, nationalism and cosmopolitanism'. Similarly, Hveem (2003) argues that that the world is in need of better governance and regional governance is essential in this regard. Hveem's main argument is that the strength of regional governance projects depends on whether or not they enjoy a comparative political advantage in resolving global governance problems. If such comparative advantage does exist, it has to do with efficacy and identity but, above all, with legitimacy and viability.

It is important to bring in here the regional dimension of multi-layered global governance. Rosenau (1997: 145) defines govern-ance as 'spheres of authority at all levels of human activity that amount to systems of rule in which goals are pursued through the exercise of control'. This over-arching definition implies that governance may come in many modes and varieties and exist at different scales and levels.

Much of the conventional discussion on governance focuses heavily on either 'global governance' or asserts that the challenge is a question of 'national governance'. Both these discourses are important and challenging. Even so, with regard to the first dis-course it is misleading to assume that global governance and mul-tilateral institutions explain the complex realities of contemporary governance. And often the second discourse about governance is state-centric and overly concerned with national 'government'. By contrast, the 'regional' dimension of global governance is crucial. Importantly, the different scales of governance are not necessarily competitive, but may be intrinsically intertwined and so influence and reshape one another. Specifically referring to ecosystems gov-ernance, Stephen Olsen, Page and Ochoa state that:

> thinking in terms of nested systems of governance is rel-evant because most environmental and societal issues both impact upon, and are impacted by, conditions and actions at both higher and lower levels in an ecosystem and governance hierarchy. Some issues can be addressed more effectively at one level, and less effectively at another. The choice of the issue or set of issues to be addressed must therefore be made in full knowledge of how responsibility and decision making authority is distrib-uted within a layered governance system. (Olsen et al. 2009)

Regarding the need for a horizontal broadening of the concept of governance, there has conventionally been a strong emphasis on formal and public modes of governance, which tends to pre-vent a more comprehensive understanding of the subject matter and the inclusion of other actors than the state. Payne (2000), an authoritative writer on regionalism and governance, concentrates on three particular modes of regional governance in the 'Triad', labelled 'multilevel governance in the EU', 'hubs and spoke gov-ernance in North America' and 'pre-governance in Asia-Pacific'. The charge that the Asia-Pacific simply has *pre-governance* reveals one limitation in this analysis. Payne's view contrasts with several observations in the field (as well as case studies earlier in this book), namely, that authority structures in East Asia or Asia-Pacific serve the interests of the dominant actors and that coalitions of state-business are organized in informal regional networks of power; that is, particular forms and modes of regional governance (Katzenstein 2000, 2005; Acharya 2010). The argument presented here is that these structures of governance will only be discovered when the concept is 'unpacked' and broadened both vertically and horizontally.

For the sake of understanding the emerging modes of governance and whose interests and purposes they serve, it must be recognized that they are more than simply formal-public systems of rule and authority structures for goal achievement. The concept of governance must be freed from wishful thinking: certain actors construct governance for certain purposes, and this implies that there can also be governance for private rather than public purposes (Jones 1998). Consequently, there is a pluralism of governance structures, which can be classified by distinguishing between public and private as well as between formal and informal dimensions of governance. Elaborating on these distinctions, Jones (2002: 2) points out that:

- *Public governance* serves an identifiable population across a range of issues of general concern.
- *Private governance* is generated by and for a specific group of actors and is concerned with a restricted range of self-interested issues.
- *Formal governance* is backed by legal treaties or constitutions.
- *Informal governance* is based upon mutual understandings and accommodations, tacit agreements, etc.

Following this, regional governance can be defined as spheres of authority at the regional level of human activity, which amounts to systems of rule – formal or informal, public or private – in which goals are pursued through the exercise of control.

Finally, to be able to speak of governance and 'systems of rule' there must still be a certain degree of control and continuity. In reality, the dividing lines between formal or informal and public or private are somewhat blurred and, as previous chapters in this book reveal, there are many examples of a small elite managing to establish a fluid and informal system of rule that serves mainly its own personal rather than the broader public interest. Regional governance can both be rather short-sighted and have very weak legitimacy. It is reasonable to demand a certain amount of legitimacy and accountability in all systems of rule, which suggests that a certain amount of 'formal' and 'public' is needed in a *functioning* system of governance. However, just as weak and harmful national governments do persist, so may weak and harmful regional governance.

Regions in Global Security Governance

At various points in the last century, including at the establishment of the United Nations in the 1940s, there was intensive discussion of the relationship between global bodies and regional agencies in the provision of security. The UN Charter was made compatible with what was loosely defined as regional arrangements or agencies. When 'the Charter made provision for a dimly conceived and vaguely apprehended regionalism' (Tavares 2009: 9), the regional approach was on an ultimately losing trajectory. As mentioned in Chapter 7, Multidimensional Regionalism a long-standing view of the global–regional relationship in global security governance saw a dominant UN delegating tasks to subordinate regional organizations. In this conception, the region is simply an intermediate actor that implements tasks decided upon at the multilateral level. According to this perspective, the main purpose of regional agencies is to contribute to a multilateral system controlled by the UN Security Council.

Since the end of the Cold War polarization, the debate about the UN and regional organizations has returned as one of the most important issues in the global security architecture, including reform of the UN Security Council. In 1992, the UN secretary-general's *Agenda for Peace* called for involvement of regional organizations in such activities as preventative diplomacy, peacekeeping, peace-making and post-conflict reconstruction. Over the next 13 years, the UN head convened six high-level meetings with regional organizations involved in security matters from every continent. Set up by the secretary-general to reflect on UN reform, the High-Level Panel on Threats, Challenges and Change acknowledged that regional groupings have made 'important contributions to the stability and prosperity of their members' (UN 2004). The secretary-general's *In Larger Freedom* (UN 2005) stated that 'the United Nations and regional organizations should therefore play complementary roles in facing the challenges to peace and security'. The High-Level Panel also urged the UN Security Council to make greater use of Chapter 8 provisions to use regional organizations in preventing and responding to threats. From a UN perspective, the critical requirements are that (1) regional action should be organized within the UN Charter and be consistent with its purposes and principles; and (2) the UN and regional organizations should collaborate more effectively and in a more integrated fashion than in the past (Thakur 2005).

This approach is orthodox in the sense of being based on the Westphalian logic and the primacy of the UN. It focuses primarily on how regional organizations are part of and can contribute to a UN system still based on the predominance of the nation-state and the hierarchy of the UN Security Council. Crucially, this orthodox approach wants to ensure that regional security operations are carried out within a UN framework under one or the other Charter mandates. Whereas the UN Charter positively encourages regional organizations to undertake non-military dispute settlement as well as conflict prevention, they are still subject to UN Security Council approval and oversight as far as a 'robust peacekeeping mandate' or 'peace enforcement' are concerned (Graham and Felicio 2006; Tavares 2009).

Those who promote the UN agenda argue that it constitutes the only possible (and desirable) foundation for a rules-based world order. For traditional multilateralists, go-it-alone strategies outside a UN framework, for instance through NATO or US unilateralism, are anathema (Thakur 2005). In the orthodox view, the UN is indispensable in providing legality and impartiality in international security operations. Some proponents of this line have in fact developed greater recognition of the role of regional organizations. Thakur (2005), for example, has acknowledged that there is an increasing gap between legality and legitimacy in multilateralism and that on its own, the UN cannot deliver a legitimate world order. In this view, closer to home, regional arrangements can counter perceptions of 'external imposition' by a distant UN. Yet this approach stresses that such regionalism must be compatible with, and contribute to, UN-based multilateralism in order to be legitimate. For Thakur, regional organizations 'may insert fresh blood into multilateralism' and fill some of its gaps, but they must do so within the UN framework (Thakur 2005; Thakur and van Langenhove 2006). In other words, it is a vertical order of multilateral sanction whereby regional security interventions are rendered legal and fully legitimate. This is similar to the emphasis on the principle of 'UN primacy in all crises' (Graham and Felicio 2006: 70). Such a view neglects the degree to which the UN-led approach and regional security governance tend to follow different logics, which results in a range of contradictions and a non-linear global security governance regime.

The Rising Relevance of Regional Security Governance

Contemporary political realities of global security governance do not accommodate this idealized hierarchical order, in which regions are reduced to an intermediary status between the global governance space (occupied by multilateral organizations such as the UN) and a national base (occupied by sovereign states). Emerging formations of contemporary regionalism assume a degree of legitimacy and actorness lacking in traditional regional agencies. A number of regional arrangements, such as the EU, ASEAN, AU, SADC and ECOWAS, have acquired some kind of institutionalized mechanism for security and conflict management. Through their regional agencies, regions have transformed from objects into subjects (*inter alia* through rising levels of regionness), making their relationship with the UN much more complex than current policy and academic debates tend to recognize. These strengthened regional arrangements get their mandate not only 'from above' (from the UN), but also 'from within' (from the cooperating states and their citizens and civil societies). This implies that states and global organizations are being locked progressively into a larger regional and interregional framework, in which 'regions' become the increasingly relevant scales and even actors in the global security architecture. This is seen in the consolidation of regional security orders and regional security architectures in Europe, Africa, Asia and Latin America (Buzan and Wæver 2003; Engel and Porto 2010; Solingen 2014).

It is unlikely that the complexity will decrease in the future. Compared to the orthodox approach by which regional agencies are subordinated to the UN Security Council, it is more realistic to think of the relationship between global and regional security governance in more horizontal and reciprocal terms. The outcome may be a 'regional multilateralism' built around regional bodies, such as ASEAN, the AU, ECOWAS, EU and SADC, as opposed to an 'orthodox multilateralism' centred on the UN and with nation-states as the basic units. Regional multilateralism expresses the ambition of groups of states to control or influence the global environment by pooling their sovereignties according to a post-Westphalian logic, rather than relying on the 'one state–one vote' procedure in the UN General Assembly or the undemocratic pluri-lateralism ('false multilateralism') of the UN Security Council.

Of course, distinct limitations to regional organizations must be acknowledged, especially in the South. As elaborated in Chapter 7, problems include resource constraints, as witnessed particu-larly severely in African cases, but also elsewhere (Söderbaum and Tavares 2009; Tavares 2009). Some regional bodies, such as ASEAN and SAARC, have suffered from organizational weak-nesses with respect to security operations. There has even been abuse of regional security mechanisms in a range of African cases (Söderbaum and Tavares 2009). In addition, regional institutions may not be strictly neutral. This is particularly true where ten-sions arise from a fear of dominance by a regional hegemon, and it has hampered the progress of regional bodies such as ECOWAS, SAARC and SADC. According to Diehl (1994: 31), such problems weigh more heavily on regional than on multilat-eral peacekeeping.

There are nevertheless many reasons why a region-centred approach could be more relevant than a UN-led approach in the emerging global security context. For instance, regional solutions are required due to the regional spillovers and regionalization of many domestic conflicts around the world. Certainly, in terms of proximity, consequences and commitments, the regional approach is more efficient than multilateral mechanisms. In many cases, regions can deal better with their own conflicts than can a distant and sometimes paralyzed UN. Moreover, regional organizations are often better than multilateral efforts at addressing conflict prevention as well as post-conflict reconstruction. In any analysis of external (including regional) involvement in protracted con-flicts it is important to make a distinction between three crucial elements: early prevention of conflict, military intervention in an ongoing conflict, and post-conflict reconstruction (Hettne and Söderbaum 2005b).

It appears that the international community is able to deal with just one major crisis at a time (Iraq, Afghanistan, etc.). This limitation is one comparative advantage of regional security governance. In many cases, however, regional interventions tend to be centred heavily on ending the actual warfare by military interventions and peace enforcement. Since interventions in ongoing conflicts are rarely successful (in the long run), there should be a stronger focus on prevention rather than forceful intervention, and such activities suit a region well. In poor regions this must be part of the international development aid system and mutually agreed on in the partnership arrangements between the global and regional domains.

The Emergence of Global–Regional Security Governance

Potentially, global and regional approaches can be competing authority structures. Insistence on the vertical UN-led approach, which subordinates regional security governance, will only reinforce competition between the two approaches. Likewise, an ideological regionalism that ignores wider multilateralism cannot address the links that exist between regional conflicts and politics further afield. Instead, complementarity can be encouraged through interregional arrangements that, nonetheless, support the values and principles associated with the idea of multilateralism. The UN would still be needed, but it would be a rather different organization compared to the present one.

A more horizontal and balanced combination of regional and global security governance structures, each with its own basis of authority, should principally provide the future governance of global security. Both the UN and regional bodies need each other and so must assume shared responsibility for resolving security problems. For its part, the UN has suffered a decline in power and authority and therefore needs the support of regional bodies. Meanwhile, many regional formations are still embryonic and need support from global arrangements. In all, an integrated global–regional strategy would provide the most feasible solution for the medium-term future.

From a policy perspective, this may mean encouraging a new role for regional peace-keeping but reinforcing the level of legality/legitimacy by multilateral sanctions and decision-making, normally through the UN. Arguably, an optimal form of

peacekeeping combines the legitimacy of multilateral (UN) interventions with the greater efficiency, in terms of proximity and
commitment, of regional actions. Such an arrangement would
need some kind of multilaterally acknowledged rules system in
order to prevent abuses. The combination of global–regional
security governance can also be sequenced, since the multilateral
operation takes longer time to organize compared to the regional.

A principle of genuinely shared responsibility stands in contrast to the orthodox approach where the UN vertically delegates
authority to and distributes mandates among regional bodies.
It is hard to conceive how the UN can maintain primacy if
regionalism continues to deepen around the world. A UN based
on nation-states is not well suited to controlling strong regions
(or countries). With increasing regional actorness, regions will
increasingly be able to manage their own conflicts. For example,
consolidated security governance in Europe around the EU will
reduce the relevance of the UN as regards European conflicts.
Similarly, if African security regionalism continues to consolidate
in the future, it would be more appropriate that the UN reconsid-
ers its own role and starts to work in more horizontal partnerships with African security mechanisms and APSA.

Regions in Global Trade Governance

The relationship between the World Trade Organization (WTO)
and management of regional economic integration is not self-
evident but complex and contradictory. Most liberals and free-
trade proponents consider multilateral free trade as the optimal
and 'first-best' option for promoting the gains from international
trade. The general assumption is that a more open and competitive international market in itself can be thought of as a global
public good (Birdsall and Lawrence 1999: 133). From this perspective regional trading arrangements are seen as a 'second-best' and
therefore judged according to whether they contribute to a more
closed or more open multilateral trading system. This particular
normative approach is embodied in the so-called 'stumbling block
versus stepping stone' dichotomy. Many of the regional trading
arrangements that existed during the era of the old regionalism in
the 1950s, 1960s and 1970s were inward-looking and protectionist.
When judged by today's economists they are often regarded as

failures and stumbling blocks – although at the time they were often seen as instruments to enhance industrial production and structural transformation.

Since the mid-1980s there has been an explosion of regional trading arrangements, and more or less every country in the world has joined one or several preferential trading schemes. Initially, in the 1980s and 1990 the GATT/WTO and its many proponents were rather sceptical of the re-emergence of regional trade integration, and mainly viewed it as new protectionism. Some influential economists, such as Bhagwati, continue to warn against protectionism, arguing that today's regional trade blocs are also 'stumbling blocks'. However, the dogmatic free-trade position has become less salient.

Since the latter half of the 2000s, the WTO has become much more positive towards the role of regionalism. As Baldwin (2008: 1) states: 'If the WTO is to survive and flourish, it must adapt because regionalism is here to stay. Embarking on a WTO Action Plan on Regionalism would be a strong step towards adapting to the new reality.' This plan is designed to enable the WTO to change from being an 'innocent bystander' to active 'engagement' with so-called regional integration arrangements (RIAs) (Baldwin 2008: 1; cf. Baldwin and Thornton 2008). But even if this perspective acknowledges certain benign aspects of economic regionalism, it is still considered a 'threat' needing regulation and control. The problem is that this will prevent economic regionalism from reaching its full potential. Active 'engagement' by the WTO still requires the *subordination* of economic regionalism to economic multilateralism, in the same way as does 'UN primacy' in the field of global security governance.

One of the main problems with the orthodox WTO approach is that it exaggerates both the benefits of multilateralism and the costs of regional arrangements. The view advanced here is that regions should not simply be assessed through the lens of multilateralism and the primacy of the WTO. Rather than subordinating regionalism under WTO multilateralism, the ambition here is to try to understand the logic of what builds the multiscalar global governance structure in trade and economic development. This does not neglect the fact that the rules of the WTO may have positive impact on regional integration agreements and set the conditions for regional trading arrangements in ways that may enhance their positive and prevent their malign effects.

Regionalism in Response to Asymmetric Multilateral Trade Governance

Even if the multilateral trading system is rather successful when viewed in historical perspective, the GATT/WTO has proved to be not only unfair but also ineffective in dealing with the economic and political challenges since the 1990s. As stated by one authority, the G8 and OECD governments 'hijacked' the WTO to protect their interests in a world where their economic and military power is being challenged by emerging economies and powers (Mistry 2003: 135). Furthermore, when viewed in terms of 'the public good', the multilateral trading system serves it in name only and not in substance (Mendoza 2003: 455). In several important respects, the WTO is neither legitimate nor effective. The welfare gains and net benefits from the multilateral trading system are extremely imbalanced and skewed in favour of the industrialized countries. The WTO only passes the minimal 'neutrality' notion of fairness but probably fails the other two: 'net benefit for all' and 'maximum rule' (Mendoza 2003: 469).

Much of contemporary regionalism, especially but not just in Africa, Asia and Latin America, has gained its strength in response to the dominance of WTO and globalization. Indeed, regionalism has been embraced since the 1990s because multilateralism no longer works (Mistry 2003: 136). Economic regionalism provides an opportunity for the market access that countries wished for but never really extracted from multilateral negotiations. Furthermore, many countries have been helped by the unilateral liberalization of neighbours and the other commitments undertaken in the context of economic regionalism.

Today there is a proliferation of bilateral, regional and assorted types of interregional trading agreements around the world, especially in Africa, the Americas and Asia-Pacific. Bilateralism is proliferating in the context of frustrations with multilateralism and because of low trust in the WTO. According to Higgott (2002: 22), many bilateral trading agreements are emerging because policy-makers want 'to create an illusion of control over one's own policy processes and policy choices'. Nonetheless, there are instances when bilateralism improves the conditions and ultimately converges into regionalism or multilateralism, or both. Overall, bilateral agreements can be seen as statements of sovereignty, which result in a fragmentation not only of multilateralism but also of regionalism. One of the more fundamental problems is that strong states often seek bilateral agreements with weaker states. Regionalism implies a more organized order compared to bilateralism. Regionalism is also more inclusive than bilateralism, since some countries will not always be able to reach relevant bilateral agreements.

The fundamental point is not to put regionalism against multilateralism, interregionalism or bilateralism. Choosing between strategies is not a simple matter and often they can be combined in creative ways. The multilateral principles and rules of the WTO may set the conditions for regional trading arrangements. If the rules of the WTO are at least adhered to that would prevent the entrenchment of inward-oriented and protectionist forms of regional trading arrangements. And multilateralism may improve the functioning of regional trading arrangements. The case of anti-dumping exemplifies how the WTO helps to reduce regional friction. Brazil and Chile (countries that are usually 'victims' of regional anti-dumping measures) are keen on stricter adherence to WTO principles and the use of such rules to 'police' regional trade activities (Tussie 2003). Increasingly, such regulatory functions and the contribution to healthy regional relations are likely to persuade members of regional trading arrangements to demand new services from the WTO. This contribution is a severely under-appreciated case of 'how regionalism is providing a substance to multilateralism' (Tussie 2003). Regionalism, thus, is quite conducive to a more useful and functional multilateralism. But more than this, regionalism may even be seen as a prerequisite for reconstructing multilateralism on a more equitable regional basis.

In several important respects there is a comparative political advantage of regionalism compared to multilateralism, at least as it is presently being practised, and this recognition is important in studying the global–regional dyad. Regionalism is here to stay. It also is likely to become a stronger force in coming decades. Regions are good vehicles for smaller countries to increase their bargaining power and voice in multilateral trade and in the context of globalization. Regionalism will often work more easily and effectively compared to a rather dysfunctional multilateralism, which is contingent on 200 or more unequal nation-states. Compared to a dysfunctional and asymmetric multilateralism based on nation-states, a 'regional multilateralism' is the most pragmatic and effective solution. Scholars have argued that regionalism will cede to multilateralism only when multilateralism is rebuilt on foundations of successful regionalism and a fairer world order (Mistry 2003: 137–8).

This is not to deny that regionalism also carries with it many risks. In Africa, but also in Latin America, regionalism can be an instrument for sustaining and reinforcing neopatrimonialism (Bach 1999a, 1999b). And in Europe there is always a discussion about the distortive effects on outsiders of strategic trade. Experience reveals that even if hegemons may provide stability in certain cases, at other times the most powerful countries may dominate regional arrangements in accordance with a myopic perception of national interest and at the expense of weaker countries (Söderbaum 2004).

Beyond Liberalization

Ontologically, the WTO has a liberal view of globalization and multilateralism, stressing the homogenizing influence of market forces in a linear drive towards an open society. According to the liberal tradition, the purpose of political order is to facilitate the free movement of economic factors (under a rules-based order). This is seen not only as a natural but also as a most beneficial condition. The optimum size of an economy (and therefore its ultimate form) is the global market. Regional economic integration arrangements distinctly are a second best, acceptable to the extent that they are 'stepping stones' rather than 'stumbling blocks' to the achievement of a world market. Seen in the broader political economy view advanced in this book, the liberal project of globalism is not realistic; the unregulated market system is analogous to political anarchy and consequently there is a need to 'politicize the global' (Hettne 2003), or to promote the 'reinvention of politics' (Beck 1997) in order to provide a more sustainable formulation of the relationships between liberal markets, equitable participation and different scales of governance. Congruently, many scholars and policy-makers have begun to press for a broader and more 'political economy' and developmentalist approach that emphasizes the need for some intervention by political institutions and room to manoeuvre in the creation of innovative development policies, which ultimately are more important than trade liberalization alone (i.e. the WTO's main emphasis) (Mendoza 2003: 473).

This political economy approach also converges with a more developmentalist understanding of trade liberalization. For instance, Rodrik (1998) emphasizes that the benefits of trade reforms for economic growth and development are often over-estimated and 'can backfire if it diverts the scarce energies and political resources ... from growth fundamentals, such as human resources, macroeconomics and fiscal policy etc.'

It seems, then, that the benefits stemming from conventional trade liberalization are less significant than what is promised in classical WTO ontology. Somewhat paradoxically, the 'success' of GATT/WTO in contributing to the reduction of tariffs and quotas implies a decrease in the potential gains from continued multilateral trade liberalization. In response, the WTO now adopts a broader approach, and tries to manage trade issues related to investments and property rights and so on. But the WTO is still heavily trade focused and has severe difficulties accepting a broader and holistic approach to economic growth and development, which goes beyond trade *per se*.

Development is a multidimensional phenomenon, which depends on positive spillover and linkages between different sectors. Such a comprehensive and multidimensional approach is not viable on the global/multilateral level or within the WTO. It can only work on a regional (or national) level, because there it is possible and viable to link trade with other sectors and issues. The comprehensive developmentalist approach posits that trade issues and trade integration need to be coupled with other forms of economic and factor market integration (such as investment, payments, monetary integration and harmonization) as well as various types of economic cooperation in specified sectors (such as transport and communications) (Robson 1993; also see Higgott 2003). The broader approach is more complex than trade liberalization but it is both fairer and more feasible politically when implemented at a regional level. In politics, it is easier to liberalize towards neighbours than it is on a multilateral basis. And from a practical point of view it is (usually) easier to deal with distribution issues within a region. Regional trade clubs can respond and deal more effectively with non-trade economic and political challenges such as environmental protection and migration (Birdsall and Lawrence 1999: 146).

Such a line of thinking can be said to be part of the EU model. It has started to have an effect in different regional models in other parts of the world, such as East and Southeast Asia (ASEAN), in Latin America (CAN, Mercosur, CACM), Caribbean (CARICOM) and Africa (SADC, EAC, ECOWAS, AU). The development strategy can only be managed through comprehensive multipurpose regional organizations, since these can exploit spillover effects and linkages between trade and non-trade issues and between economic and political sectors/benefits. This would be considerably more difficult in other types of organizations. NAFTA for instance is mainly a trade agreement and not a functioning political region, which implies that it is more difficult to exploit such linkages. Similarly, most countries in EFTA found membership in the EC/EU more rewarding. This reveals the general trend towards more multidimensional forms of regionalism and towards multipurpose regional organizations with a greater actorness. It also depends on a change of attitude by the political regimes involved, away from old-fashioned competitive Westphalian thinking towards a more cooperative post-Westphalian political rationale.

In summary, insistence on a vertical WTO-led approach will only reinforce competition between multilateralism and regionalism in the global trading system. Such an approach fails to understand the complex relationship between global and regional trade governance. As advanced here, a more nuanced view suggests instead that the multilateral and regional modes of governance have different logics. Experiencing a decline in power and authority, the WTO needs the support of regional bodies. It is somewhat difficult to conceive how the WTO will maintain primacy if RIAs continue to deepen and strengthen around the world. As formal macro-regions emerge and take a political actor role, there will be a need for more organized contacts between these regions through interregionalism (see previous chapter). Strong regions are likely to be able to manage their own development and trading problems just as the EU has done historically. Thus, further consolidation of economic regionalism in Africa as well as Asia and Latin America may reduce the relevance of the WTO. If so, it would imply a more balanced relationship between the WTO and the needs of RTAs. The WTO would still be required, but compared to the present, it would be a rather different organization. Meanwhile, many regional economic arrangements are still embryonic and indeed need support from the WTO. In this future, an integrated global–regional strategy would provide the most feasible solution.

Regions in Global Health Governance[1]

Health has become part of global governance over the last few decades and, seen as a global public good, this is another reflection of the emergence of a post-Westphalian order (Woodward and Smith 2003; Fidler 2004). Quite obviously, germs do not recognize borders and 'germ globalization is permanent while the borders are the transitory phenomenon' (Fidler 2004: 14). In short, confronting a borderless public bad needs borderless governance in order to create a global public good, be it better control of AIDS, Ebola, SARS or 'old' infectious diseases such as malaria, smallpox and tuberculosis.

Infectious diseases are always threatening, but particularly when unknown. Confronting this, existing actors tend take on new roles, and so increase their actorness. For instance, the WHO is a global actor, but by its constitution it is Westphalian rather than post-Westphalian in character: the WHO reflects the principle of 'international' governance (between states) rather than 'global' governance, which among other things would include actors besides states, such as TNCs and NGOs, and at various scales of governance. In the triangle drama played out between state, market and civil society, the WHO represents the state whereas market and civil society might be represented by, for example ASTRA and Médecins Sans Frontières respectively. At its formation in 1948, regular relations with NGOs were planned for in the constitution of the WHO, but this official communication process now is anachronistic, as most contacts take place via informal networking (Fidler 2004: 52). There is substantial tension between NGOs and TNCs, as exemplified by the Campaign for Access to Essential Medicines (organized by Médecins Sans Frontières) and the International Baby Food Action Network, both relatively successful. This major struggle between two types of non-state actors shows the extent to which a post-Westphalian logic reigns supreme. On other occasions, partnerships are created between state-actors and NGOs, one important example being the Global Fund to Fight AIDS, Tuberculosis, and Malaria (the Global Fund). According to Fidler (2004: 55) 'the concept and structure of the Global Fund are as un-Westphalian as one could imagine'.

---

[1] This section draws on research collaboration with Björn Hettne (Hettne and Söderbaum 2006).

Even if communicable disease control has become increasingly centralized and globalized over time, there also is a growing regional dimension. This transformation and the gradual strengthening of the regional dimension is seen in a variety of cases, such as AIDS, avian influenza or 'bird flu' (which originated in Southeast Asia and infected humans in Thailand and Vietnam), and SARS. AIDS is a global challenge but has distinctive regional characteristics. It must be approached globally, but strategies must maintain a view on the regional peculiarities wherever the disease appears (which was also underlined in Chapter 7, Multidimensional Regionalism). In contrast, the avian influenza epidemic is a communicable local and regional disease, spreading between birds, and from birds to people, but with significant uncertainties about infection between humans. SARS is another disease that jumped the species divide to become a relatively localized human disease. Thanks to global air travel, the virus became a regional challenge with global impacts. The case of the SARS epidemic in the spring of 2003 and the regional context in which the outbreak took place provides a relevant case study for the changing dynamics of global health governance. Of course, this focus is not because of the relative medical importance of SARS compared with AIDS and other diseases. AIDS has a comparatively long epidemiological history but as a relative newcomer, SARS is the first post-Westphalian pathogen, and so SARS is particularly relevant for illustrating the transition of public health governance on infectious diseases from the traditional Westphalian framework to something new. At issue here is whether the new implies global or regional governance, or a combination of the two. The answer here is the latter.

The Case of SARS

SARS is a respiratory illness first recognized as a global threat in March 2003. SARS is caused by a previously unknown coronavirus, called SARS Coronavirus (SARS-CoV) and the primary infection vector appears to be close person-to-person contact. SARS-CoV is believed to be transmitted most readily by respiratory droplets (droplet spread) produced when an infected person coughs or sneezes, and this puts health workers at high risk. In addition, it remains possible but unknown if SARS-CoV can be airborne spread, or dispersed in other ways. SARS-CoV typically incubates between 2 and 7 days but infected persons are most likely contagious only when they present symptoms, such as fever or cough. Patients are most contagious during the second week of illness.

First appearing in Southern China in November 2002, SARS travelled to Toronto where, in terms of being outside the region of origin, a large number of people became infected. According to the WHO, between November 2002 and July 2003, a total of 8,096 people worldwide contracted SARS which was accompanied by either pneumonia or respiratory distress syndrome (probable cases). Cases occurred in almost 30 countries, 5,327 of which were in China (with 1,755 additional cases in Hong Kong), 346 in Taiwan, 238 in Singapore, and 63 in Vietnam. Outside the region, Canada had 251 and United States 33 (WHO 2015). Of the 8,096 infected, a total of 774 died.

The outbreak took the world by surprise and panic was near. Damage limitation was achieved in spite of, rather than because of, the prevailing form of international health governance. Policy measures were on the whole reactive rather than proactive. Remarkably, the most important national actor took measures to hide rather than disclose on the outbreak: China delayed reporting from November 2002 to February 2003. Other countries in the region appeared more concerned with the potential for damage to tourism than the damage to public health. In retrospect, the outbreak was managed in an effective way and all the lessons learnt are important for the future development of health governance in situations where global, regional and national modes of governance intersect with one another.

Criticism of China by the WHO was very frank, not only for hiding the extent of the outbreak, but also for allocating too few resources to national public health. This 'radical break with traditional diplomacy' (Fidler 2004) shows that international actors can take on global roles; that is, to move beyond the Westphalian logic in a situation of emerging crisis when the old rules do not apply. It is hard to find any policy area where national secrecy, justified by sovereignty, is more damaging for all interests involved than is the case with infectious diseases. It may be possible to cover up and deny starvation, torture, even genocide, but communicable diseases are potentially part of the globalized condition. Fortunately, this was ultimately realized in Beijing. But what if this had happened in North Korea or in a collapsed state, or for that matter in a system rejecting modern science and a rational scientific approach to public health such as the Taliban? The Chinese *volte face* was a genuine embarrassment for the regime, but the alternative of trying to cover up the outbreak of disease would have led to worse.

SARS was reported in 21 of China's 31 provinces and, as this accounted for at least half the cases of the world, the disease can be described as a regional disease. Mitigatory measures taken in China were massive. The political system was well-suited to the situation (once the danger was acknowledged); as has been said: 'China is as good at fighting SARS as at hiding it' (Chen 2003: 107). As far as institutional efficiency goes, the same can be said about other authoritarian countries such as Singapore and Vietnam. Paradoxically, the measures taken (surveillance, isolation and quarantine) to combat the spread were the traditional; it was the organizational (post-Westphalian) approach that was new. China acted in a Westphalian manner to a fundamentally post-Westphalian phenomenon (Chen 2003: 107). Despite attempting to, China could not control the flow of information and information leaked out (Internet, email, mobile phone). Significantly, China's initial actions, whilst doubtless misguided, were not wrong in terms of international law. This in particular underlines the need for a qualitative transformation of global health governance, for the sake of dealing effectively with similar, future outbreaks.

What are the implications of SARS for global and regional governance? Some described the epidemic as a threat to regional security (Curley and Thomas 2004) and the ASEAN was one of the actors of this drama. This is particularly interesting because, for many, ASEAN was seen as the guardian of Westphalian principles of non-intervention. Coming after the Asian Financial Crisis (AFC) discussed in Chapter 7 (as well as the forest fires in Indonesia – 'the haze'), SARS was another eye-opener.

It has to be acknowledged that the initial regional response was feeble and, above all, late. Once China admitted its mistake in hiding the disease and changed political strategy, however, impressive regional diplomatic activity began soon after. And in that respect, SARS gives an opportunity to study 'the effectiveness of the organizational response at the regional level' (Curley and Thomas 2004: 21).

Thailand in particular among the countries of ASEAN understood the regional nature of the crisis and called for regional responses. But this was not as rapid as those taken by the individual countries, and that has to do with the confusion regarding the competence of competing regional organizations: ASEAN, APEC, ASEAN Plus Three (APT). SARS was a new type of challenge, which in its aftermath left behind a new institutional framework to deal with regional crises. Lessons from the 1998 AFC were also carried over to the fight against SARS. One of these was the need to find the relevant national network. In effect, the urgency of the crisis forced ASEAN to increase its actorness and to move beyond the Westphalian framework. Of the array of regional organizations, APT was most relevant, since it involved China. APEC proved to be irrelevant due to a more narrow concern with free trade – which shows the limits of single-purpose regional organizations in the face of new issues. A second lesson was to accept putting pressure on slow reacting or reluctant countries for the sake of effectiveness. And a third lesson was to develop sectoral and intersectoral mechanisms both nationally and regionally, i.e. allow the needed institutionalization.

The last lesson is reflected by the number of meetings held between ministers, bureaucrats and experts within ASEAN and APT. A special meeting of Ministers of Health from the APT countries was held in Kuala Lumpur on 26 April and announced a number of measures to be carried out regionally and in individual countries. On 29 April, there was a Special ASEAN Leaders' Meeting in Singapore with further announcements about establishing networks for information and arrangements for health control (in spite of objections from Cambodia, Laos and Myanmar). On 8–9 May, the annual ASEAN Labour Ministers' meeting was devoted to the SARS threat, and they also met their counterparts in the APT countries (China, South Korea and Japan). On 15–16 May, APT Airport Officials met in Pampanga in the Philippines and discussed how to prevent the spread of SARS through civil aviation. APEC trade ministers met in Khon Kaen in Thailand on 2–3 June to assess the economic damages. The list of actual meetings is much longer, but it suffices to make the point that SARS was a mobilizing event with respect to regional governance. Significantly, civil society organizations and business were also drawn into the emerging networks, suggesting a particular style of regional health governance.

Limited as it, thankfully, proved to be, the SARS epidemic had major consequences for global public health governance and control of communicable diseases as a public and regional good. It revealed the weaknesses of the orthodox Westphalian health system. It underlined the need for a substantive strengthening of the global infrastructure and a regional dimension of global health governance, in terms of both effectiveness and actorness. Crucially, a functioning global public health system needs effective organizations on the national, regional and global levels – that is, a nested and multilayered global governance structure with effective capacity and actorness at each level with respect to necessary and specific tasks.

Conclusion

This chapter began by stating that the Westphalian nation-state approach to governance is undergoing transformation, yet the ultimate manifestation of the post-Westphalian model – fully-fledged globalization or multilateral governance – is also contested, or even premature. The basic argument is that contemporary global governance has regional governance as an essential ingredient, albeit not always the most important one.

Too many observers are locked into linear thinking whereby regional governance is considered a step (stepping stone) towards the 'superior' solution of fully-fledged global and multilateral governance. Such thinking has at least two major weaknesses. Firstly, it is built on an ideological and theoretical perspective that is biased in favour of multilateral governance at the expense of other notions about the regulation of transnational politics. Secondly, it is built around binary distinctions, which neglects the diversity of relationships that exist between multilateral/global and regional governance. A need to transcend binary distinctions is one of the major messages of this chapter; such distinctions are reinforced by the 'primacy of the UN' in global security and the misleading analogy of stumbling block vs. stepping stone in the trade controversy. Instead, there is a need to acknowledge and understand the diversity of relationships that exist between global and regional governance. In the field of security and trade, there are combinations of global–regional modes of governance that interact in complex and non-linear ways. From a normative standpoint, these are in many respects also the preferred solutions. The field of health is particularly interesting in that it has been dominated by Westphalian modes of government. Confronted by many transnational health challenges, nested forms of governance are emerging whereby national, regional and global modes of governance interact and shape one another.

13
Conclusion

The starting point of this book was that all too often regionalism is too narrowly understood. The book emphasizes a number of conceptual, theoretical and methodological deficits in the field, which are caused by, among other things, the many divides and conflicts between different participating disciplines, theoretical traditions and regional and thematic specializations. This book has tried to transcend some of the intellectual divides in the field, searching for more creative and synthetic ways to think about regions and regionalism.

The book offers a four-fold approach to rethinking regionalism that is rooted in constructivist and reflectivist scholarship. Despite criticism of rationalist and problem-solving theories of regionalism, the goal is not to prove these theories wrong or irrelevant, but rather to justify alternative ways of thinking about the issues.

The first component of 'rethinking' is a concern that the deep roots and global history of regionalism are not understood properly if one adopts a view that regionalism 'commenced' in Europe after the First or Second World Wars. It is necessary to adopt a longer historical perspective, which acknowledges the pluralism of regionalism in time and space.

The distinction drawn between old and new regionalism inserted a certain historical perspective into the debate. Clearly, this distinction was relevant in the late 1980s as a means to identify regionalism past and present. One result of this distinction, however, was confusion, not least because it inhibited deeper historical analysis to some extent. And the confusion was reinforced further by the fact that the labels of 'old' and 'new' were sometimes misused in the criticism of others.

After several decades of 'new regionalism', it is fruitful to move ahead and unbundle the binary distinction between old and new regionalism. There are continuities as well as discontinuities over time. Importantly, however, the most recent wave of regionalism differs from earlier phases of regionalism. For instance, while the very existence of a meaningful regionalism was questioned just a few decades ago, that today seems improbable. Today, regionalism has become a structural component of global politics, deepening and expanding into an increasing number of policy fields, beyond the conventional focus on trade and security to health and environment and social policy (Fawn 2009). Regionalism is increasingly complex, with multifold interactions between state and non-state actors, institutions and processes.

As an empirical phenomenon, regionalism has become increasingly complex and this has changed the intellectual landscape of the study of it. Importantly, there is an increasing acceptance that a multitude of analytical standpoints and perspectives on regionalism are both necessary and plausible. In a theoretical and methodological sense, we have moved beyond the new regionalism into an era which, in terms of intellectual history, can be referred to as 'comparative regionalism'. Despite the undoubted progress, in some important respects the study of regionalism remains underdeveloped and fragmented. One of the most important of these weaknesses is an embryonic understanding of regional space; i.e., the second component of rethinking regionalism.

Rethinking regional space begins with the realization that scholars still place too much focus on states-led regional organizations and 'formal' mechanisms. On the whole, the field has failed to embrace one of the central arguments emphasized in the new regionalism approach (NRA): the study of regionalism must not be reduced to the scholarship of regional organizations. In many ways, the focus on interstate and supranational regional organizations is rooted in Eurocentric theory-building and ambitions to solve the problem of what types of regions are the most functional, instrumental and efficient 'to rule' or govern. This book avoids the obsession with regional organizations by favouring a societal understanding of regional space. From such social constructivist perspective, the purpose is to understand and explain the processes by which regions are made and unmade by the different participating actors and formal as well as informal institutions.

Transcending the excessive attention paid to sovereignty transfer and formal/formalistic political unification within inter-state and supranational regional organizations, such as the AU, ASEAN, ECOWAS, EU, NAFTA and SADC, is an obvious necessity. But this is not an argument that scholars should cease analysing regional organizations or 'institutional design'. It simply implies that the overwhelming dominance of a rather narrow and particular interpretation of the logic of states-led regional organizations has prevented alternative answers about how and why regions are formed and who are the relevant region-builders.

Closely linked to the rejection of states-led regional organizations as the only focus is a rejection of both 'state-centrism' and 'methodological nationalism'. Again, the solution is not to ignore the state. Instead, attention must be drawn to the fundamental transformation that is underway in the political and institutional landscape. There is a need to deal with more complex and multi-layered governance structures and spatialities, in which the nation-state is 'unbundled,' reorganized and assumes different functions and where non-state actors also contribute at various scales of action. Methodologically, the issue is to transcend Western conceptions of the unitary and Westphalian state and open up to a broader, social understanding of what is regionalism and region-alization in the different policy fields and parts of the world where it occurs. A focus on 'regional space' instead of states-led regional organizations is still rare in the study of regionalism. 'Few are the works that seriously challenge the convenient practice of relying on spaces that are either formally predefined by regional organiza-tions and treaties or tangible in terms of material flows' (Mattheis 2014: 63). Differently expressed, the fundamental methodologi-cal problem concerns the prevalent view of regional space as just another 'container', with predefined views about inside/outside and how regions 'become regions'.

Drawing on the sociological notion of regional space, sev-eral chapters of the book look beyond the reductionist focus on (formal) regional organizations towards how a variety of state, market, civil society and external actors come together to con-struct regions in a series of overlapping, contradictory and some-times competing organizations, networks and modes of regional governance.

Regions are political and social projects. The study shows that region-builders may be motivated by material incentives as well as by ideas, identities and other cognitive factors. Regions are not only material but also exist in imaginations. Arising from this, what exactly a region should be is permanently disputed. Different actors may use regionalism for satisfying a range of different interests, goals and identities. It follows that region-building is not a harmonious process; both integration and disintegration are part of it. Regionness is a concept and heuristic tool that seeks to grasp the conditions when the many varieties and strategies of regionalization and regional agencies solidify and converge within a particular regional space. This idea is not part of a stage theory, because there is nothing evolutionary about the emergence, spread and consolidation of regionalism. Regionness can either increase or decrease, and there are clearly different pathways to regionness. Even if developed originally for understanding the evolution and consolidation of European integration, the basic idea of the regionness framework is to provide a heuristic tool for comparing the consolidation of regions in time and space. This links to the third element of rethinking offered in this book: comparing regions.

Arguably, the consolidation of 'comparative regionalism' constitutes one of the core intellectual characteristics of the most recent phase in the study of regionalism, 'beyond' the era of the new regionalism. Comparative regionalism is a core contribution of this book. Today, there is a trend to avoid having to make a simple choice between qualitative and quantitative methodologies and sources of information, and instead to use whatever methods and data are needed to answer the research question. Perhaps more importantly, there is also a trend to try to overcome the conflict between Eurocentrism and anti-Eurocentrism with intensified debate between students of European integration and those of regionalism in the rest of the world. Once again, although there has been progress in the past decade, the comparative perspective in studying regionalism remains immature. In response, this book tries to contribute to a more eclectic comparative approach to the study of regions and regionalism without becoming trapped in either parochialism or false universalism. One of the main arguments here is that we need to move towards a non-Eurocentric discourse on comparative regionalism, built around general concepts and theories, but which is still culturally sensitive.

In offering a way out of these pitfalls, the book acknowledges the richness of comparative studies – in time and across different units of analysis. All regions and regional organizations may be compared in some or other way, even if it may be difficult to compare regions at every stage of their development. Hence, there is still a need for regions to be situated historically and contextually. The eclectic comparative perspective outlined here does not reject the idea that the EU (and potentially also other regions) can be compared to other federal polities (e.g. the US, Germany, Canada) or old empires.

Since regionalism is closely linked to global transformation and world order change, it cannot be understood merely from the point of view of the region under study. Understanding the role of regions in global transformation requires integrating regional theory with a 'global' approach: and that is the fourth component of rethinking offered in this book. In other words, 'comparative regionalism' is not enough to address the essential logic of how regions affect global governance. Fortunately, a global approach does not prevent a particular focus on the regions. 'Global social theory' means a comprehensive social science that abandons state-centrism and methodological nationalism, but at the same time takes regional peculiarities into consideration. It is clear that the Westphalian nation-state has lost some of its historical importance. In many parts of the world, there is no return to the Westphalian nation-state as it was once known, while elsewhere, people have yet to experience a functioning nation-state, able to provide security and welfare. In these cases, it is unlikely that they ever will experience a Westphalian nation-state in the way it functioned in the nineteenth and twentieth century.

Even if states remain important actors, it is quite clear that they lack capacity to handle transnational challenges to national interests and increasingly respond through global and regional governance. Through these processes, states intentionally or unwittingly yield sovereignty, autonomy and decision-making power to some or other degree and, ultimately, may end up as semi-independent parts of larger transnational and regional political communities. In this emerging, multilayered and 'multiplex' system of governance, actors other than the state gain strength (Acharya 2014). This is seen in most policy fields, ranging from trade, economic development and the environment to social policy and security. Thus, the emerging global social theory must rise to the challenge of accommodating the simultaneous involvement of state as well as non-state actors and global, regional, national and local-level processes in the course of global transformation. Stating which level is dominant is not relevant, because actors and processes at the various levels interact and their relative importance differs in time and space.

Global social theory must demystify the concept of globalization, and distinguish the new aspects from the old and specify the different repercussions in various parts of the world. Global social theory has to be a theory about the world order in transformation and the emergence of a multilayered pattern of governance, which accounts for the role of regions and regionalism. Indeed, regions have become crucial ingredients of global transformation – which explains why they have moved into centre place in current international relations (Katzenstein 2005; Acharya 2014). At present, the globalized world order is hierarchic; a future world of regions or 'regional worlds' appears more likely and may possess a stability and equality that the globalized order lacks (Hettne et al. 1999; Acharya 2014).

A more symmetric, or horizontalized, world of regions would necessarily mean a reduced role for the West, whereby different regional worlds could have some autonomy (Acharya 2014). A regionalized world order and a more complex globality, rather than continued uni-linear globalization, would not only be more efficient in resolving conflicts, but also facilitate a genuine global cultural pluralism. A region-based inter-civilizational dialogue would give a new meaning to history, in contrast with the 'end of history' thesis that is inherent in views of ultimate Western dominance or the alternative 'clash of civilizations'. This kind of dialogue on a global level presupposes that the parties possess a material base, which could be guaranteed only from within a regionalist 'protective' framework (new forms of political community and new governance structures). To date, there is not that much experience of constructive interregional relations to draw upon, but as illustrated by the last chapters in this book, there is comfort to be drawn from the fact that there are few clashes between regions.

Bibliography

Acharya, A. (1997) 'Ideas, Identity and Institution-Building: from the "ASEAN Way" to the "Asia-Pacific Way"?', *The Pacific Review*, Vol 10, No. 3, pp. 319–46.

Acharya, A. (2001) *Constructing a Security Community in Southeast Asia: ASEAN and the Problem of Regional Order*. London: Routledge.

Acharya, A. (2002) 'Regionalism and the Emerging World Order: Sovereignty, Autonomy, Identity', in Breslin, S., C. Hughes, N. Phillips and B. Rosamond (eds), *New Regionalisms in the Global Political Economy* (London: Routledge).

Acharya, Amitav (2004), 'How Ideas Spread: Whose Norms Matter? Norm Localization and Institutional Change in Asian Regionalism', *International Organization*, Vol. 58, No. 2, pp. 239–75.

Acharya, A. (2006) 'Europe and Asia: Reflections on a Tale of Two Regionalisms', in Fort, B. and D. Webber (eds), *Regional Integration in Europe and East Asia: Convergence or Divergence?* (London and New York: Routledge).

Acharya, A. (2007) 'The Emerging Regional Architecture of World Politics', *World Politics*, Vol. 59, No. 4, pp. 629–52.

Acharya, A. (2012) 'Comparative Regionalism: A Field Whose Time has Come?' *The International Spectator*, Vol. 47, No. 1, pp. 3–15.

Acharya, A. (2014) *The End of American World Order* (Cambridge: Polity Press).

Acharya, A. and A. I. Johnston (eds) (2007a) *Crafting Cooperation. Regional International Institutions in Comparative Perspective* (London: Oxford University Press).

Acharya, A. and A. I. Johnston (2007b) 'Comparing Regional Institutions: An Introduction', in Acharya, A. and A. Johnston (eds), *Crafting Cooperation. Regional International Institutions in Comparative Perspective* (London: Oxford University Press).

Acharya, A. and A. I. Johnston (2007c) 'Conclusion: Institutional Features, Cooperation Effects, and the Agenda for Further Research on Comparative Regionalism', in Acharya, A. and A. Johnston (eds), *Crafting Cooperation. Regional International Institutions in Comparative Perspective* (London: Oxford University Press).

ADB (2008) *Emerging Asian Regionalism. A Partnership for Shared Prosperity* (Manila: Asian Development Bank).

Adler, E. (1997a) 'Seizing the Middle Ground: Constructivism in World Politics', *European Journal of International Relations*, Vol. 3, No. 3, pp. 319–63.

Adler, E. (1997b) 'Imagined (Security) Communities: Cognitive Regions in International Relations', *Millenium: Journal of International Studies*, Vol. 26, No. 2, pp. 249–77.

Adler, E. and M. Barnett (eds) (1998a) *Security Communities* (Cambridge: Cambridge University Press).

Adler, E. and M. Barnett (1998b) 'A Framework for the Study of Security Communities', in Adler, E. and M. Barnett (eds), *Security Communities* (Cambridge: Cambridge University Press).

Aggarwal, V. K. and E. A. Fogerty (2004) 'Between Regionalism and Globalism: European Union Interregional Trade Strategies', in Aggarwal, V. K. and E. A. Fogerty (eds), *EU Trade Strategies: Between Regionalism and Globalism* (Basingstoke: Palgrave Macmillan).

Agnew, J. (1998) 'Political Power and Geographical Scale', Paper for *Third Pan-European IR Conference and Joint Meeting with ISA*, Vienna, Austria, 16–19 September.

Alter, K. J. and Helfer, L. R. (2010) 'Nature or Nurture? Judicial Lawmaking in the European Court of Justice and the Andean Tribunal of Justice'. *International Organization*, Vol. 64, pp. 563–92.

Anderson, B. (1983) *Imagined Communities: Reflections on the Origin and Spread of Nationalism* (London/New York: Verso).

Archer, C. (1992) *International Organizations*. London: Routledge.

Armstrong, D., Bello, V., Gilson, J. and Spini, D. (eds) (2011) *Civil Society and International Governance: The Role of Non-state Actors in Global and Regional Regulatory Frameworks* (London: Routledge).

Asante, S. K. B. (1997) *Regionalism and Africa's Development. Expectations, Reality and Challenges* (Basingstoke: Macmillan).

Axline, W. A. (1977) 'Underdevelopment, Dependence and Integration: The Politics of Regionalism in the Third World', *International Organization*, Vol. 31, No. 1, pp. 83–105.

Axline, W. A. (1994a) 'Cross-Regional Comparison and the Theory of Regional Cooperation: Lessons from Latin America, the Caribbean, South East Asia and the South Pacific', in Axline, W. A. (ed.), *The Political Economy of Regional Cooperation. Comparative Case Studies* (London: Pinter Publishers).

Axline, W. A. (1994b) 'Comparative Case Studies of Regional Cooperation among Developing Countries', in Axline, W. A. (ed.), *The Political Economy of Regional Cooperation. Comparative Case Studies* (London: Pinter Publishers).

Azarya, V. (1994) 'Civil Society and Disengagement in Africa', in Harbeson, J. W. (ed.), *Civil Society and the State in Africa* (Boulder: Lynne Rienner).

Ba, A. A. (2009) *[Re]Negotiating East and Southeast Asia: Region, Regionalism, and the Association of Southeast Asian Nations* (Stanford, CA: Stanford University Press).

Bach, D. C. (1999a) *Regionalisation in Africa. Integration & Disintegration* (London: James Currey).

Bach, D. C. (1999b) 'Regionalism Versus Regional Integration: The Emergence of a New Paradigm in Africa', in Grugel, J. and W. Hout (eds), *Regionalism Across The North–South Divide: State Strategies and Globalization* (London: Routledge), pp. 136–47.

Bach, D. C. (2005) 'The Global Politics of Regionalism: Africa', in Farrell, M., Hettne, B. and L. van Langenhove (eds), *Global Politics of Regionalism. Theory and Practice* (London: Pluto Press).

Baert, F., T. Scaramagli and F. Söderbaum (eds) (2014) *Intersecting Interregionalism. Regions, Global Governance and the EU* (Dordrecht: Springer).

Balassa, B. (1961). *The Theory of Economic Integration* (London: Allen and Unwin).

Baldersheim, H., Haug, A. V. and M. Øgård (eds) (2011) *The Rise of the Networking Region: The Challenges of Regional Collaboration in a Globalized World* (Basingstoke: Ashgate).

Baldwin, R. (2008) 'Multilateralising Regionalism: The WTO's Next Challenge', vox, 29 February 2008. [http://www.vowEU.org]. Retrieved 1 April 2008.

Baldwin, R. and P. Thornton (2008) *Multilateralising Regionalism: Ideas for a WTO Action Plan on Regionalism* (London: Centre for Economic Policy Research).

Bartlett, R. (1993) *The Making of Europe: Conquest, Colonization and Cultural Change, 950–1350* (Penguin Books).

Beck, U. (1997) *The Reinvention of Politics* (Cambridge: Polity Press).

Bhagwati, J. (1993) *The World Trading System at Risk* (Princeton, NJ: Princeton University Press).

Binder, L. (1958) 'The Middle East as a Subordinate International System', *World Politics*, Vol. 10, No. 3, pp. 408–29.

Birdsall, N. and R. Z. Lawrence (1999) 'Deep Integration and Trade Agreements: Good for Developing Countries?', in Kaul, I., I. Grunberg and M. A. Stern (eds), *Global Public Goods. International Cooperation in the 21st Century* (New York: UNDP and Oxford University Press).

Börzel, T. (2016) 'Theorizing Regionalism: Cooperation, Integration and Governance', in Börzel, T. and T. Risse (eds), *The Oxford Handbook of Comparative Regionalism* (Oxford. Oxford University Press).

Börzel, T. and T. Risse (eds) (2016) *The Oxford Handbook of Comparative Regionalism* (Oxford. Oxford University Press).

Bourne, A. (2003) 'Regional Europe', in Cini, M. (ed.) *European Union Politics* (Oxford: Oxford Univerity Press).

Breslin, S. and R. Higgott (2000) 'Studying Regions: Learning from the Old, Constructing the New', *New Political Economy*, Vol. 5, No. 3, pp. 333–52.

Breslin, Shaun, Richard Higgott and Ben Rosamond (2002) 'Regions in Comparative Perspective', in Breslin, S., C. W. Hughes, N. Phillips and B. Rosamond (eds), *New Regionalisms in the Global Political Economy: Theories and Cases* (London: Routledge).

Breslin, S. and R. Higgott (2003) 'New Regionalism(s) in Historical Perspective', *Asia-Europe Journal*, Vol. 1, 2 (May).

Breslin, S. and G. D. Hook (eds) (2002) *Microregionalism and World Order* (Basingstoke: Palgrave).

Bretherton, C. and J. Vogler (1999) *Europe as a Global Actor* (London: Routledge).

Bull, H. (1977) *The Anarchical Society. A Study of Order in World Politics* (Basingstoke: Macmillan).

Buzan, B. (1991) *People, States and Fear: An Agenda for International Secruity Studies in the Post-Cold War Era* (Boulder, CO: Lynne Rienner).

Buzan, B. (2003) 'Regional Security Complex Theory in the Post-Cold War World', in Söderbaum, F. and T. M. Shaw (eds), *Theories of New Regionalism. A Palgrave Reader* (Basingstoke: Palgrave).

Buzan, B. and O. Wæver (2003) *Regions and Powers. The Structure of International Security* (Cambridge: Cambridge University Press).

Buzdugan, S. R. (2013) 'Regionalism from Without: External Involvement of the EU in Regionalism in Southern Africa', *Review of International Political Economy*, Vol. 20, No. 4, pp. 917–46.

Bøås, M. (2000) 'Security Communities: Whose Security', *Cooperation & Conflict*, Vol. 35, No. 3, pp. 309–19.

Bøås, M. (2003) 'Weak States, Strong Regimes: Towards a "Real" Political Economy of African Regionalization', in Andrew, J. A. and F. Söderbaum (eds), *The New Regionalism in Africa* (Aldershot: Ashgate).

Bøås, M., M. H. Marchand and T. M. Shaw (2003) 'The Weave-World: The regional Interweavig of Economies, Ideas and Identitites', in F. Söderbaum and T. M. Shaw (eds), *Theories of New Regionalism. A Palgrave Reader* (Basingstoke: Palgrave).

Bøås, M., M. H. Marchand and T. M. Shaw (eds) (1999), *New Regionalisms in the New Millennium*, special issue of *Third World Quarterly*, Vol. 20, No. 5 (October).

Bøås, M., M. H. Marchand and T. M. Shaw (2005) *The Political Economy of Regions and Regionalism* (Basingstoke: Palgrave Macmillan).

Cable, V. and D. Henderson (eds) (1994) *Trade Blocs? The Future of Regional Integration* (London: Royal Institute of International Affairs).

Camroux, D. (2010) 'Interregionalism or Merely a Fourth-Level Game? An Examination of the EU–ASEAN Relationship', *East Asia*, Vol. 27, No. 1, pp. 57–77.

Cantori, L. J. and S. L. Spiegel (1970) *The International Politics of Regions: A Comparative Approach* (Englewood Cliffs, NJ: Prentice-Hall).

Caporaso, J. A. (1971) 'Theory and Method in the Study of International Integration', *International Organization*, Vol. 25, No 2, pp. 228–53.

Caporaso, J. A. (1997) 'Does the European Union Represent an n of 1?', *ECSA Review*, Vol. X, No. 3, pp. 1–2.

Carbone, M. (ed.) (2013) *The European Union in Africa: Incoherent Policies, Asymmetrical Partnership, Declining Relevance?* (Manchester: Manchester University Press).

Castells, M. (1996) *The Rise of the Network Society* (Blackwell: Cambridge).

Chazan, N. (1999) *Politics and Society in Contemporary Africa* (Boulder, CO: Lynne Rienner).

Checkel, J. T. (2007) 'Social Mechanisms and Regional Cooperation: Are Europe and the EU Really all that Different?', in Acharya, A. and A. Johnston (eds), *Crafting Cooperation. Regional International Institutions in Comparative Perspective* (London: Oxford University Press).

Chen, K. (2003) 'China is as Good at Fighting SARS as at Hiding It', *Wall Street Journal*, 4 June.

Cheru, F. and Obi, S. (eds) (2010) *The Rise of China and India in Africa: Challenges, Opportunities and Critical Interventions* (London: Zed).

Chiuta, T. M. (2000) 'Shared Water Resources and Conflicts: The Case of the Zambezi River Basin Institutions', in Tevera, D. and S. Moyo (eds), *Environmental Security in Southern Africa* (Harare: SAPES).

Choi, Y. J. and J. A. Caporaso (2002) 'Comparative Regional Integration', in Carlsnaes, W., T. Risse and B. Simmons (eds), *Handbook of International Relations* (London: Sage).

Christiansen, T. (2001a) 'European and Regional Integration', in Baylis, J. and S. Smith (eds), *The Globalization of World Politics: An Introduction to International Relations* (Oxford: Oxford University Press).

Christiansen, T. (2001b) Intra-institutional politics and inter-institutional relations in the EU: towards coherent governance? *Journal of European Public Policy*, Vol. 8, No. 5, pp. 747–69.

Christiansen, T. and S. Piattoni (eds) (2004) *Informal Governance in the European Union* (Cheltenham: Edward Elgar).

Christiansen, T., K. E. Jørgensen and A. Wiener (eds) (1999) 'The Social Construction of Europe,' Special Issue of *Journal of European Public Policy*, Vol. 6, No. 4.

Cini, M. (2003) 'Intergovernmentalism', in Cini, M. (ed.) *European Union Politics* (Oxford: Oxford University Press).

Clapham, C. (1996) *Africa and the International System. The Politics of State Survival* (Cambridge: Cambridge University Press).

Clapham, C. (1999) 'Boundaries and States in the New African Order', in D. C. Bach (ed.) *Regionalization in Africa: Integration and Disintegration* (Oxford: James Currey).

Coleman, W. D. and G. R. D. Underhill (eds) (1998) *Regionalism and Global Economic Integration. Europe, Asia and the Americas* (London: Routledge).

Collins, A. (2007) 'Forming a Security Community: Lessons from ASEAN', *International Relations of the Asia-Pacific,* Vol. 7, No. 2, pp. 203–25.

Combaz, E. (2013) 'Regional development programmes and poverty reduction', *GSDRC Helpdesk Research Report 1023.* (Birmingham, UK: GSDRC, University of Birmingham).

Cooper, A., C. Hughes and P. De Lombaerde (eds) (2008) *Regionalization and the Taming of Globalization* (London: Routledge, forthcoming).

Costa, O. and C. Dri (2014) 'How does the European Parliament contribute to the construction of the EU's interregional dialogue?', in Baert, F. Scaramagli, T. and F. Söderbaum (eds.), *Intersecting Interregionalism* (Dordrecht: Springer).

Cox, R. W. (1981) 'Social Forces, States, and World Orders: Beyond International Relations Theory', *Millennium: Journal of International Studies,* Vol. 10, No. 2, pp. 126–55.

Cox, R. W. (1996) *Approaches to World Order* (Cambridge: Cambridge University Press).

Curley. M. and N. Thomas (2004) 'Human Security and Public Health in South East Asia', *Australian Journal of International Affairs,* Vol. 58, No. 1.

De Lombaerde P. (2011) 'Comparing Regionalisms: Methodological Aspects and Considerations', in Shaw, T. M., J. A. Grant and S. Cornelissen (eds), *The Ashgate Companion to Regionalisms* (Farnham-Burlington: Ashgate).

De Lombaerde, P. and M. Schulz (eds) (2009) *The EU and World Regionalism. The Makability of Regions in the 21st Century* (Farnham: Ashgate).

De Lombaerde, P. and F. Söderbaum (eds) (2013) *Regionalism,* Vols. 1–4 (London: SAGE).

De Lombaerde, P., F. Söderbaum, L. Van Langenhove and F. Baert (2010) 'The Problem of Comparison in Comparative Regionalism', *Review of International Studies,* Vol. 36, No. 3, pp. 731–53.

de Melo, J. and A. Panagariya (1995) 'Introduction', in de Melo, J. and A. Panagariya (eds), *New Dimensions in Regional Integration* (Cambridge-New York: Cambridge University Press).

Deacon, B., M. C. Macovei, L. Van Langenhove and N. Yeates (eds) (2010) *World-Regional Social Policy and Global Governance: New Research and Policy* (London: Routledge).

Delputte, S. and F. Söderbaum (2012) 'European aid Coordination in Africa: Is the Commission Calling the Tune?', in Gänzle, S., S. Grimm and D. Mahkan (eds), *The European Union and Global Development: An Enlightened Superpower in the Making?* (Basingstoke: Palgrave Macmillan).

Deutsch, K. W., Burrell, S., Kann, R., Lee, M., Lichtermann, M., Lingren, R., Loewenheim, F. and van Wanegen, R. W. (1957) *Political Community and the North Atlantic Area: International Organization in the Light of Historical Experience* (Princeton, NJ: Princeton University Press).

Diehl, P. F. (1994) *International Peacekeeping* (Baltimore, MD: Johns Hopkins University Press).

Doidge, M. (2007) 'Joined at the Hip: Regionalism and Interregionalism', *Journal of European Integration,* Vol. 29, No. 2, pp. 229–48.

Doidge, M. (2011) *The European Union and Interregionalism: Patterns of Engagement* (Farnham: Ashgate).

Doidge, M. (2014) 'Interregionalism and the European Union: Conceptualizing Group-to-Group Relations', in Baert, F., T. Scaramagli and F. Söderbaum (eds), *Intersecting Interregionalism* (Dordrecht: Springer).

Duina, F. (2005) *The Social Construction of Free Trade. The EU, NAFTA, and Mercosur* (Princeton, NJ: Princeton University Press).

Duina, F. (2013) *Institutions and the Economy* (Cambridge: Polity Press).

ECLA (1959) *The Latin American Common Market and the Multilateral Payments System* (Santiago: United Nations Publications).

ECLAC (1994) *Open Regionalism in Latin America and the Caribbean: Economic Integration as a Contribution to Changing Production Patterns with Social Equity* (Santiago: ECLAC).

Elgström, O. (2009) 'Trade and Aid? The Negotiated Construction of EU Policy on Economic Partnership Agreements', *International Politics*, Vol. 46, No. 4, pp. 451–68.

Elgström, O. and M. F. Larsén (2008) 'The Role of Commission and Council (Dis-) Unity in International Trade Negotiations: A Case Study of the EPA Negotiations', Paper for the *Fourth Pan-European Conference on EU Politics*, University of Latvia, Riga, 25–27 September.

Emerson, G. (2014) 'An Art of the Region: Towards a Politics of Regionness', *New Political Economy*, Vol. 19, No. 4, pp. 559–77.

European Commission (1995) 'European Community support for regional economic integration efforts among developing countries', Communication from the Commission, COM (95) 219 (Brussels: Commission of the European Communities).

European Commission (2001) 'Europe and Asia: A strategic framework for enhanced partnerships'. Communication from the European Commission COM(2001) 469 final (Brussels: Commission of the European Communities).

European Commission (2004) 'A World Player: The European Union's External Relations' (Brussels: DG for Press and Communication, European Commission).

European Commission (2005), *EU Strategy for Africa: Towards a Euro-African Pact to Accelerate Africa's Development*, COM(2005) 489 final (Brussels: Commission of the European Communities).

European Commission (2013) 'Study on Blue Growth, Maritime Policy and EU Strategy for the Baltic Sea Region', Background Paper for the Maritime Stakeholder Conference, September, [http://www.partiseapate.eu/wp-content/uploads/2013/11/02b_AngelaSchultz-Zehden_BlueGrowth.pdf].

Farrell, M. (2006) 'A Triumph of Realism over Idealism? Cooperation Between the European Union and Africa', in Söderbaum, F. and P. Stålgren (eds), *The European Union and the Global South* (Boulder/London: Lynne Rienner Publishers).

Farrell, M. (2010) 'A Move Toward Hybrid Interregionalism in Asia', in Söderbaum, F. and P. Stålgren (eds), *The European Union and the Global South* (Boulder, CO: Lynne Rienner).

Farrell, M., B. Hettne and L. van Langenhove (eds) (2005) *The Global Politics of Regionalism. Theory and Practice* (London: Pluto Press).

Fawcett, L. (2005a) 'Regionalism From a Historical Perspective', in Farrell, Mary, M., B. Hettne and L. van Langenhove (eds), *Global Politics of Regionalism. Theory and Practice* (London: Pluto Press).

Fawcett, L. (2005b) 'Origins and Development of Regional Ideas in the Americas', in Fawcett, L. and M. Serrano (eds), *Regionalism and Governance in the Americas* (Basingstoke: Palgrave).

Fawcett, L. (2012) 'Between West and Non-West: Latin American Contributions to International Thought', *International History Review*, Vol. 34, No. 2, pp. 679–704.

Fawcett, L. (2015) 'History and Concept of Regionalism: A Call for a Post-Revisionist Synthesis', Paper for the *International Studies Association Conference 2015*, New Orleans: ISA, pp. 1–19.

Fawcett, L. and A. Hurrell (1995) *Regionalism in World Politics: Regional Organization and International Order* (Oxford: Oxford University Press).

Fawn, R. (2009) 'Regions and Their Study: Wherefrom, What for and Where to?', *Review of International Studies*, Vol. 35, Supplement S1, pp. 5–34.

Fidler, D. P. (2004) *SARS. Governance and the Globalization of Disease* (Basingstoke: Palgrave Macmillan).

Fioramonti, L. (ed.) (2012) *Regions and Crises. New Challenges for Contemporary Regionalisms* (Basingstoke: Palgrave).

Fioramonti, L. (ed.) (2014) *Civil Society and World Regions. How Citizens Are Reshaping Regional Governance in Times of Crisis* (Lanham: Lexington Books).

Fourutan, F. (1995) 'Regional Integration in Sub-Saharan Africa: Past Experience and Future Prospects', in de Melo, J. and A. Panagariya (eds), *New Dimensions in Regional Integration* (Cambridge: Cambridge University Press).

Froitzheim, M., F. Söderbaum and I. Taylor (2011) 'The Limits of the EU as a Peace and Security Actor in the Democratic Republic of the Congo', *Africa Spectrum,* Vol. 46, No. 3, pp. 45–70.

Gamble, A. and A. Payne (eds) (1996a) *Regionalism and Global Order* (Basingstoke: Macmillan).

Gamble, A. and A. Payne (1996b) 'Conclusion: The New Regionalism', in Andrew Gamble and Anthony Payne (eds), *Regionalism and World Order.* Basingstoke: Macmillan.

Gamble, A. and A. Payne (2003) 'The World Order Approach', in Söderbaum, F. and T. M. Shaw (eds), *Theories of New Regionalism. A Palgrave Reader* (Basingstoke: Palgrave).

Genna, G. and De Lombaerde, P. (2010) 'The Small N Methodological Challenges of Analyzing Regional Integration', *Journal of European Integration*, Vol. 36, No. 6, pp. 583–95.

Gilpin, R. (1987) *The Political Economy of International Relations* (Princeton, NJ: Princeton University Press).

Gilson, J. (2002) *Asia Meets Europe* (Cheltenham: Edward Elgar).

Gilson. J. (2005) 'New Interregionalism? EU and East Asia', *Journal of European Integration*, Vol. 27, No. 3, pp. 307–26.

Giordano, M. and Wolf, A. (2003) 'Sharing Waters: Post-Rio International Water Management', *Natural Resources Forum*, Vol. 27, pp. 163–171.

Godsäter, A. (2013) *Civil Society Regionalization in Southern Africa: The Cases of Trade and HIV/AIDS* (Gothenburg: School of Global Studies, University of Gothenburg).

Godsäter, A. and F. Söderbaum (2011) 'Civil Society in Regional Governance in Eastern and Southern Africa', in Armstrong, D., V. Bello, J. Gilson and D. Spini (eds), *Civil Society and International Governance. The Role of Non-State Actors in Global and Regional Regulatory Frameworks* (London: Routledge).

Goh, G. (2003) 'The 'ASEAN Way': Non-Intervention and ASEAN's Role in Conflict Management', *Stanford Journal of East Asian Affairs*, Vol. 3, No. 1, pp. 113–18.

Graham, K. and T. Felicio (2006) *Regional Security and Global Governance: A Study of Interaction Between Regional Agencies and the UN Security Council with a Proposal for a Regional-Global Security Mechanism* (Brussels: VUB Brussels University Press).

Grant, A. J. and F. Söderbaum (eds) (2003) *The New Regionalism in Africa* (Aldershot: Ashgate).

Gratius, S. (2011) 'The EU and the 'Special Ten': Deepening or Widening Strategic Partnerships', *FRIDE Policy Brief*, p. 76.

Gray, J. (2013) 'Can Foreign Aid Buy Cooperation? External Funding and International Organizational Adaptation' (Pittsburgh, PA: University of Pittsburgh, draft).

Grevi, G. (2010) 'Making EU Strategic Partnerships Effective', *FRIDE Working Paper,* December, p. 102.

Grieco, J. M. (1997) 'Systemic Sources of Variation in Regional Institutionalization in Western Europe, East Asia and the Americas', in Mansfield, E. D. and H. V. Milner (eds), *The Political Economy of Regionalism* (New York: Columbia University Press).

Griffith-Jones, S. (2003) 'International Financial Stability and Market Efficiency as a Global Public Good', in Kaul, I., P. Conceicao, K. Le Goulven and R. Mendoza (eds), *Providing Global Public Goods. Managing Globalization* (Oxford: UNDP & Oxford University Press).

Grimm, S. (2010) 'EU Policies Toward the Global South', in Söderbaum, F. and P. Stålgren (eds), *The European Union and the Global South* (Boulder, CO: Lynne Rienner Publishers).

Haas, E. B. (1958) *The Uniting of Europe: Political, Social and Economic Forces 1950–1957* (Stanford, CA: Stanford University Press).

Haas, E. B. (1961) 'International Integration: The European and the Universal Process', *International Organization*, Vol. 15, No. 3, pp. 366–92.

Haas, E. B. (1964) *Beyond the Nation-State* (Stanford, CA: Stanford University Press).

Haas, E. B. (1967) 'The Uniting of Europe and the Uniting of Latin America', *Journal of Common Market Studies,* Vol. 5, No. 4, pp. 315–43.

Haas, E. B. (1970) 'The Study of Regional Integration: Reflections on the Joy and Anguish of Pretheorizing', *International Organization*, Vol. 24, No. 4, pp. 607–46.

Haas, E. B. (1975) *The Obsolescence of Regional Integration Theory* (Berkeley, CA: Institute of International Studies).

Haas, E. B. (1976) 'Turbulent Fields and the Theory of Regional Integration', *International Organization*, Vol. 30, No. 2, pp. 173–212.

Haas, E. B. and P. Schmitter (1964) 'Economics and Differential Patterns of Integration: Projections about Unity in Latin America', *International Organization,* Vol. 18, No. 4, pp. 259–99.

Hänggi, H. (2006) 'Interregionalism as a Multifaceted Phenomenon: In Search of a Typology', in Hänggi, H., R. Roloff and J. Rüland (eds), *Interregionalism and International Relations* (London: Routledge).

Hardacre, A. (2010) *The Rise and Fall of Interregionalism in EU External Relations* (Dordrecht: Republic of Letters Publishing).

Hardacre, A. and M. Smith (2009) 'The EU and the Diplomacy of Complex Interregionalism', *The Hague Journal of Diplomacy*, Vol. 4, No. 2, pp. 167–88.

Hardacre, A. and Smith, M. (2014) 'The European Union and the Contradictions of Complex Interregionalism', in Baert, F., T. Scaramagli and F. Söderbaum (eds), *Intersecting Interregionalism* (Dordrecht: Springer)

Hearn, J. (2007) 'African NGOs: The New Compradors?', *Development and Change* Vol. 38, No. 6, pp. 1095–110.

HELCOM (Helsinki Commission – Baltic Marine Environment Protection Commission) (2010) 'Ecosystem Health of the Baltic Sea. Initial Holistic Assessment', *Baltic Sea Environment Proceedings*, No. 122.

Hentz, J. J. and M. Bøås (eds) (2003) *New and Critical Security and Regionalism: Beyond the Nation State* (Aldershot: Ashgate).

Hentz, J., F. Söderbaum and R. Tavares (2009) 'Regional Organizations and African Security: Moving the Debate Forward', *African Security*, Vol. 2, No. 2–3, pp. 206–17.

Herbst, J. (2007) 'Crafting Regional Cooperation in Africa', in Acharya, Amitav and Alastair Johnston (eds), *Crafting Cooperation. Regional International Institutions in Comparative Perspective* (London: Oxford University Press).

Hettne, B. (1994) 'The New Regionalism: Implications for Development and Peace', in Hettne, B. and A. Inotai, *The New Regionalism: Implications for Global Development and International Security* (Helsinki: UNU/WIDER).

Hettne, B. (1997) 'Development, Security and World Order: A Regionalist Approach', *European Journal of Development Research*, Vol. 9, No. 1, pp. 83–106.

Hettne, B. (1999) 'Globalization and the New Regionalism: The Second Great Transformation', in B. Hettne, A. Inotai and O. Sunkel (eds), *Globalism and the New Regionalism* (Basingstoke: Macmillan).

Hettne, B. (2002) 'The Europeanization of Europe: Endogenous and Exogenous Dimensions', *Journal of European Integration,* Vol. 24, No. 4, pp. 325–40.

Hettne, B. (2003) 'The New Regionalism Revisited', in Söderbaum, F. and Shaw, T. (eds), *Theories of New Regionalisms: A Palgrave Reader* (Basingstoke: Palgrave).

Hettne, B. (2005) 'Beyond the New Regionalism', *New Political Economy,* Vol. 10, No. 4, pp. 543–71.

Hettne, B. (2014) 'Regional Actorship: A Comparative Approach to Interregionalism', in Baert, F., T. Scaramagli and F. Söderbaum (eds), *Intersecting Interregionalism. Regions, Global Governance and the EU* (Dordrecht: Springer).

Hettne, B. and F. Söderbaum (1998) 'The New Regionalism Approach', *Politeia,* Vol. 17, No. 3, pp. 6–21.

Hettne, B. and F. Söderbaum (2000) 'Theorising the Rise of Regionness', *New Political Economy,* Vol. 5, No. 3, pp. 457–74.

Hettne, B. and F. Söderbaum (2005a) 'Civilian Power or Soft Imperialism: the EU as a Global Actor and the Role of Interregionalism', *European Foreign Affairs Review,* Vol. 10, No. 4, pp. 535–52.

Hettne, B. and F. Söderbaum (2005b) 'Intervening in Complex Humanitarian Emergencies: The Role of Regional Cooperation', *The European Journal of Development Research,* Vol. 17, No. 3, pp. 449–61.

Hettne, B. and F. Söderbaum (2006) 'Regional Cooperation: A Tool for Addressing Regional and Global Challenges', in ITFGPG *Meeting Global Challenges: International Cooperation in the National Interest* (Final Report, Stockholm).

Hettne, B., Inotai, A. and O. Sunkel (eds) (1999) *Globalism and the New Regionalism* (Basingstoke: Macmillan).

Hettne, B., A. Inotai and O. Sunkel (eds) (2000a) *National Perspectives on the New Regionalism in the North* (Basingstoke: Macmillan).

Hettne, B., A. Inotai and O. Sunkel (eds) (2000b) *National Perspectives on the New Regionalism in the South* (Basingstoke: Macmillan).

Hettne, B., A. Inotai and O. Sunkel (eds) (2000c) *The New Regionalism and the Future of Security and Development* (Basingstoke: Macmillan).

Hettne, B., A. Inotai and O. Sunkel (eds) (2001) *Comparing Regionalisms: Implications for Global Development* (Basingstoke: Macmillan).

Heydon, K. and S. Woolcock (2009) *The Rise of Bilateralism. Comparing American, European and Asian Approaches to Preferential Trade Agreements* (New York: UNU Press).

Higgott, R. (1997) '*De Facto* and *De Jure* Regionalism: The Double Discourse of Regionalism in the Asia Pacific', *Global Society,* Vol. 11, No. 2, pp. 165–83.

Higgott, R. (1998) 'The International Political Economy of Regionalism: the Asia-Pacific and Europe Compared', in William D. Coleman, W. D. and G. R. D. Underhill (eds), *Regionalism and Global Economic Integration. Europe, Asia and the Americas* (London: Routledge).

Higgott, R. (2002) 'From Trade-Led to Monetary-Led Regionalism: Why Asia in the 21st Century will be Different to Europe in the 20th Century', *UNU/CRIS e-Working Papers* 2002/1, Bruges: UNU/CRIS.

Higgott, R. (2006) 'The Theory and Practice of Region: the Changing Global Context', in Fort, B. and D. Webber (eds), *Regional Integration in Europe and East Asia: Convergence or Divergence?* (London and New York: Routledge).

Hix, S. (1994) 'The Study of the European Community: The Challenge to Comparative Politics', *West European Politics,* Vol. 17, No. 1, pp. 1–30.

Hodgson, G. (1988) *Economics and Institutions* (Cambridge: Polity Press).

Hoffmann, S. (1966) 'Obstinate or Obsolete? The Fate of the Nation-state and the Case of Western Europe', *Daedalus,* Vol. 95, No. 3, pp. 862–915.

Holden, M. (2001) 'Is a Free Trade Agreement the Answer for Southern Africa? Insigths from Development Economic Theory', in Vale, P., L. Swatuk and B. Odén (eds), *Theory, Change and Southern Africa's Future* (Basingstoke: Palgrave).

Holland, M. (2006) '"Imagined" Interregionalism. Europe's relations with the Africa, Caribbean and Pacific states (ACP)', in Hänggi, H., R. Roloff and J. Rüland (eds), *Interregionalism and International Relations* (London: Routledge).

Hooghe, L. and G. Marks (2001) *Multi-level Governance and European Integration* (Boulder-Lanham: Rowman and Littlefield).

Hook, G. and I. Kearns (eds) (1999) *Subregionalism and World Order* (Basingstoke: Macmillan).

Howell, J. (2000) 'Making Civil Societies from the Outside – Challenges for Donors', *European Journal of Development Research*, Vol. 12, No. 1, pp. 3–22.

Hurrell, A. (1995) 'Explaining the Resurgence of Regionalism in World Politics', *Review of International Studies*, Vol. 21, No. 4, pp. 331–58.

Hurrell, A. (2005) 'The Regional Dimension in International Relations Theory', in Farrell, M., B. Hettne and L. Van Langenhove (eds), *Global Politics of Regionalism. Theory and Practice* (London: Pluto Books).

Hurt, S. R. (2003) 'Co-operation and Coercion? The Cotonou Agreement between the European Union and ACP States at the End of the Lomé Convention', *Third World Quarterly*, Vol. 24, No. 1, pp. 161–76.

Hveem, H. (2000) 'Explaining the Regional Phenomenon in an Era of Globalization', in Stubbs, R. and G. R. D. Underhill (eds) *Political Economy and the Changing Global Order* (Oxford: Oxford University Press, 2nd Edition).

ITFGPG (2006) *Meeting Global Challenges: International Cooperation in the National Interest* (Final Report. Stockholm).

Jenkins, C. and L. Thomas (2001) 'African Regionalism and the SADC', in Telò, M. (ed.), *European Union and New Regionalism. Regional Actors and Global Governance in a Post-Hegemonic Era* (Aldershot: Ashgate).

Jessop, R. (2003) 'The Political Economy of Scale and the Construction of Cross-Border Regions', in Söderbaum, F. and T. M. Shaw (eds), *Theories of New Regionalism. A Palgrave Reader* (Basingstoke: Palgrave).

Jones, B. (2002) 'Governance and the Challenges of Changing *Political Space*', in Ferguson, Y. H. and R. J. Jones (eds) *Political Space: Frontier of Change and Governance in a Globalizing World* (Albany, NY: State University of New York Press).

Jönsson, C., S. Tägil and G. Törnqvist (2000) *Organizing European Space* (London: Sage).

Journal of European Public Policy, Vol. 12, No. 2, 2005, 'Special Issue: The Disparity of European Integration: Revisiting Neofunctionalism in Honour of Ernst Haas.'

Katzenstein, P. J. (1996) 'Regionalism in Comparative Perspective', *Cooperation and Conflict*, Vol. 31, No. 2, pp. 123–59.

Katzenstein, P. J. (2000) 'Regionalism and Asia', *New Political Economy*, Vol. 5, No. 3 (November), pp. 353–68.

Katzenstein, P. J. (2005) *A World of Regions: Asia and Europe in the American Imperium* (Ithaca, NY: Cornell University Press).

Katzenstein, P. J. and T. Shiraishi (eds). (1997) *Network Power: Japan and Asia* (Ithaca, NY: Cornell University Press).

Kaul, I., Conceicao, P., Le Goulven, K. and R. Mendoza (eds). (2003) *Providing Global Public Goods. Managing Globalization* (Oxford: UNDP & Oxford University Press).

Kearns, I. and G. Hook (1999) 'Conclusion: Subregionalism – An Assessment' in Hook, G. and I. Kearns (eds) *Subregionalism and World Order* (Basingstoke: Macmillan).

Keating, M. and Loughlin, J. (eds) (1997) *The Political Economy of Regionalism* (London: Frank Cass).

Keohane, R. O. and S. Hoffmann (1991) 'Institutional Change in Europe in the 1980s', in Keohane, R. O. and S. Hoffmann (eds), *The New European Community. Decision-Making and Institutional Change* (Boulder, CO: Westview Press), pp. 1–40.

Kohli, A., P. Evans, P. J. Katzenstein, A. Przeworski, S. Hoeber Rudolph, R. J. C. Scott and T. Skocpol, (1995) 'The Role of Theory in Comparative Politics: A Symposium', *World Politics*, Vol. 48, pp. 1–49.

Lammich, G. (2014) 'China's Impact on Capacity Building in the African Union', paper presented at the *Workshop: South-South Development Cooperation Chances and Challenges for the International Aid Architecture*, September 26–27, 2014 at Heidelberg University.

Laursen, F. (ed.) (2003) *Comparative Regional Integration. Theoretical Perspectives* (Aldershot: Ashgate).

Laursen, F. (ed.) (2010) *Comparative Regional Integration: Europe and Beyond* (Aldershot: Ashgate).

Lenz, T., J. Bezuijen, L. Hooghe and G. Marks (2014) 'Patterns of International Organization: General Purpose vs. Task Specific', Research Paper 128, Robert Schuman Centre for Advanced Studies (RSCAS), Florence: European University Institute.

Lenze, N. and C. Schriwer (eds) (2014) *Converging Regions: Global Perspectives on Asia and the Middle East* (Basingstoke: Ashgate).

Lorenz-Carl, U. and M. Rempe (eds) (2013) *Mapping Agency. Comparing Regionalisms in Africa* (Farnham: Ashgate).

Malamud, A. (2003) 'Presedentialism and Mercosur: A Hidden Cause for a Successful Experience', in Laursen, F. (ed.), *Comparative Regional Integration. Theoretical Perspectives* (Aldershot: Ashgate).

Mamdani, M. (1995) 'A Critique of the State and Civil Society Paradigm in Africanist Studies', in Wamba-dia-Wamba, E. and M. Mamdani (eds), *African Studies in Social Movements and Democracy* (Dakar: Codesria).

Mansfield, E. D. and R. Bronson (1997) 'The Political Economy of Major-Power Trade Flows', in Mansfield, E. D. and H. V. Milner (eds), *The Political Economy of Regionalism* (New York: Columbia University Press).

Mansfield, E. D. and H. V. Milner (eds) (1997) *The Political Economy of Regionalism* (New York: Columbia University Press).

Marchand, M. H. (2001) 'North American Regionalisms and Regionalization in the 1990s', in Schulz, M., F. Söderbaum and J. Öjendal (eds), *Regionalization in a Globalizing World. A Comparative Perspective on Actors, Forms and Processes* (London: Zed Books).

Marchand, M. H., M. Bøås, M. and T. M. Shaw (1999) 'The political economy of new regionalisms', *Third World Quarterly*, Vol. 20, No. 5, pp. 897–910.

Marks, G. (1997) 'Does the European Union Represent an n of 1?', *ECSA Review*, Vol. X, No. 3, pp. 2–3.

Marks, G., L. Hooghe and K. Blank (1996) 'European Integration from the 1980s: State-Centric v. Multi-Level Governance', *Journal of Common Market Studies*, Vol. 34, No. 3, pp. 341–78.

Mattheis, F. (2014) *New Regionalism in the South – Mercosur and SADC in a Comparative and Interregional Perspective* (Leipzig: Leipziger Universitätsverlag).

Mattli, W. (1999) *The Logic of Regional Integration: Europe and Beyond* (Cambridge: Cambridge University Press).

Mattli, W. (2005) 'Ernst Haas's Evolving Thinking on Comparative Regional Integration: Of Virtues and Infelicities', *Journal of European Public Policy*, Vol. 12, No. 2, pp. 327–48.

Mendoza, R. (2003) 'The Multilateral Trade Regime: A Global Public Good for All?', in Kaul, I., P. Conceicao, K. Le Goulven and R. Mendoza (eds), *Providing Global Public Goods. Managing Globalization* (Oxford: UNDP & Oxford University Press).

Meyer, A. (2009) 'Regional Conflict Management in Central Africa: From FOMUC to MICOPAX', *African Security*, Vol. 2, No. 2–3, pp. 158–74.

Mistry, P. S. (1999) 'The New Regionalism: Impediment or Spur to Future Multilateralism?' in Hettne, B. et al. (eds), *Globalism and the New Regionalism* (Basingstoke: Macmillan).

Mistry, P. S. (2003) 'New Regionalism and Economic Development', in Söderbaum, F. and Shaw, T. M. (eds), *Theories of New Regionalism. A Palgrave Reader* (Basingstoke: Palgrave).

Mitrany, D. (1943) *A Working Peace System: An Argument for the Functional Development of International Organization* (London: Royal Institute of International Affairs).

Mittelman, J. H. (1999) 'Rethinking the "New Regionalism" in the Context of Globalization', in Hettne, B., A. Inotai and O. Sunkel (eds), *Globalism and the New Regionalism* (Basingstoke: Macmillan).

Mittelman, J. H. (2000) *The Globalization Syndrome. Transformation and Resistance* (Princeton, NJ: Princeton University Press).

Moravcsik, A. (1993) 'Preferences and Power in the European Community: A Liberal Inter-governmentalist Approach', *Journal of Common Market Studies*, Vol. 31, No. 4, pp. 473–524.

Moravcsik, A. (1997) 'Does the European Union Represent an n of 1?', *ECSA Review*, Vol. X, No. 3, pp. 3–4.

Moravcsik, A. (1998) *The Choice for Europe. Social Purpose and State Power from Messina to Maastricht* (Ithaca, NY: Cornell University Press).

Muchie, Mammo (ed.) (2003) *The Making of the Africa-nation: Pan-Africanism and the African Renaissance* (London: Adonis & Abbey).

Murithi, T. (2005) *The African Union. Pan-Africanism, Peace-Building and Development* (Aldershot: Ashgate).

Murphy, A. B. (1991) 'Regions as Social Constructs: The Gap between Theory and Practice', *Progress in Human Geography*, Vol. 15, No. 1, pp. 23–35.

Nesudurai, H. E. S. (2005) 'The Global Politics of Regionalism: Asia and the Asia Pacific' in Farrell, M., B. Hettne and L. van Langenhove (eds), *The Global Politics of Regionalism. Theory and Practice* (London: Pluto Press).

Neumann, I. B. (1994) 'A Region-Building Approach to Northern Europe', *Review of International Studies*, Vol. 20, No. 1, pp. 53–74.

Neumann, I. B. (2003) 'The Region-Building Approach', in Söderbaum, F. and Shaw, T. M. (eds), *Theories of New Regionalism. A Palgrave Reader* (Basingstoke: Palgrave).

Nicol, A. et al. (2001) *Transboundary Water Management as an International Public Good* (Prepared for Development Financing 2000 Study 2001: 1. Stockholm: Ministry for Foreign Affairs).

Niemann, M. (2000) *A Spatial Approach to Regionalisms in the Global Economy* (Basingstoke: Macmillan).

Niemann, M. (2001) 'Unstated Places – Rereading Southern Africa', in Vale, P., L. A. Swatuk and B. Odén (eds), *Theory, Change and Southern Africa's Future* (Basingstoke: Palgrave).

Nye, Joseph S. (1968) 'Comparative Regional Integration: Concept and Measurement', *International Organization*, Vol. 22, No. 4, pp. 855–80.

Nye, Joseph S., Jr. (1970) 'Comparing Common Markets: A Revised Neo-Functionalist Model', *International Organization*, Vol. 24, No. 4, pp. 796–835.

Nye, Joseph (1971) *Peace in Parts: Integration and Conflict in Regional Organization* (Boston: Little, Brown and Company).

Obi, C. (2009) 'ECOWAS on the Ground: Comparing Peacekeeping in Liberia, Sierra Leone, Guinea Bissau and Côte d'Ivoire', *African Security*, Vol. 2, No. 2–3, pp. 119–35.

Ohmae, K. (1995) *The End of the Nation-State. The Rise of Regional Economies* (London: HarperCollins).

Öjendal, J. (2001) 'Southeast Asia at a Constant Crossroads. An Ambiguous New Region', in Schulz, M., F. Söderbaum and J. Öjendal (eds), *Regionalization in a Globalizing World. A Comparative Perspective on Forms, Actors and Processes* (London: Zed Books).

Olsen, S. B., Page, G. G. and Ochoa, E. (2009) *The Analysis of Governance Responses to Ecosystem Change: A Handbook for Assembling a Baseline*. Land-Ocean Interactions in the Coastal Zone (LOICZ) Reports and Studies No. 34. (Geesthacht: GKSS Research Center).

Paasi, Anssi (2001) 'Europe as a Social Process and Discourse: Considerations of Place, Boundaries and Identity', *European Urban and Regional Studies*, Vol. 8, No. 1, pp. 7–28.

Parsonage, J. (1997) 'Trans-state Developments in South-East Asia – Subregional Growth Zones', in Rodan, G., K. Hewison and R. Robison (eds), *The Political Economy of South-East Asia – An Introduction* (Oxford: Oxford University Press).

Pastor, R. A. (2005) 'North America and the Americas', in Farrell, M., B. Hettne and Luk van Langenhove (eds), *The Global Politics of Regionalism. Theory and Practice* (London: Pluto Press).

Payne, A. (1998) 'The New Political Economy of Area Studies', *Millennium: Journal of International Studies*, Vol. 27, No. 2, pp. 253–73.

Payne, A. (2000) 'Globalisation and Modes of Regionalist Governance', in Pierre, J. (ed.), *Debating Governance* (Oxford: Oxford University Press).

Payne, A. and A. Gamble (1996) 'Introduction: The Political Economy of Regionalism and World Order', in Gamble, A. and A. Payne (eds), *Regionalism and World Order* (Basingstoke: Macmillan).

Pempel, T. J. (ed.) (2005) *Remapping East Asia: The Construction of a Region* (Ithaca, NY: Cornell University Press).

Perkmann, M. and Sum, N-L (eds) (2002) *Globalisation, Regionalisation and the Building of Cross-Border Regions* (Basingstoke: Palgrave).

Phillips, N. (2005) 'The Americas', in Payne, A. (ed.), *The New Regional Politics of Development* (Basingstoke: Palgrave).

Poku, N. (2001) *Regionalization and Security in Southern Africa* (Basingstoke: Palgrave).

Polanyi, K. (1944) *The Great Transformation: The Political and Economic Origins of Our Time* (Boston: Beacon Press).

Pollack, Mark A. (2003) *The Engines of European Integration. Delegation, Agency, and Agenda Setting in the EU* (Oxford: Oxford University Press).

Prebisch, R. (1959) *The Latin American Common Market and the Multilateral Payments System* (Santiago: United Nations Publications).

Prodi, R. (2000) 'Europe and Global Governance', Speech to the Second COMECE Congress, Brussels, 31 March 2000. SPEECH/00/115.

Puchala, D. J. (1971) 'Of Blind Men, Elephants and International Integration', *Journal of Common Market Studies*, Vol. 10, No. 3, pp. 267–84.

Ravenhill, J. (2003) 'The New Bilateralism in the Asia Pacific', *Third World Quarterly*, Vol. 24, No. 2, pp. 299–317.

Regelsberger, E. (1990) 'The dialogue of the EC/twelve with other regional groups: A new European identity in the international system?', in Edwards, G. and E. Regelsberger (eds.), *Europe's Global Links: The European Community and Interregional Cooperation* (London: Pinter).

Reynaert, V. (2012) 'The European Union's Foreign Policy since the Treaty of Lisbon: The Difficult Quest for More Consistency and Coherence', *The Hague Journal of Diplomacy*, Vol. 7, No. 2, pp. 207–26.

Riggirozzi, P. (2012) 'Region, Regionness and Regionalism in Latin America: Towards a new synthesis', *New Political Economy*, Vol. 17, No. 4, 421–43.

Riggirozzi, P. (2014) 'Regionalism through social policy: collective action and health diplomacy in South America', *Economy and Society*, Vol. 43, No. 3, pp. 432–54.

Riggirozzi, P. and D. Tussie (eds) (2012) *The Rise of Post-hegemonic Regionalism. The Case of Latin America* (Dordrecht: Springer).

Robles, A. C. Jr. (2008) *The Asia–Europe Meeting: The Theory and Practice of Interregionalism* (London: Routledge).

Robson, P. (1993) 'The New Regionalism and Developing Countries', *Journal of Common Market Studies*, Vol. 31, No. 3, pp. 329–48.

Robson, P. (1998) *The Economics of International Integration* (London: Routledge).

Rodrik, D. (1998) 'Trade Policy and Economic Performance in Sub-Saharan Africa', *EGDI Studies in Brief 1/98*, Stockholm: EGDI.

Rosamond, B. (2000) *Theories of European Integration* (Basingstoke: Palgrave Macmillan).

Rosamond, B. (2005) 'The Uniting of Europe and the Foundation of EU Studies: Revisiting the Neofunctionalism of Ernst B. Haas', *Journal of European Public Policy*, Vol. 12, No. 2 (April), pp. 237–54.

Rosenau, J. (1997) Along the Domestic-Foreign Frontier: Exploring Governance in a Turbulent World (Cambridge: Cambridge University Press).

Ruggie, J. G. (1998) *Constructing the World Polity* (London: Routledge).

Rüland, J. (2006) 'Interregionalism: an unfinished agenda', in Hänggi, H., R. Roloff and J. Rüland (eds), *Interregionalism and International Relations* (London: Routledge).

Rüland, J. (2014) 'Interregionalism and International Relations: Reanimating an Obsolescent Research Agenda?', in Baert, F., T. Scaramagli and F. Söderbaum (eds), *Intersecting Interregionalism* (Dordrecht: Springer).

Russett, B. M. (1967) *International Regions and the International System. A Study in Political Ecology* (Chicago, IL: Rand & McNally & Co).

Sandholtz, W. and A. Stone Sweet (1998) *European Integration and Supranational Governance* (Oxford: Oxford University Press).

Santander, S. (2010) 'The Ups and Downs of Interregionalism in Latin America' in Söderbaum, F. and P. Stålgren (eds), *The European Union and the Global South* (Boulder, CO: Lynne Rienner Publishers).

Santander, S. (2014) 'The Impact of the Iberian States on Europan Union-Latin American Interregionalism', in Baert, F., T. Scaramagli and F. Söderbaum (eds), *Intersecting Interregionalism* (Dordrecht: Springer)

SAPSN (2000) 'Making Southern African Development Cooperation and Integration a People-centered and People-driven Regional Challenge to Globalisation', Declaration to the Governmental Summit of the Southern African Development Community (SADC), Windhoek, Namibia, 1–7 August 2000.

Sbragia, A. M. (1992) 'Thinking about the European Future: The Uses of Comparison', in Sbragia, A. M. (ed.), *Euro-Politics. Institutions and Policy-Making in the 'New' European Community* (Washington, DC: The Brookings Institution), pp. 257–91.

Schmitter, P. C. and S. Kim (2008) 'Comparing Processes of Regional Integration: European 'Lessons' and Northeast Asian Reflections', *Current Politics and Economics of Asia*, Vol. 17, No. 1, pp. 11–36.

Schoeman, M. and M. Muller (2009) 'SADC as Regional Peacekeeper: Myth or Reality?' *African Security*, Vol. 2, No. 2–3, pp. 175–92.

Scholte, J. A. (2002) Civil Society and Governance', in Ougaard, M. and R. Higgott (eds), *Towards a Global Polity* (London: Routledge).

Schulz, M., F. Söderbaum and J. Öjendal (eds) (2001) *Regionalization in a Globalizing World. A Comparative Perspective on Actors, Forms and Processes* (London: Zed Books).

Shaw, T. M., J. A. Grant and S. Cornelissen (eds) (2011) *The Ashgate Research Companion to Regionalisms* (Aldershot: Ashgate).

Sida (2002) 'Strategi för svenskt stöd till regionalt utvecklingssamarbete i Afrika söder om Afrika', AFRA (Stockholm: Sida).

Smis, S. and S. Kingah (2014) 'The Court of Justice of the European Union and Other Regional Courts', in Baert, F., T. Scaramagli and F. Söderbaum (eds), *Intersecting Interregionalism* (Dordrecht: Springer).

Smith, S. (1997) 'New Approaches to International Theory', in Baylis, John and Steve Smith (eds), *The Globalization of World Politics: An Introduction to International Relations* (Oxford: Oxford University Press).

Söderbaum, F. (2004) *The Political Economy of Regionalism. The Case of Southern Africa* (Basingstoke: Palgrave Macmillan).

Söderbaum, F. (2005) 'Exploring the Links between Micro-regionalism and Macro-regionalism', in Farrell, M., B. Hettne and L. van Langenhove (eds), *Global Politics of Regionalism. Theory and Practice* (London: Pluto Press).

Söderbaum, F. (2007) 'Regionalisation and Civil Society: The Case of Southern Africa', *New Political Economy*, Vol. 12, No. 3 (September), pp. 319–37.

Söderbaum, F. (2009) 'Comparative Regional Integration and Regionalism', in Landman, T. and N. Robinson (eds), *The SAGE Handbook of Comparative Politics* (London: SAGE).

Söderbaum, F. (2011) 'Formal and Informal Regionalism', in Shaw, T. M., A. J. Grant, and S. Cornelissen (eds), *Ashgate Research Companion to Regionalisms* (Aldershot: Ashgate).

Söderbaum, F. (2013) 'What's Wrong with Regional Integration? The Problem of Eurocentrism'. *EUI Working Papers 64,* Robert Schuman Centre for Advanced Studies, European University Institute, pp. 1–15.

Söderbaum, F. (2015) 'Rethinking the Politics of Transboundary Water Management: The Case of the Zambezi River Basin', *International Journal of Water Governance*, Vol. 3, No. 3, pp. 1–12.

Söderbaum, F. and I. Taylor (2001) 'Transmission Belt for Transnational Capital or Facilitator for Development – Problematising the Role of the State in the Maputo Development Corridor'. *Journal of Modern African Studies,* Vol. 39, No. 4, pp. 675-95.

Söderbaum, F. and A. Sbragia (2010) 'EU Studies and the "New Regionalism": What Can Be Gained from Dialogue?', *Journal of European Integration*, Vol. 32, No. 6, pp. 563–82.

Söderbaum, F. and J. Granit (2014) 'The Political Economy of Regionalism. The Relevance for International Waters and the Global Environment Facility', *STAP Issues Paper Series*. Washington, DC: Global Environmental Facility.

Söderbaum, F. and L. Van Langenhove (eds) (2006) *The EU as a Global Player. The Politics of Interregionalism* (London: Routledge).

Söderbaum, F. and T. M. Shaw (eds) (2003) *Theories of New Regionalism. A Palgrave Reader* (Basingstoke: Palgrave).

Söderbaum, F. and P. Stålgren (eds) (2010a) *The European Union and the Global South* (Boulder, CO: Lynne Rienner Publishers).

Söderbaum, F. and P. Stålgren (2010b) 'The Limits to Interregional Development Cooperation in Africa', in Söderbaum, F. and P. Stålgren (eds), *The European Union and the Global South* (Boulder, CO: Lynne Rienner Publishers).

Söderbaum, F. and R. Tavares (2008) *The African Union and the Regional Economic Communities: 3 Scenarios for 2018–2028.* Report commissioned by the Swedish Armed Forces, Stockholm: Swedish Armed Forces.

Söderbaum, F. and R. Tavares (eds) (2009) 'Regional Organizations in African Security', Special Issue of *African Security*, Vol. 2, No. 2–3, pp. 69–217.

Söderbaum, F. and I. Taylor (eds) (2003) *Regionalism and Uneven Development in Southern Africa. The Case of the Maputo Development Corridor* (Aldershot: Ashgate).

Söderbaum, F. and I. Taylor (eds) (2008) *Afro-regions: The Dynamics of Cross-border Micro-regionalism in Africa* (Uppsala: Nordic Africa Institute).

Solingen, E. (1996) 'Democracy, Economic Reform and Regional Cooperation', *Journal of Theoretical Politics*, Vol. 8, No. 1, pp. 79–114.

Stone Sweet, A. and W. Sandholtz (1997) 'European Integration and Supranational Governance', *Journal of European Public Policy*, Vol. 4, No. 3, pp. 297–317.

Strange, S. (1999) 'The Westfailure System', *Review of International Studies*, Vol. 25, No. 3, pp. 345–54.

Steiner, T. (2000) 'Europe meets Asia. 'Old' vs. 'New' Inter-regional Co-operation and ASEM's Prospects.' *Working Paper, 22*, Department of International Relations, Hebrew University.

Swatuk, L. (2000) 'Power and Water: The Coming Order in Southern Africa', in Björn Hettne et al. (eds), *The New Regionalism and the Future of Security and Development* (Basingstoke: Macmillan).

Tavares, R. (2009) *Regional Security: The Capacity of International Organizations* (London and New York: Routledge).

Taylor, I. (2003) 'Globalisation and Regionalisation in Africa: Reactions to Attempts Neo-liberal Regionalism', *Review of International Political Economy*, Vol. 10, No. 2, pp. 310–30.

Taylor, I. (2005) *NEPAD. Toward Africa's Development or Another False Start?* (Boulder, CO: Lynne Rienner).

Taylor, I. and P. Williams (2001) 'South African Foreign Policy and the Great Lakes Crisis: African Renaissance Meets Vagabonde Politique', *African Affairs*, Vol. 100, pp. 265–86.

Taylor, I. (2008) *China's New Role in Africa* (Boulder, CO: Lynne Rienner).

Telò, M. (ed.) (2014) *European Union and New Regionalism. Competing Regionalism and Global Governance in a Post-Hegemonic Era* (3rd edn) (Aldershot: Ashgate).

TFGPG (2004) 'Meeting Global Challenges: International Cooperation in the National Interest', Working Paper for the Secretariat of TFGPG.

Thakur, R. (2005) *The United Nations, Peace and Security: From Collective Security to the Responsibility to Protect* (Cambridge: Cambridge University Press).

Thakur, R. and L. Van Langenhove (2006) 'Enhancing Global Governance Through Regional Integration', *Global Governance: A Review of Multilateralism and International Organizations*, Vol. 12, No. 3, pp. 233–40.

Thompson, G., J. Frances, R. Levacic and J. Mitchell (eds) (1991) *Markets, Hierarchies & Networks. The Co-ordination of Social Life* (London: Sage and the Open University).

Thompson, W. R. (1973) 'The Regional Subsystem: A Conceptual Explication and a Propositional Inventory', *International Studies Quarterly*, Vol. 17, No. 1, pp. 89–117.

Tsoukalis, L. (1997) *The New European Economy Revisited* (Oxford: Oxford University Press).

Tussie, D. (2003) 'Regionalism: Providing a Substance to Multilateralism?', in Söderbaum, F and T. M. Shaw and Timothy M Shaw (eds), *Theories of New Regionalism. A Palgrave Reader* (Basingstoke: Palgrave).

UN (2004) *A More Secure World: Our Shared Responsibility*, Report of the Secretary-General's High Level Panel on Threats, Challenges and Change (New York: UN, 2004).

UN (2005) *In Larger Freedom: Towards Development, Security and Human Rights for All* (New York: UN).

Van Langenhove, L. (2011) *Building Regions. The Regionalization of the World Order* (Aldershot: Ashgate).

Vasconcelos, A. (2007) 'European Union and Mercosur', in Telò, M. (ed.) *European Union and New Regionalism. Regional Actors and Global Governance in a Post-Hegemonic Era* (2nd edn) (Aldershot: Ashgate).

Vivares, E. (ed.) (2013) *Exploring the New South American Regionalism* (Aldershot: Ashgate).

Warleigh, A. (2004) 'In Defence of Intra-disciplinarity: "European Studies", the "New Regionalism" and the Issue of Democratisation', *Cambridge Review of International Affairs,* Vol. 17, No. 2, pp. 301–18.

Warleigh-Lack, A. (2006) 'Towards a Conceptual Framework for Regionalisation: Bridging "New Regionalism" and "Integration Theory"', *Review of International Political Economy*, Vol. 13, No. 5, pp. 750–71.

Warleigh-Lack, A. and L. Van Langenhove (2010) 'Rethinking EU Studies: The Contribution of Comparative Regionalism', *Journal of European Integration*, Vol. 32, No. 6, pp. 541–62.

Warleigh-Lack, A. and B. Rosamond (2010) 'Across the EU Studies–New Regionalism Frontier: Invitation to a Dialogue', *Journal of Common Market Studies*, Vol. 48, No. 4, pp. 993–1013.

Warleigh-Lack, A., N. Robinson and B. Rosamond (eds) (2011) *New Regionalism and the European Union. Dialogues, Comparisons and New Research Directions* (London: Routledge).

Wendt, A. (1992) 'Anarchy is What States Make of It: The Social Construction of Power Politics', *International Organization*, Vol. 46, No. 2, Spring (1992), p. 391–425.

WHO (2015) 'Summary of propbable SARS cases with onset illness from 1 November 2002 to 31 July 2003', WHO. [http://www.who.int/csr/sars/country/table2004_04_21/en/]. Retrieved 20 April 2015.

Wiener, A. and T. Diez (ed.) (2003) *European Integration Theory* (Oxford: Oxford University Press).

Woodward, D and R. D. Smith (2003) 'Global Public Goods and Health: Concepts and Issues', in Smith, R., R. Beaglehole, D. Woodward, and N. Drager (eds), *Global Public Goods for Health: Health Economic and Public Health Perspectives* (Oxford: Oxford University Press).

World Bank (2011) *Partnering for Africa's Regional Integration – Progress Report on the Regional Integration Assistance Strategy for Sub-Saharan Africa* (Washington, DC: World Bank).

Wunderlich, J.-U. (2012) 'The EU as an Actor Sui Generis? A Comparison of EU and ASEAN Actorness', *Journal of Common Market Studies*, Vol. 50, No. 4, pp. 653–69.

Index